KENT

IN PREHISTORIC TIMES

KENT

IN PREHISTORIC TIMES

PAUL ASHBEE

TEMPUS

*To Richmal amoris causa and The Kent Archaeological Society, as well as all
who have pursued, or are pursuing, prehistory in Kent*

First published 2005

Tempus Publishing Limited
The Mill, Brimscombe Port,
Stroud, Gloucestershire, GL5 2QG
www.tempus-publishing.com

British Library Cataloguing in Publication Data.
A catalogue record for this book is available from the British Library.

ISBN 0 7524 3136 6

Typesetting and origination by Tempus Publishing Limited
Printed in Great Britain

CONTENTS

PREFACE

Although Kent in its every dimension always loomed large for those fortunate enough to grow to maturity within its bounds, travel in Britain and upon the European mainland brought personal appreciation of prehistory into a broader perspective. Sadly, for many years it seemed that Kent, when viewed against the splendours of Wessex, appeared, despite its geographical situation, as something of a backwater. The substance and erstwhile size of the Medway's megalithic long barrows mitigated against this view, as did the monuments and potential of the chalklands of East Kent. Recent developments in archaeology at large have shown that this pessimistic view was erroneous and it has emerged that in Kent, from early Neolithic times onward, there was an intensity of settlement likely to have been in advance of, though differing from, much of wider southern England. This change of view, developed during the past half-century, has in great measure been brought about by the advent and progress of rescue archaeology. Begun by Brian Philp, largely in western Kent, a half-century ago, this now includes various units and associations, led by talented people, who have, by their continuing endeavours, given us a variety of insights into a remarkable range of primary evidence concerning the nature of Kent's prehistoric past.

The greater number of Kent's prehistoric sites have been known to the present writer since his school days. Norman Cook, in Maidstone's Museum, had allowed the copying of his *Sites, Monument and Antiquities* record, and, armed with its details, forays by bicycle and bus were made. War service permitted appraisals of prehistory and field monuments in various parts of England, Scotland and Wales. Although some of Ronald Jessup's Belgian barrows were seen when blanketed with snow, the peaceful post-war summer allowed the scrutiny of long barrows and their megalithic chambers in Germany and Holland. Down the years much more has been seen of Germany, various European museums and of the antiquities and field monuments of Ireland. This belated return to Kent has shown that, while there are affinities with aspects of the various manifestations of prehistory on the European mainland, its early past, although it has individual qualities, is for the most part in harmony with the record of southern England.

Despite the nature of Kent, a clear geographic entity and the territory of a tribe named by Caesar, there has been but one comprehensive consideration of its prehistory. This was *Early Man* by George Clinch, in the initial volume of the *Victoria County History* (1908). Ronald Jessup's *Archaeology of Kent* (1930) was a valuable contribution to the county's prehistory, as was his later *South-East England* (1970). The *Research Report* published by the Council for British Archaeology (No.48,1982) was a collection of papers, concluding at AD 1500, from a conference at Broadstairs, held in 1979 A recurrent theme was the alleged neglect of Kent's prehistory. A study of the *South East to AD 1000* (1988), by Peter Drewett and his friends, explored much the same territory, for the most part the Weald, as did Ronald Jessup in 1970. They were, however, able to incorporate the research themes they had developed while working under rescue conditions. Indeed, rescue archaeology pertaining to the Channel Tunnel base and its new railway has given us a range of dramatic and intimate insights. A recent, exciting, issue of *Current Archaeology* (May 2000) was devoted to Kent and depicts samples of the sites examined prior to the great undertaking.

Archaeologica Cantiana, the journal of the Kent Archaeological Society, the initial issue of which appeared in 1859, has in its many volumes much pertaining to prehistory. Its re-exploration and pursuit through the distinctive blue-bound volumes (there are now 1235) has been a heady pleasure, for there are so many diverting byways. Apart from early excavations, such as Ringwould's round barrow, the various communications reflect that, until the years after World War II, Kent was an agricultural county and many reports, articles, and observations were, with exceptions, of accidental discoveries. Of especial note are the nineteenth-century coloured engravings of such as Aylesford's gold torques, from the Medway, and the historic hillfort excavations of the 1930s, Bigberry and Oldbury. Indeed, the coloured engravings in the early issues of *Archaeologia Cantiana*, which also extended to the grave furniture from the Ringwould round barrow, are unique. Another aspect of *Archaeologia Cantiana* is that each volume is comprehensively indexed and that appropriate, detailed, efficient, index volumes have been produced. Indeed, writing as one who frequently consults archaeological journals of all kinds, those from Kent are rarely inaccurate and their handling has a modicum of aesthetic pleasure.

When writing a book of this kind, one becomes more than ever conscious that radiocarbon dating, and its many complexities, has been with us for half-a-century. Indeed, apart from the remote Palaeolithic past, its constraints are a matrix for much of the narrative, and dates are cited when existent or appropriate. As has been stressed in the text, radiocarbon years have been calibrated with the annular rings of America's long-lived bristle-cone pine trees. Therefore, when a date is cited, lower-case letters (bc) indicate radiocarbon years while higher-case (BC) denotes calibration into solar years. In some circles years before the present (bp and BP) are cited. By current convention the present is AD 1950.

Any narrative treating the prehistoric past of a particular region must perforce make use of the work of fellow prehistorians, their excavation reports of primary material, classifications and interpretations. The bibliography of this volume is a tribute to them. Nonetheless, the recital, with its nuances and fortes which have been distilled from the rich fabric of emergent prehistory, is my own. The many and necessary qualifications, which should condition the narrative, have been largely omitted.

Always, when abroad in Kent, and elsewhere, or when writing and drawing, my work has benefited from Richmal's, my wife's, constant help and searching critical observations. In the words of William Stukeley, who, during the eighteenth, century drew and described such as Kit's Coty House, the Lower Kit's Coty House and the Coffin Stone, which are monuments central to any appraisal of Kent's prehistory, 'Nor could travailing curiosity or Antiquarian Researches be rendered so agreeable as with a fair and witty Companion and Fellow laborer'.

ACKNOWLEDGEMENTS

Beyond the continuous, arduous, checkreading undertaken by Richmal, my talented and supportive wife, friends, individual and institutional, have sustained my endeavours. Use of the library resources of the Society of Antiquaries of London has been facilitated by the unflagging energy and unfailing patience of Adrian James, the Assistant Librarian. During the past decade, papers pertaining to remarkable megalithic long barrows have appeared in *Archaeologia Cantiana*. Many owe much to the skilled, perceptive editorship exercised by Terry Lawson. His comments and precepts have spilled into the narratives to their considerable benefit. During early days, also the Kent Archaeological Society's library whose serried periodicals have sustained my endeavours since my schooldays.

Attributions and appreciations of the many whose comments and particular illustrations pertaining to Kentish prehistory have been of great value are listed below. They range from William Stukeley's Lambarde's insights concerning Kit's Coty House, penned at the end of the sixteenth century, to the comprehensive *Historical Atlas of Kent*, edited by Terry Lawson and David Killingray, which appeared at the end of 2004.

From the eighteenth century, there is the depiction of William Lambarde (*1*) by George Vertue. William Stukeley (*2*), painted in oils during the 1720s, reproduced by the kind permission of the Society of Antiquaries of London; the Margate palstaves are illustrated by John Lewis, Thanet's historian (*51*). There are also John Thorpe's (*3* and *4*) depictions of the Coffin Stone and the Lower Kit's Coty House. Nineteenth-century sources have yielded details of the excavation of east Kent's round barrows from papers by J.Y. Akerman (*47*) and C.H. Woodruff (*48* and *66*) besides a portrait of Sir Joseph Prestwich (*5*), from his wife's biography, and W. Scott-Robertson's illustration (*58*) of Dover's golden twisted bar-torque.

With the advent of the troubled twentieth century one looks to a muster of distinguished names, largely those who forged the practice of British prehistory. These, in alphabetical order, begin with the accurate delineations of the flint implements, Palaeolithic and Mesolithic, studied by J.P.T. Burchell (*18* and *21*). They are followed by the disciplined drawings of J.P. Bushe-Fox (*69*) and the pioneer earthwork plans of I. Chalkley Gould (*59, 63* and *64*). The reproduction of such surveys is now largely the prerogative of official bodies and few authors can afford their rapacious fees. Hubert Elgar's photographs (*32* and *41*) and Sir Edward Harrison's portrait of Benjamin Harrison (*6*) are memorable, as are the illustrations marshalled by Ronald Jessup for his *Archaeology of Kent* (1930), and subsequent studies (*20, 56* and *67*). George Payne's plate of the Twydall handaxes (*14*) and W.B.Wright's map (*12*) reflect Kent's preeminence in Palaeolithic studies, as do the illustrations of material from the famous Barnfield Pit, by courtesy of the Royal Anthropological Institute (*16* and *17*) and of the Swanscombe area from the studies of J.P.T. Burchell. Detailed, forward-looking, Bronze Age considerations are reflected in the illustrations of C.M. Piggott (*53*) and C.F.C. Hawkes (*54*) as does the pottery from Minnis Bay so well illustrated by F.H. Worsfold (*55*). W.G. Klein's sensitive drawings of the miniature Iron Age ritual shields from Worth (*71*) are well known to specialists and should be studied by all concerned with that dimension of Kent's prehistory.

World War II was to some extent a watershed for the pursuit of prehistory during the twentieth century and the new standards are notable and reassuring. Kent's geology, which has determined many things, was sensitively illustrated by C.P. Burnham and S. McRae (*7*). D.A. Roe's map (*15*) vividly shows the great number of palaeoliths from Kent and its gravels. A notable undertaking was the excavation of the Chestnuts long barrow and an examination of its Mesolithic industry by John Alexander (*22*), which has been supplemented by A.G. Woodcock (*23*). G.C. Dunning's illustrations of Kentish Neolithic and Bronze Age pottery (*27, 46* and *49*) are memorable, as was O.G.S. Crawford's drawing of the Birchington globular urn (*52*). Brian Philp has most kindly allowed the reproduction of the Baston Manor late Neolithic pottery (*42*). J.D.Cowen studied the Folkestone sword (*56*), while earlier material was included in Sabine Gerloff's wider considerations (*44*), as were Kent's collared urns by I.H. Longworth (*50*). The barbed spearheads from Broadness, Swanscombe, were detailed by Colin Burgess (*57*).

Bigbury Camp, Harbledown, was studied by F.H. (Hugh) Thompson and two of his lucid illustrations are reproduced with the kind permission of the Society of Antiquaries of London (*60* and *61*). David Kelly, while at Maidstone's Museum, excavated part of the Quarry Wood earthwork at Loose, and has most kindly allowed the use of his survey (*62*). A number of Aylesford's pedestal urns are from Ann Birchall's comprehensive study (*68*), while to Keith Parfitt one is most grateful for his long barrow map and drawing of the bronze mirror from the Chilham burial (*29* and *70*). Hammill's ritual shaft, one of the first of its kind to be recognised, drawn by J.D. Ogilvie (*72*), is reproduced by the kind permission of the Kent Archaeological Society, while Elizabeth Pirie has allowed the use of her historic photograph (*73*) of the Boughton Aluph bronze bucket mount.

To all these individuals and institutions I am most grateful for their permission to publish photographs and line illustrations taken from their works. Although one can illustrate aspects of one's own endeavours pertaining to Kent, many wider aspects must perforce be based upon the the insights and illustrations of those who pursue parallel objectives. Let these words express my sincere and continued indebtedness.

PROLOGUE

When, a lifetime ago, in 1931, Dr R.E.M. Wheeler (he became Sir Mortimer in 1952) reviewed Ronald Jessup's *Archaeology of Kent* (1930) he said:

> Kent is one of the rare counties which can claim some real territorial and historic unity. Blocked towards the south-west by the great barrier of the Weald; open along an extended coastline to the shortest channel-crossings; and covering the whole Thames estuary up to the lowest natural bridge-head at Southwark – these and other special factors combined to give ancient Kent a certain isolation and prestige which facilitates a separate treatment of its archaeology.

He was impressed by the massive megalithic long barrows of the Medway valley, but saw Kentish archaeologists' attention to its prehistory, apart from many considerations of Pleistocene flints, as having fallen short of that of some of those of neighbouring counties. Sadly this situation persisted for a long time. However, the rescue archaeology, which began in West Kent and later developed in East Kent, plus the researches of various concerned individuals, has redressed the balance. As in much of Britain, our Kentish landscape is a palimpsest from which can be wrested a detailed past, from prehistory to the present.

Pleistocene flint artifacts from Kentish river gravels and related deposits, apart from the hominid remains which have been found at Swanscombe, are the principal evidence of human life and its endeavours during the aeons of time that was the Palaeolithic. Men had moved out of Africa, into Europe. Kent could not have had a geographical identity, yet its modest rivers and the Thames-side region may well have proffered favourable circumstances for early humankind. Their modes may have been more sophisticated than is commonly thought, while flint of quality from the chalk could have promoted the emergence of various tool forms. With the onset of the last, the Devensian, glaciation, only the lands that are now the south of France would have been habitable. With the retreat of the ice and the consequential climatic amelioration Europe became afforested and at its forefront and in its depth were the ingenious adaptations, termed the Mesolithic, which had their genesis in the rapid and remarkable advances of the later Palaeolithic. It was during this time that the terrain which was to become Kent became an entity in some measure separated from the Euro-Asian landmass. This was because of isostatic land adjustments and a eustatic rise of sea-level consequent upon the great glacial recessions. Nonetheless, movement across tranquil, island-protected waters was the rule. Initially the identifiable Mesolithic communities were pan-European and it is only after more than a millenium that a sense of insular individuality, brought about by sea-level rises and separation, can be detected. For the most part they moved, and had their being in woodland, which from time to time was cleared by the employment of fire. Only recourse to the chalk and greensand heights, where they looked upon rivers and considerable land areas, could have fuelled a sense of territoriality.

Skin boats, laden with seed-corn, animals and eager immigrants, have for long been considered as the inception of the British Neolithic. An alternative notion, that of acculturation combined with changes to an organised pattern of food production, farming, has for long been inadequately explored. Archaeologically observable innovation is complemented by the palaeobotanical evidence of human interference with forest and plant cover, which, although contemporary, cannot be directly related to it. It is, nonetheless, manifest that much of the evidence of earlier Neolithic occupation, scattered hearths, pits, occasional post-structures with pottery, flints, stones and other debris might be indicative of enduring Mesolithic lifestyles. An aspect of the fundamental changes that came about was the construction of causewayed enclosures, long barrows and, from time to time, timber houses, largely unsubstantial. The location and identification of our Kentish causewayed enclosures has come about from recent researches into our prehistory, aided by aerial reconnaisance. One such enclosure is at no great distance from the Medway's megalithic long barrows, while another is indicative of low-lying lost lands now submerged by the Thames estuary. Further earthen long barrows might still be discovered in the vicinity. At least seven ruined but recognisable stone-chambered long barrows, Kit's Coty House being the best known, still remain in the Medway valley where that river cuts through the chalk of the North Downs. They had exceptionally high rectangular chambers, proportional façades and stone kerbs. They are distinct from other groups and are likely to have had affinities with the stone-built long barrows of Holland and northern Germany. Like others of their kind they emerge as surrogate long houses, with the lineaments of those inhabited by the first farmers of the European heartlands, while their chambers were repositories for human remains. There were centuries of recourse to them before they were finally sealed with occupation debris. A rectangular timber long house's post-holes have been found at a point central to the series. Some of their sarsen stones were of almost Stonehenge calibre and they cannot but have fulfilled a central role for the Neolithic communities of the terrain that was to become Kent. Three earthen long barrows are known upon the high chalklands flanking East Kent's River Stour. Julliberrie's Grave, at Chilham, was excavated during the later 1930s. A broken polished flint axe of Northern European affinity was found within its loam core while there was recourse to it culminating in early Romano-British burials in its ditch. The long mounds at Boughton Aluph and Elmsted have the appropriate lineaments. So far overt later Neolithic earthworks have not been found within the county. Traces of a cursus are possible near Ramsgate while a henge may have preceded the ampitheatre at Richborough. Ebbsfleet, the type-site for the distinctive later Neolithic pottery style, awaits further investigation. There are more incidences of this later impressed pottery within the county as there are of the Grooved wares. Flint axes, many polished beyond functional necessity, have been collected in numbers, as have imported axes fashioned from hard, fine-grained rocks. These changes, termed the Neolithic, were slow, piecemeal processes and proximity to the European mainland was a fundamental factor.

Metallurgy, copper and later bronze, began with the artifacts which furnished some of Kent's Beaker burials. The earliest of these are likely to have been beneath low barrows but as time passed more massive mounds became the norm. Burials accompanied by daggers and a single axe, various ceramics, trinkets and recently a gold cup, one of a kind which has affinities with a southern English series of amber and shale cups, show that the 'Wessex' phenomenon of central southern England, notably Stonehenge's supportive landscape on Salisbury Plain, may have been more extensive than is commonly thought. The barrows of Kent, notably on the eastern chalklands, may prove to have been as numerous, and thus comparable, with particular areas of middle southern England. Collared urns, which echo in enhanced form the pronounced rims of the later Neolithic impressed wares, are few in number but may increase as barrow sites are excavated by rescue operations. Urns at no great remove from the Deverel-Rimbury series have been found but, as yet, cemeteries as, for example, in the Bournemouth area, are lacking. Middle Bronze Age hoards, supplemented by single bronzes have been found in varying circumstances and many may be votive. An even greater weight of Late Bronze Age bronzes has been found, particularly in Thanet. Some have been termed founder's hoards, as scrap metal and tools are not unknown. Nonetheless, votive intent, perhaps a specific circumstance, may have determined their interment. The remains of a boat and bronze artifacts from the sea point to

Dover as a point of Bronze Age landfall, a function which other havens in their earlier form may have fulfilled. Certain installations, now earthworks, commonly considered Iron Age, may have had their origin at this time.

With the move to iron technology it would be surprising were not the resources of the Weald examined and exploited. The change was gradual and bronze types were initially copied. Although, because of its frequency in nature, production and forging rapidly became a domestic craft. Nonetheless, what appears to have been an entreprenurial mode of iron production emerged within the Weald, where processing sites are known and the indications are that finished material may have been exported. The main centres of this lay between the headwaters of the Medway and Rother and the indications are that it was an enterprise largely in the hands of the *Cantiaci*. It is salutary to remember that the last Wealden furnace, that at Ashburnham, closed early in the nineteenth century. The later prehistoric sites were at no great distance from their sources of raw materials. Eventually production involved water-power and the hammer-ponds as they are known are in their numbers evidence of a considerable industry. Wealden hillforts are likely to have been sentinels for the security of the enterprises.

In as much as hillforts, often, as in Kent, of considerable size, can be excavated, those in the county have been. During the 1930s Bigbury and Oldbury were investigated and this work continued in the post-war world with Keston, Squerryes, the stronghold of the Loose, dispersed *oppidum* and the Wealden sites by Tonbridge and Tunbridge Wells. There has also been an inventory made of the metalwork dug up at Bigbury during the nineteenth century. In the century between Caesar's incursions and the Claudian annexation there was a move from Bigbury to the site of modern Canterbury and from Loose to Rochester, where enclosed oppida emerged. Dover, from Bronze Age times onwards, is likely to have been a port, protected by a considerable hillfort, upon which, in later times, a castle was sited. Recently it has emerged that a haven at Margate may have been dominated by an enditched installation. Research geared to rescue archaeology has provided valuable insights into the countryside of the pre-Roman Iron Age and the sites of farms in the Woodbury tradition have been identified and examined. It is likely that in particular areas their density was not inconsiderable. At Aylesford late in the nineteenth century prestigious grave furniture and pottery was unearthed by gravel diggers and salvaged and published by Sir Arthur Evans in 1890. Gravel digging at Swarling, near Canterbury, encountered a not dissimilar cemetery in 1921. It was systematically excavated and the nature of its graves defined. Those sites featured frequently in the archaeological literature of the twentieth century. More recently and of note are the bucket burials found at Alkham and those from Deal, inhumations, some sword-furnished and one crowned. A significant cult site was investigated at Worth-next-Sandwich during the 1920s while that on Blue Bell Hill is likely to have had early origins. Others may be as yet unrecognised, within earthwork enclosures or beneath Roman developments. A pioneer excavation disclosed the nature of the Hammill shaft, and others in the Wilsford tradition have been found. Coinage came early to Kent and the density of Gallo-Belgic gold coins that have come to light is remarkable. They cannot be casual losses and thus ritual intent may be an explanation for their presence in the ground. Various notable artifacts, ranging from particular brooches to the Aylesford bucket, have been considered as 'Early Celtic Art' and it should not be overlooked that the term 'art' often betokens arbitrary selection. Taken together this material – objects entailing skilled, intricate, workmanship, exercised for a considerable time – is indicative of the wealth of the *Cantiaci*. Indeed, it was during the pre-Roman Iron Age that Kent's coastal geography was observed and its people named.

It is tempting to see the iron of the Weald, which was of high quality, as a source of wealth for the elite of the *Cantiaci* expended in funerary furnishings, principally those from Aylesford, Swarling and, latterly, Deal. They have been unfavourably compared with the status of certain graves of the tribes north of the Thames and the notion that Kent may have been peripheral to pre-Claudian economic expansion has had currency. The graves of various principals may have, by the standards obtaining at the time of the interments, been sumptious, but they are not in any way comparable with, for example, the *fürstengräber* of the timber merchants of southern Germany. Apart from iron, a source of revenue could have been the control by the *Cantiaci* of the short sea routes to the European mainland, primarily from Dover to a visible opposite coast.

Caesar's incursions were the point at which our county stepped upon the stage of written history, and he remarked, rather patronisingly, that it was not without civilisation comparable with that of Gaul. A century later, the Claudian task force had an unopposed landing: by the end of the summer, after an opposed encounter across the Medway, the prestigious *Catuvellauni* had been crushed and their capital taken. In spite of Romanisation, Britain, and even Kent, close by the European mainland, was never entirely severed from its earlier past. The end of antiquity has been thought of as coming with the failure and decline of the Roman imperial system. Nonetheless, the Roman world was so esteemed and prestigious that, in the years to come, its glories continued to be envied, exalted and emulated. An origin myth has been created which forgets the pattern of continuity with our prehistory, the societies of the *Cantiaci*, and their forbears. Indeed, Kent's agrarian, administrative and social modes may be rather more ancient than is commonly thought.

Prehistoric archaeology is about things and is essentially the study of the material relics that mankind has left behind him in past times, for example tools, weapons, houses, cult sites, tombs, farms, fields and forts. From such remains it is possible to distill an historical record of times often long before the advent of written records. Such a narrative is primarily technological, for it is not difficult to discuss how things were made or built. Thereafter there are economic considerations, the exploitation of an environment and the lifestyle obtained therefrom. This may involve collaboration with other disciplines such as palaeobotany, climatology and even palaeopathology. The nature of social structures and the ideologies that lubricated them are, however, less direct, more subjective and difficult. There may be no logical relationship between some aspects of human activity and the evidence remaining for a prehistorian. Moreover, it has from time to time been asserted that there is no guarantee that observed material distinctions are a true reflection of social differences. Despite these strictures it is generally accepted that archaeological endeavour is a source of reasoned, plausible prehistory and that the evidence therefore has been subjected to the process of interpretation. Indeed, archaeological evidence is our creation because we apply our explicative methodology to the materials that we study. To cite Robin Collingwood, the eminent philosopher and archaeologist of the 1930s, there is a past-in-itself which we can never grasp, as a prehistorian can only perceive a past-as-known to him as an individual, conditioned by the nature of the evidence available to him.

To conclude this introduction, it must be stressed that this book is but a beginning and Kent has emerged as a fruitful, rewarding area for research into prehistory. This is because it looks to the Low Countries and the Rhine, the route into the heartland of mainland Europe, as well as north-eastern France. Whereas powerful, prestigious prehistoric societies emerged in Wessex, it is not unlikely that Kent was in some measure seminal and that the patent links with the European mainland, to be seen in Wessex, were via our shores. The *Cantiaci*, encountered by Caesar and, later on, the Claudian task force, had already an established, deep-rooted, prehistoric past.

ONE

ANTIQUARIES AND PIONEER PREHISTORIANS

William Lambarde (1536-1601) (*1*), the Elizabethan antiquary and jurist (Warnicke, 1973), author of the famous *Perambulation of Kent* (1576-96), the first topographical survey published in England, was mindful of Kit's Coty House and Julliberrie's Grave. The first, on Blue Bell Hill, is the well-known stone-built long barrow of the Medway Valley series, the second the earthen long barrow near Chilham standing above the Stour. Lambarde, who had seen Stonehenge in 1578, wrote in the 1596 edition of his *Perambulation* (p. 369)

> The Britons ... erected to the memory of Catigerne (as I suppose) that monument of
> foure huge and hard stones, which are yet standing in this parish [Aylesford], covered
> after the manner of Stonage (that famous sepulchre of the Britons upon Salisburie
> plaine) and now termed of the common people heere Citscotehouse ...

A side note adds 'Citscote house in Totington guund' as the location. The legend that Julliberrie's Grave was the burial place of Q. Laberius Durus, Caesar's tribune, killed by the Britons (BG, V, XV), was initially recounted by Lambarde (1576, 256). He cited Camden saying that

> (not without reason) some have called it Iulham, the place of Iulius: even as others call
> the Greene hillocke at Chilham, Iullaber of Laberius Durus, one of Caesar's Colonels,
> that was slaine by the Britaines upon the rising of that his Campe.

Camden's *Britannia* (Piggott, 1976, 33-55), in its many editions, carried details of Kit's Coty House and Julliberrie's Grave which were cited by Edward Hasted (Black, 2001) and William Henry Ireland (Ashbee, 1996, 5).

Above left: 1 William Lambarde (1536-1601), Kent's Elizabethan antiquary. This portrait is probably from George Vertue's *Heads of Illustrious Persons of Great Britain* (1743-51)

Above right: 2 A formal portrait in oils, by an unknown artist, of William Stukeley during the 1720s. In the possession of the Society of Antiquaries of London and is here reproduced with their kind permission

Among the material assembled by John Aubrey (1626-97) (Powell, 1948; rev.ed., 1963) for his *Monumenta Britannica*, the first English work to rely entirely upon material remains for a view of the past, is a drawing of Kit's Coty House (Fowles (ed.) 1980, 814-5) given to him by the classical scholar Thomas Gale (Piggott, 1989, 33, 125). On the same page is a transcript of Thomas Philipot's (1659, 48) description and statement that it is a memorial to Catigern. Aubrey, between 1671 and 1679, made frequent visits to Kent, staying at Hothfield Place with his friend and patron, Nicholas Tufton, 3rd Earl of Thanet. To get there he sometimes took a boat to Gravesend, where he was met with horses (Tylden-Wright, 1991, 170). From there he would have crossed Rochester Bridge, to join the eastward road through Bearsted, passing Kit's Coty House and the other ruined long barrows. Although no record has survived, it is inconceivable that he did not visit them and make comparisons with such Wiltshire 'sepulchres' (his term for long barrows) as West Kennet (Piggott, 1962, 1, Pl.1), well known to him.

William Stukeley (1687-1765) (2) was a pioneer unmatched in the history of archaeology, noted for his work on Stonehenge and Avebury, as well as his later-life obsession with the Druids (Piggott, 1950; 1985); he made major excursions into Kent (Ashbee, 2001) and in his published works, and many surviving papers, there are details of the principal prehistoric monuments of Kent, as seen by him during the earlier years of the eighteenth century. His closest friends were John Gray, the Canterbury physician and, from about 1720, Lord Winchelsea of Eastwell Park. Stukeley's Kentish drawings, the engravings in *Itinerarium Curiosum* I (1724) and II (1776) are, apart from his records of Stonehenge and Avebury, some of the most informative of their kind. Among the 35 engravings, there are four of Kit's Coty House and its fellows and three of Julliberrie's Grave.

The 'Prospect of Kit's Coty House' of 15 October 1722 is Stukeley's appreciation of a relict landscape, comparable with his vistas from Stonehenge (1740, Tabs. VIII, IX, X). An original field drawing is in Oxford's Bodleian Library (MS Top. Gen. B. 53 f19v) and it was from this that the published plate was composed. Kit's Coty House, with its long barrow, is the distant focal point, the Lower Kit's Coty House, reconstructed as a cove, has been inserted (Ashbee, 1993b) and the Coffin Stone is indicated. Stukeley's notions regarding coves are the substance of his second plate (*I.C.* (ii), 1776, 32. 2d). This depicts the structure of Kit's Coty House and the misleading reconstruction of the Lower Kit's Coty House. The 'Prospect of the Country from Kit's Coty House 15 October 1722', the third plate, is a reversal of the initial plate. Kit's Coty House, with its considerable long barrow, is in the foreground, together with 'The General's Tomb', and the related monuments, lower down the hillside, are in their appropriate places. The final plate (*I.C.* (ii), 1776, 34. 2d) portrays, from the south, the Lower Kit's Coty House. It can be seen clearly as a fallen rectangular chamber. At the eastern end, a massive lozengiform boulder, inclined at about 45 degrees, would appear to have been the portal stone (Ashbee, 2000, 333, fig.4). The 'Upper Coty House', is skylined on the upper hill-slope and the long barrow appears substantial. From this engraving it is clear that Stukeley's notions of this fallen chamber as a cove was an exercise of his enthusiasm for these enigmatic structures (Burl, 1988).

Julliberrie's Grave is the vantage point for Stukeley's initial depiction of this long barrow (*I.C.* (ii), 1776, 54). He noted the traces of Lord Winchelsea's excavations of 1702, and the thrown-down northern end (Ashbee, 1996, 5, fig.1). The drawing was dated 10 October 1722 and, when Stukeley returned to Kent in 1724, the long barrow, which had been further surveyed and measured by Lord Winchelsea in 1723, was the subject of a careful portrayal of its setting and character (*I.C.* (ii), 1776, 56.2). This presentation and that made in 1725, a 'Prospect' with Julliberrie's Grave in the middle distance, made from the

Woolpack Inn, in Chilham (*I.C.* (ii), 1776, 57, 2d), are clearly comparable with those of the long barrows in the vicinity of Avebury (Stukeley, 1743, Tab. 22), also drawn in 1724.

Edward Hasted (1732-1812), the historian of Kent (Black, 2001), included antiquities in his volumes, the work for which had occupied 40 years. Earthworks interested him and there is record of his digging, with the Revd Bryan Faussett, the investigator of East Kent's Saxon graves (Jessup, 1964, *passim*), into an earthwork at Heppington (Black, 2001, 123). His *History and Topographical survey of the County of Kent* initially appeared in four magisterial folios between 1778 and 1799 and was followed by 12 octavo volumes, the second edition, between 1797 and 1801. His lucid accounts of Kit's Coty House and the Lower Kit's Coty House are illustrated by lively engravings (Hasted, 1782, 177-9). A particular friend of Edward Hasted was John Thorpe (1715-92), the son of Dr John Thorpe (1682-1750) who practised medicine in Rochester and studied its antiquities (Black, 2001, *passim*, Pl. 15). His *Custumale Roffense* (1788), a folio which complemented his father's *Registrum Roffense* published in 1769, contains (pp. 67-75) a lively account of the Medway Valley's stone-built long barrow remnants illustrated by maps and engravings (1,*3* and *4*).

It has been said that Kent never attracted the attentions of 'openers' of barrows as in Wiltshire and Dorset, where Sir Richard Colt Hoare and William Cunnington investigated more than 450 mounds, between 1800 and 1810 (Grinsell, 1992, 356). However, those pursuing prehistory overlook the work of the Revd Bryan Faussett (Hawkes 1990) who, between 1760 and 1773, unearthed some 750 Anglo-Saxon burials. At that time the concept of pagan Saxon antiquities had not been formulated (Leeds, 1913, 40) and Faussett thought that he had encountered the remains of 'Britons Romanised' and 'Romans Britonised'. This belief could only have emerged from an acquaintance with the beliefs of his age regarding the 'Ancient Britons', the pre-Roman inhabitants of our island (Piggott, 1989). Thus he should be numbered amongst the pioneers of the pursuit of our prehistory, indeed the burials on the downs at Barfriston, Beakesbourne, Bishopsbourne, Chartham, Kingston and Sibertswold were marked by small barrows (Hawkes, 1990, Pl. 1.1). The graves were emptied by workmen and, as they neared the bottom, Faussett finished the work, made notes and removed the artifacts for further examination. He had an incisive knowledge of human anatomy, was able to age and sex some of the skeletons that he encountered while observing the wear on, and loss of, their teeth. His great collection of antiquities languished at Heppington for three generations, until seen by the Canterbury Congress in 1844.

A romantic, rather picturesque antiquary of the later eighteenth and early nineteenth century was James Douglas (1753-1819); soldier, antiquary, artist and

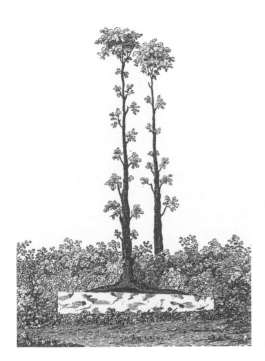

Left: 3 John Thorpe's illustration of the Coffin Stone (1788. Pl.III, fig.2). He said that William Stukeley gave it this name because the edge, seen in a lane-side bank, resembled an exposed coffin

Above: 4 Lower Kit's Coty House as depicted by John Thorpe, *Custumale Roffense*, London, 1788

eventually a divine (Jessup, 1975). Having been a cadet in the Austrian army, he was at home in mainland Europe and, indeed, some of his archaeological work was carried out in Belgium. He is to be remembered for his *Nenia Britannica or A Sepulchral History of Great Britain from the earliest period to its General Conversion to Christianity*. It was published, in London, in parts, between 1786 and 1793. Although the relics dug up during the construction of Chatham Lines against the Napoleonic threat played their part, he carried out purposeful excavations upon ancient sites. In Kent there were Rochester, Chatham Lines, Canterbury, Barham Downs, St Margaret's-at-Cliffe, Ash-by-Sandwich, Sibertswold, Greenwich Park and Kit's Coty House. Ahead of his time, he was concerned with geology, the nature of soils determining farming and settlement. He also thought of the preservation of antiquities in various soils besides the meanings of soil and crop marks. At Kit's Coty House, Douglas (1793, 181) set a man to dig on the west side of the monument and recalls that 'the spot had been, by the appearance of the soil, previously explored.' He left us a fine watercolour of a workman, *c.*1783, digging (Jessup, 1975, Pl. 34 (lower), 291). A full decade before John Frere wrote to the Secretary of the Society of Antiquaries of London enclosing the Acheulian handaxes found at Hoxne, near Diss, in Suffolk (Daniel, 1975, 26), Douglas read to the Royal Society his *Dissertation on the Antiquity of the Earth* (1785). In 1773 the fossil bones of what may have been a mammoth were found at a depth of some 12ft in the hitherto undisturbed sand and gravel of the River Medway at Chatham. He stressed the undisturbed stratification, the relative age of the bones and challenged the concept of a universal deluge (Jessup, 1975, 81-3). These observations were received in silence and Douglas, then in Holy Orders, lost all the chances of preferment that his manifold abilities would have allowed.

A number of barrow excavations were carried out in East Kent during the earlier part of the nineteenth century, by which time the so-called 'Three Age System' had emerged in Denmark (Daniel, 1975, 45-8). They were summarised by C.H. Woodruff FSA in *Archaeologia Cantiana* (IX, 16-30). Two are of special interest as excavation methodologies considerably in advance of the standards of the time (Wheeler, 1954, 7, Pl. 1) obtained. In Iffin's Wood, Chartham, Matthew Bell of Bourne Park, Bishopsbourne, in January 1842, examined a barrow 150ft in circumference and 6ft in height. Details of the work were communicated to the Society of Antiquaries of London by John Yonge Akerman, FSA (1806-73). Akerman was initially secretary to William Cobbett (1762-1832), the agricultural essayist and politician, and later Lord Alfred Conyngham FSA, the President of the new British Archaeological Association which met at Canterbury in 1844. He was an enthusiastic numismatist, founder of the Numismatic Journal in 1830, and a founder member, from 1837, of the Numismatic Society. His narrative (Akerman, 1844) recounts how Bell trenched the barrow and found five inverted collared urns containing cremated bones. An 'Horizintal Section of the Barrow', and a lively isometric representation of the sectioned mound, illustrated the paper. Cumberland Henry Woodruff FSA, whose father, the Revd John Woodruff, had investigated the Upchurch Roman potteries, made detailed mention of the Iffin's Wood barrow in his 'Celtic Tumuli' papers (1874; 1877) and in 1872 undertook the excavation of a considerable barrow at Ringwould, near Dover (Grinsell 1992, 369).

Faience beads accompanied the Ringwould burials, which were beneath an oval bowl barrow some 70ft in diameter and between 4-5ft in height. Woodruff's accounts of his excavation (1874, 21-27; 1877, 53-6) are illustrated by a schematic plan, as prepared by Bell (1877, 53-6) for Iffin's Wood, and a careful drawing labelled 'Section of central portion of West Tumulus'. The four urns were inverted over cremations in small grave-pits, one of which contained a slotted miniature vessel. Coloured plates in *Archaeologi Cantiana* (IX (1874), 23, Pl, I, opp; 24, Pl.11 opp.) depict the pottery and beads and dimensions are given. This material is now in Maidstone's Museum.

The earlier decades of the nineteenth century saw the emergence of the county archaeological societies (Piggott, 1976, 17 1-95; Wetherall, 1998), although ecclesiology and the medievalism of Sir Walter Scott's novels made their contribution. There was, via geology and the various speculations regarding the antiquity of man, current since the 1820s, a wide intellectual concern regarding the remains of our nation's past. The then new railways also played a part: the travellers, largely from the new leisured class thrown up by the industrial revolution, sought the mild intellectual stimulus proffered by a combination of ingenious antiquarianism and agreeable landscapes, catered for by a nationwide proliferation of popular guide books (Ashbee, 1996, 15). A book that was designed for this genre was Thomas Wright's *Wanderings of an Antiquary* (1854). Five of its 16 chapters, all of which in concise and general terms describe areas and places where antiquities had been found and monuments were to be seen, pertain to Kent and Chapter IX deals with 'The Valley of Maidstone – Kit's Coty House and the Cromlechs around'. The ruined long barrows on both sides of the Medway are commented upon, the flint-filled pits on Blue Bell Hill mentioned, as is his trenching of what proved to be a Roman barrow at Holborough, above Snodland. Thomas Wright (1816-77) (Roach Smith, 1883, 76-85) was our first professional archaeologist in that he supported himself by his antiquarian researches, books and involvement with archaeological and publishing societies.

As Frank Jessup wrote (1956) 'The Kent Archaeological Society was born in the old State Bed Room at Mereworth Castle on the 19 September, 1857' two years before the publication of Charles Darwin's *Origin of Species*. The midwives were 11 Kentish noblemen and gentlemen invited to the castle by Viscount and Viscountess Falmouth. This nascence was curiously late in the day, for the Sussex Archaeological Society was established in 1845 and within the next decade there emerged societies in Surrey, Somerset, Wiltshire, and elsewhere (Piggott, 1976, 175). Prehistory did not loom large in the early days of Kent's society. There was Lord Stanhope's romantic suggestion that the second Annual General Meeting should dine in a tent at Kit's Coty House, a notion which many felt as lacking practicality. Nonetheless, it should not be forgotten that the society was instrumental in obtaining and preserving the later Bronze Age gold *armillae* from the Medway at Aylesford (Pretty, 1863; Roach Smith, 1874). Later in its history the Society supported Bennett's excavations (1913) at Coldrum, R.F. Jessup's work at Bigbury (1933b; 1936) and that by J.B. Ward-Perkins (1939; 1944) at Oldbury.

Late eighteenth- and early nineteenth-century geology produced a perspective of earth history that extended immeasurably into a past far before the appearance of man. A particular dimension was consideration of the age of mankind and this emerged first in caves where patently man-made flint implements were found, beneath sheets of stalagmite, associated with the bones of extinct animals such as mammoths, rhinoceros and reindeer. Later in the century, from about 1837, Jacques Boucher Crêvecoeur de Perthes, a scientifically minded customs official at Abbeville, in France, began to collect, from the gravels of the River Somme, the flaked flint implements that are today termed handaxes, again associated with the bones of extinct animals.

The best-known bone-cave is Kent's cavern, near Torquay, in Devon. Here, in 1825, Father J. MacEnery began to excavate and found flint tools together with the bones of extinct animals in an undisturbed layer sealed by a considerable sheet of stalagmite. His conclusions were that man and these creatures must have co-existed, a view unacceptable in those days. He died in 1841 and his work was followed by that of William Pengelly, who confirmed his conclusions and published them in 1869. Following up on his work in Kent's Cavern, Pengelly investigated another cave, near Brixham, also in Devon, where again flint implements and the bones of extinct fauna were in undisturbed conditions. The work was supported by the Royal and Geological societies and lasted from July 1858 until the summer of 1859 and was in every dimension supervised by Pengelly (Garrod, 1926, 24-48). The evidence from the Brixham cave was convincing. Joseph Prestwich (1812-96) (Prestwich, 1899) and Sir Charles Lyell (1797-1875), the geologists, accepted it and included it with comments in their various publications (Prestwich, 1899, *passim*; Lyell, 1863, 96-102). Although the solid geology of Kent is far removed from that of Devon, the nature of Oldbury Hill's rock-shelters was seen during the 1860s by Benjamin Harrison (Harrison, 1925, 68), while what have been termed ossiferous fissures have also been encountered in the vicinity of Ightham (Bennett, 1907, 101-18) and there are caves, perhaps remaining from early ragstone quarrying, near Otham Church (Bennett, 1907, 133).

The discoveries by Boucher de Perthes of the regularly flaked implements associated with the bones of extinct animals that he had found in the gravels of the River Somme were exhibited, in 1838, to The Societe Impériale d'Emulation de la Somme at Abbeville and, a year later, to the Institut de France. Thereafter, they were published in detail (Daniel, 1975, 59) and despite derision and being labelled as a dangerous deviationist, for belief in diluvial catastrophes was widespread, Boucher de Perthes persisted in the pursuit of his haches antédiluviennes and their association with the bones of extinct animals. Eventually there were some who came to accept his views, notably Dr Rigollot from Amiens and Albert Gaudry, the French palaeontologist (Prestwich 1899, *passim*). Fate, however, relented!

In November 1858, Hugh Falconer (1808-65) the geologist, who had already recognised the significance of worked flints and the bones of cave bear and rhinoceros being found together in the Brixham cave in Devon, visited Abbeville, en route to the caves of Sicily. He saw the flaked flint handaxes and was convinced by all that he saw and considered Boucher de Perthes' claims for them as correct. He wrote at once to his friend Joseph Prestwich (1812-96) (5), one of England's leading geologists, and one of a firm of family wine merchants, and on his return told his opinion to John Evans (1823-1908) who, besides being,

5 Sir Joseph Prestwich (1812–1896) who, with John Evans, visited Abbeville in 1859 and viewed the flint implements found by Boucher de Perthes in the gravels of the River Somme, and confirmed their authenticity. *After G.A. Prestwich, 1899*

at that time, England's leading archaeologist, was a busy papermaker at Hemel Hempstead, in Hertfordshire. Prestwich reached Abbeville on 27 April 1859 and Evans arrived there late in the evening of the same day. Boucher de Perthes, now past 70 and who, in the style of an earlier age, still wore a wig, called upon them soon after seven o'clock the next morning to take them to the gravel pits from whence his great collection of flint implements had been derived. At Amiens they located an implement *in situ* and photographed the section. They were greatly impressed by all that they saw and thought that the implements and all pertaining to them were obviously convincing. On the evening of 30 April they returned to England, wholly converted by the evidence that Boucher de Perthes had put before them.

On the evening of 5 May, Joseph Prestwich entertained a number of geologists and antiquaries with his legendary sherry and a view of the flint implements that he and John Evans had brought back from France, interesting them greatly. Meanwhile, John Evans came upon John Frere's letter of sixty years before in the *Archaeologia* (1800, 204–205) regarding Hoxne, in Suffolk. In Evans' words:

> I at once communicated so remarkable confirmation of our views to Mr Prestwich, who lost no time in proceeding to Hoxne …
>
> During the winter of 1858–9 the workmen had discovered two of the flint implements (to which they gave the appropriate name of fighting stones), one of which Mr Prestwich removed from a heap of stones in the pit …

At Hoxne, however, as well as at Amiens, I have had ocular testimony .... in the gravel thrown out from a trench dug under our own supervision, I myself found one of the implements of the spearhead type, from which, however, the point had been unfortunately broken by the workmen in digging …

Thus, when Joseph Prestwich gave his paper (1861) to the Royal Society a month after the momentous visit, the title was 'On the occurrence of Flint-implements, associated with the Remains of Animals of Extinct Species in Beds of a Late Geological Period in France at Amiens and Abbeville, and in England at Hoxne'. At times his voice was hardly audible but, notwithstanding, the assertions regarding the finding of the flint implements were accepted. On 2 June, John Evans read his own account of the discoveries to the Society of Antiquaries of London, which was entitled: 'On the Occurrence of Flint Implements in undisturbed beds of Gravel, Sand and Clay'.

Prestwich's paper is published in the *Philosophical Transactions of the Royal Society*, 150 (1861), pp. 277-317 and that by Evans is in *Archaeologia* XXXVIII (1860) pp. 280-307. These pronouncements coming from scholars of such high repute had a great effect upon scientific opinion throughout the world. Indeed, by the autumn of 1859 the notion of the antiquity of man was widely accepted.

The year 1859 has often been described as the greatest in the history of science, for in the Spring, the discovery of man as contemporary with the extinct animals was revealed and in November of the same year Charles Darwin, writing at Downe House, Downe, published his *Origin of Species* (Desmond & Moore, 1991, *passim*). This furnished, among other things, a framework for the evolution of man and a system for the progression of his early technology. The discovery of what came to be termed the Old Stone Age was sensational, for archaeology had provided the evidence for the cultural evolution of man by the recognition of his most ancient implements. Darwin's Downe had on its outskirts High Elms, the considerable house of Sir John Lubbock (1834-1913), later Lord Avebury (Duff (ed.) 1934; Collins, 1986, 19), one of a banking family more interested in science than money. In October 1865, he produced the first edition (there were to be six more) of his *Prehistoric Times* (London): the book that first used the terms 'Palaeolithic' and 'Neolithic' for the two newly recognised divisions of the Stone Age, the Old and New, and also gave wide currency to the term 'Prehistoric'. During 1865, Joseph Prestwich moved from London to Darent Hulme, on the hills above Shoreham, John Evans at that time preparing *Ancient Stone Implements* (London) (1st ed. 1872; 2nd ed. 1897) was a frequent visitor and river-drift sites in Kent, where handaxes were found, were often jointly examined. Indeed, the emergence of early prehistory became in great part an enactment for which Kent was the stage.

6 Benjamin Harrison of Ightham (1837-1921), famous for his pioneer work on palaeoliths from local deposits and his later promotion of eoliths. *After Sir E.R. Harrison, 1928*

Complementing and, because of his effective fieldwork, accentuating the comprehensive concerns of Evans, Prestwich, and their various associates, was Benjamin Harrison (1837-1921) (6), archaeologist, geologist, historian and topographer, who lived at Ightham for all of his 83 years and, for 54 of them, kept the village's general shop (Harrison, 1928). As early as 1854 he thought of the cavities in Rose Wood, where numerous flint flakes and implements were to be found, as 'pit dwellings' (Cook & Jessup, 1933). Stirred by the story of Boucher de Perthes' palaeoliths, he found one in the vicinity of Rose Wood in 1863. Later, he searched the Oldbury and Shode Gravels, amassing a considerable number therefrom. From 1885 onwards, he found numerous weathered examples high on the North Downs, largely in the vicinity of Ash (Harrison, 1928, 137). With notions of Darwinian evolution in mind, he found, in the ocherous gravels near South Ash, in 1865, thermal flakes with damaged edges which often produced points which he thought were primitive human handiwork terming them 'eoliths' (Jessup, 1930, 1-11). Joseph Prestwich was convinced by the nature of the eoliths and later claims were made for various eolithic manifestations, particularly in East Anglia (Moir, 1927, 4-51; Kendrick & Hawkes, 1932, 1-12). As well as the eoliths, Benjamin Harrison's contribution to emergent prehistory in Kent was considerable. Although his son's comprehensive biography (1928) tells us much, his papers, letters and notebooks deposited in Maidstone's Museum await analysis. His kindliness and magnetic personality attracted many and there emerged, during the first decade of the twentieth century, what has been termed the Ightham circle. F.J. Bennett, a one-time member of H.M. Geological Survey, wrote the story of Ightham (1907), which is prefaced by a portrait of Harrison and contains a parish place names list which he had compiled. F.W. Shilling and L.H. de Barri Crawshay in 1921, the last year of Benjamin Harrison's life, made an excavation into the ocherous gravel at South Ash and found eoliths, which he sketched for his notebook. His memorial in Ightham Church has an inset eolith and records his contribution to the concept of the considerable antiquity of man, while the Coldrum stone-built long barrow remains were restored, vested in the National Trust, and dedicated to his memory.

Mention should also be made of Flaxman Charles John Spurrell who, in 1880, was living at Belvedere, Lesness Heath. He exchanged letters with and visited Benjamin Harrison from that time onwards (Harrison, 1928, *passim*). His interest was the Palaeolithic and he contributed details of discoveries, in West Kent and Crayford especially, besides observations on their manufacture, to early issues of *Archaeologia Cantiana*. For a meeting held at Dartford in 1867 he prepared a paper, illustrated by a distribution map of Dartford Antiquities (1889). He was a Fellow of the Society of Antiquaries of London and is recorded as having resigned therefrom on St George's Day, 1910. Sir John Evans' *Ancient Stone Implements* (2nd ed. 1897), provides an insight into the wide nature of his interests in stone artifacts while P.J. Tester (1950, 130) gives an insight into his work on Dartford Heath's gravels. R.F. Jessup (1930, 21) refers to the 'late' F.C.J. Spurrell's researches in North Kent as being 'not nearly so well known as they deserve to be'. More recently, John Wymer (1968, 320) refers to the discovery in 1879 of 'one of the most famous Palaeolithic sites in Britain, a buried land surface with a rich Levalloisian industry'. Some flakes were directly upon the bones of butchered animals. In 1898 he has an address in Norwich and, thereafter, he severed his connections with Kent. He appears to have known Norfolk, as Reid Moir (1927, 66) records his discovery of an ocherous palaeolith from a gravel hill-capping near Sheringham.

In 1899 the *Victoria History of the Counties of England,* known to all as the V.C.H., was launched. It was a monument to Queen Victoria's Diamond Jubilee and was to be England's counties' history in 160 volumes. Kent's initial volume appeared in 1908 and the third and last in 1932. It has been said (Yates, 1994, 212) that they are dated and were, at the time of their publication, not particularly well received. Naturally one cannot evaluate certain aspects of them but in Vol. 1 (1908), the contribution by George Clinch (1860-1921) on Early Man, and the inventory of Ancient Earthworks by I. Chalkley Gould, were well in accord with their time, while R.A. Smith's work on the Anglo-Saxon remains was unparalleled until well into the century. Likewise in Vol III (1932), Dr R.E.M. (later Sir Mortimer) Wheeler's account of Roman Kent, that begun by Francis Haverfield (1924), was authoritative (Jessup, 1930, vi). One is puzzled that this sterling work was never continued and updated.

George Clinch was born at Borden, near Sittingbourne, and his archaeology began with the collection of flint implements from the fields around his father's house. After schooling, he obtained a post in the library of the British Museum and was able to write about London's topography, flint implements from West Wickham, possible pit-dwelling at Hayes and numerous books and papers pertaining to the Bromley district. In 1895 he became Clerk to the Society of Antiquaries of London, and, in 1910, Librarian. His work on Early Man for Kent's 1908 *Victoria County History* followed the pattern of prehistory established by Sir John Lubbock in *Prehistoric Times* (1863 and subsequent eds.), namely the Palaeolithic, Neolithic, Bronze Age and, as he termed it, Prehistoric Iron Age. For the first he discussed the more important sites, with illustrations, and a list of river gravels with observations upon the implements therefrom. This includes the Ightham district, Oldbury and the many implements and flakes from the area of the rock shelters. Neolithic Kent begins with surface industries and alleged hut-stances, arrowheads and axes. There is, however, beneath the sobriquet 'Megalithic Remains' an account of the ruins of stone-built long barrows of the Medway Valley, which includes a valuable series of photographs of fallen chambers taken in wintertime. Incidental Bronze Age implements are seen as from the vicinity of rivers, some hoards are listed, implements and beakers, besides gold *armillae*, are illustrated. The Early Iron Age begins with Arthur Evans' material from Aylesford (1890) together with illustrations for which dimensions are provided. Some paragraphs on coins supplement the sections, as does a list of barrows and some observations regarding prehistoric roads. All is concluded by a 'Topographical List of Prehistoric Antiquities in Kent', while an appendix describes the gold bracelets found at Bexley. At the outset a distribution map depicts 'Prehistoric Remains'. Chalkley Gould's 'Ancient Earthworks' lists the earthworks of all ages and has in it a valuable series of pioneer plans, which demand further investigation, survey and record. Until his death in October 1907, I. Chalkley Gould FSA was Hon. Secretary of the Committee on Ancient Earthworks and Fortified Enclosures, set up by the Congress of Archaeological Societies of which his friend J. Horace Round FSA was a member. At the outset of the twentieth century he was probably England's leading field archaeologist and his list in Kent's *Victoria County History* (I, 1908) was one of his last achievements.

In 1881, Frederick V. James (Bowden, 1991, 105) left his post as Assistant Curator at Maidstone's Chillington House Museum and became an archaeological assistant to General Pitt Rivers, who is considered to have revolutionised the processes of excavation and the recording of its results (Wheeler, 1954, 9-14). He trained all his assistants, who were selected for their probity and professional capabilities. There are especial tributes to Frederick James in the prefaces of the first three of the volumes of *Excavations in Cranborne Chase* (1887, 1888 and 1892), who was the principal assistant and who, accordingly, received a superior salary. After a decade with the General, Frederick James left Rushmore in 1891 to return to Maidstone's Museum as curator. Besides his rearrangements of the displays, he made various contributions to Kentish prehistory, notably Bronze Age burials at Aylesford (James 1899; Ashbee, 1997, 150-4). He was also an art historian and a competent linguist. Sadly his tenure (1891-1902) was overshadowed by the overweening George Payne (1848-1920), who, from 1884, became Secretary and curiously, 'Chief Curator' of the Kent Archaeological Society, a position he held until 1904. It would seem that Frederick James was borne down by the pressures exerted upon him and perhaps by a lack of support from his Committee. It appears that he took to drink, left the Museum in 1902, was hospitalised and passed into oblivion. Frederick James, presumably as befitting his decade as Secretary and Principal Excavation Assistant to General Pitt Rivers, always presented himself in a dark suit, topped by a bowler hat. He carried his style into later life and is readily identifiable in certain of H. W. Elgar's photographs of the Medway Valley's sarsen-stone-built long barrows (Ashbee, 1993a, 87, Pl. V).

Payne, in 1893, published his *Collectania Cantiana* which carries on the title-page his styles. Although largely an epitome of his various discoveries, it has in it a useful account, with illustrations, of the Neolithic material from Grovehurst. Despite what may have been personality defects (Woodruff, 1921) he was well thought of and was mooted to assist Pitt Rivers as Assistant Inspector of Ancient Monuments, an appointment that never came to pass.

Sand and gravel extractions since the 1870s, produced the huge pit, now a lake, at Aylesford, north-west of the Church. In November 1886, Arthur Evans (later Sir Arthur) together with his father Dr John Evans (later Sir John) paid a visit to this pit, to search for Palaeolithic implements. However, their attention was taken by

> another and highly interesting discovery that had just been made whilst removing the surface earth ... this consisted of a bronze pail or situla (Evans, 1890, fig. 11) and a small fragment of another, an oenochôe (1890, fig. 14), a long-handled pan or patella (1890, fig. 16) and two filbulae (1890, figs. 17, 18), also of bronze, together with calcined bones and fragments of earthenware vases.

They were, it was alleged by the workmen, in a circular pit, some 5ft 6in in depth. The burned bones were in the bucket, with the other objects close by and the pots, some containing cremated bones, were 'around'. There were, it was claimed, a circle of urns and a large pit filled with animal bones which were 'thrown over a neighbouring field'. The oft repeated illustration of the grave-pit which contained the situla and patella is clearly labelled 'Diagrammatic sketch from account given' (Evans, 1890, 4, fig. 1).

In a sense the archaeology of the pre-Roman Iron Age began in 1890, for Arthur Evans was able to show that the origins of the artifacts were deep in mainland Europe. His conclusions were widely accepted by such as Reginald Smith when he published grave groups encountered at Welwyn (1912). A cemetery at Swarling, close by Canterbury, excavated in 1921 (Bushe-Fox, 1925), led to the concept of the Aylesford-Swarling culture as an intrusive phenomenon prior to the Roman incursions.

A minor revolution in British prehistory began when, in 1920, O.G.S. Crawford became Archaeology Officer of the Ordnance Survey. He was, in 1927, the founder and editor of the journal *Antiquity*. His years with the Ordnance Survey are entertainingly delineated in his autobiography (Crawford, 1955, 154-278) and he edited *Antiquity* until his death in 1957. During the last two years of his life, after a visit, with R.L.S. Newall, to the present writer's excavations at Amesbury in 1956, he became an archaeological uncle who sent searching letters upon European matters that had to be given careful answers. Last encountered at the Fussell's Lodge long barrow excavations, his demise left a considerable gap in our national ranks. His mind was much concerned with maps (Crawford, 1955, 216) and his contribution to Kentish prehistory was, in 1924, *Ordnance Survey, Professional Papers – New Series No. 8, Notes on Archaeological Information incorporated in the Ordnance Survey Maps, Part 2, The Long Barrows and Megaliths in the Area covered by sheet 12 of the ¼ inch map (Kent, Surrey and Sussex)*. Prefaced by a full-sized reproduction of Stukeley's engraving of the Kit's Coty House long barrow, there is a succinct descriptive text and a tabulation of the long barrows of Kent and Sussex. He listed four readily recognisable Kentish long barrows, namely Addington, Coldrum, Kit's Coty House and Julliberrie's Grave. Thereafter he had the category 'Burial Chambers', sites where no remains of a mound were visible or recorded, followed by two instances of 'Megalithic Remains' probably burial chambers. Hubert Elgar, of Maidstone's Museum, provided most of the bibliographical references and accompanied Crawford on his scrutiny of the various sites. There were plans and a map excerpt of the Medway Valley with symbols denoting the various sites. There were plans of the earthen long barrows on the Downs of Sussex, with plans by Herbert Toms (Bradley, 1989) who, like Frederick James, had been an assistant of General Pitt Rivers and was, in 1924, curator of Brighton's Museum. For Kent there was a map excerpt showing the sites and their relationship with gaps and rivers. Crawford was not unacquainted with Kent beyond the stone-built long barrows. In *Wessex from the Air* (Crawford and Keiller, 1928, 254-6) there is a chapter on kite-shaped earthworks, which is illustrated by a detailed plan, by A.H.A Hogg, of such an earthwork in Mangravet Wood, near Maidstone (1925, 255, fig.61), showing that a Roman road was aligned upon it. It was an outlier of the Loose *oppidum* (Kelly, 1971).

He also traced the Roman road southwards from Rochester into the Weald and photographed the paved ford at Benenden. In his foreword to I.D. Margary's book (1948) on such roads, he commended the pursuit of lesser roads and terrace-ways, which could be of earlier origins. He found East Kent attractive and, in the 1930s, little known, and his 'Field Notes in the Canterbury District' (1934) reflect his interest. He attracted a *Festschrift* (Grimes (ed.) 1951) and its papers, many of which are relevant even to today's endeavours, depict prehistory in action at the outset of the 1950s.

A remarkable book, romantically entitled *In Kentish Pilgrimland* by William Coles Finch, the Rochester topographical writer, who had written about water and the countryside, appeared in 1927. Its 300 pages were illustrated by about 100 plates of mostly ancient and historical monuments and, more importantly, some 10 of these were of the remnants of the stone-built long barrows, on both sides of the Medway Valley, depicting them as they were at the conclusion of the First World War. The two final chapters describe them in general terms, which were pleasant and, as an introduction, informative. The plate opposite p. 267, scaled by the author's son, is the first, and probably the last, picture of the Coffin Stone to be published before another great stone was set upon it.

A near forgotten landmark, indeed, a benchmark, in the progress of Kent's prehistory was the publication in 1930, of *The Archaeology of Kent* by Ronald F. Jessup. It was the second of a county Archaeologies series of which only eight appeared. Considered as progeny of the Victoria County Histories, they proceeded, period by period, following the format of Sir John Lubbock's *Prehistoric Times* (1865). It was unique among the series in that Kent is likely to have been a distinctive territory in earlier prehistory, emerging as the territory of the *Cantiaci*, when Caesar sailed from Gaul. Reviewed in *Archaeologia Cantiana* (XLIII (1931), 304-7) by R.E.M. Wheeler, (later Sir Mortimer) it was for the most part highly commended. It was felt, however, that much more might have been made of environmental factors to the extent of a map depicting their basis, for it was clear that Jessup was alive to them. He concluded by saying that the book was 'The first substantive work of a young and able archaeologist who should go far in the service of his county'. As is noted in the preface, Hubert Elgar provided photographs, inexplicably over-reduced, and it is noted that Norman Cook, then Keeper of Archaeology and Sub-Curator at Maidstone's Museum, had in mind work upon aspects of Kentish prehistory. Apart from the Roman Occupation and the Anglo-Saxons, pagan and Christian, the book was a survey of Kent's prehistory, supplemented by a Gazetteer, replete with accurate references. It is said that some 60,000 Palaeolithic implements are known from Swanscombe alone, the Mesolithic and Neolithic are compounded from flints, the megalithic long barrow remains are comprehensively described, as is the Bronze Age, by beakers and later bronzes, while the Early Iron Age has all the characteristics of a launching pad for further research. Later in 1933 that research came to pass, for Ronald Jessup led an investigation of Bigbury Camp, at Harbledown (Jessup, 1933b; Jessup and Cook, 1936), supported by, besides Norman Cook, Stuart Piggott. Plate 1 of the 1936 narrative is historic in that recognisable figures are at work above the orchard. The plan, sections and pottery drawings were in advance of anything that had gone before in the county. Later, during 1936 and 1937, the seemingly solitary earthen long barrow, Julliberrie's Grave, at Chilham, above East Kent's Stour Valley, was investigated (Jessup, 1937; 1939; Ashbee, 1996). It was without burials, its northern end had been truncated, and there was a broken 'Northern' flint axe from the loam core, while it had Romano-British burials at its southern end. Recently two more apparent long barrows have been found in the Stour Valley, at Boughton Aluph and Elmstead.

Ronald Jessup (1906-91) was a busy banker until 1967. After war service, his primary interests moved to Romano-British and Anglo-Saxon archaeology. A notable undertaking was his excavation of the Roman barrow, at Holborough, Snodland, (Jessup, 1954), trenched by Thomas Wright in 1844, and left isolated by a great chalk quarry. Notable also was his work on Anglo-Saxon jewellery, published in 1974. During the 1930s, Ronald Jessup and L.V. Grinsell, listed the barrows of Kent with a joint paper in mind. Sadly the notes were destroyed during World War 2 by enemy action but, however, Leslie Grinsell (1992) has given us a view of what the paper might have been.

Ronald Jessup (1930, 28-34) made reference to various human bones found in North Kent and here, usually because they were dug from gravels, as 'remains of men of the Old Stone Age'. These have long since been shown as from more recent interments. However, in 1935 at Swanscombe, part of a human occipital bone was found in the Upper Middle Gravel, with handaxes, by A.T. Marston of Clapham, who visited the pit, from time to time, in search of implements. They were 24ft from the surface and a preliminary notice of their discovery appeared in Nature (Oct. 19, 1935, 637). He kept a look out for further pieces and, on 15 March 1936, Marston found a left parietal bone, which articulated with the occipital, which was again reported in Nature (August 1936).

On the eve of World War 2, the many enterprises and investigations by J.P.T. Burchell (Jacobi, 1982, 22) led to his finding of 'Decorated prehistoric pottery from the bed of the Ebbsfleet, Northfleet' in 1938 (Burchell and Piggott, 1939). Ebbsfleet ware, as it came to be called (Piggott, 1954,308), subsequently recognised at a number of sites, emerged as the prototype for the later Mortlake tradition. Despite the war, the Kent Archaeological Society continued to issue *Archaeologia Cantiana*. In 1941 this contained valuable accounts of earthworks in Joyden's Wood, Bexley and on Hayes and West Wickham commons (Hogg,

1941; 1971; Hogg, O'Neil and Stevens, 1941) and was followed in 1942 by details of 'Two Burial Groups of Belgic Age, Hothfield Common' encountered during the digging of a military drainage sump. A map reference was given and the contributor was J.G.S. Brinson Lt. R.E. (1943). Photographs with scales illustrated the vessels, as did a plan. Another paper, by C.F.C. Hawkes (1942), was published in the *Proceedings of the Prehistoric Society*, entitled 'The Deverel Urn and the Picardy pin: a phase of Bronze Age settlement in Kent'. Emerging from this was the observation that later Bronze Age Kent, by adopting pins and bracelets, was different from southern England in that these artifacts indicated mainland European usages. A year later, in the same national journal, there appeared F.H. Worsfold's (1943) details of pits, pottery, a later Bronze Age hoard, wooden structural remains and palaeobotanical material from a wetland foreshore site at Minnis Bay, in Thanet.

During the 1930s, when Norman Cook was Sub-Curator and Keeper of Archaeology, Maidstone's Museum was, in a sense, the nerve centre of Kentish prehistory. R.F. Jessup paid tribute to it, and to Norman Cook, at the outset of his book, while such as Stuart Piggott, Grahame Clark and others who constructed British prehistory were visitors. With the untimely demise of Hubert Elgar, the museum's direction had fallen into the hands of A.C. Golding (Cook, 1950). In 1937 Norman Cook was invited by Alexander Keiller to succeed Stuart Piggott as Principal Archaeologist at Avebury. He was conscious that his future at Maidstone would be bleak and thus the invitation was accepted. Thereafter Maidstone's Museum became a static institution, library and sources of reference closed off and inaccessible, until Golding's retirement in 1948. However, in 1948, a visit found hitherto barred book-stacks open, tables and chairs piled high with albums, files and papers, all backed by Allen Grove's friendly, welcoming, smile.

With the advent of Allen Grove, the museum at Maidstone, which houses also the Kent Archaeological Society's library and collections, became once again a live institution, promoting whenever possible, prehistory in the county. One of his first contributions (Grove, 1952) was the discovery of Beale Poste's details of his barrow excavations at Whiteheath, Hollingbourne, together with depictions of Bronze Age urns and various Anglo-Saxon pieces. Subsequently (Kelly, 1976, 232) the Whiteheath artifacts came to light when the residue of the Leeds Castle estate was sold and the three earlier Bronze Age urns (Champion, 1982, 33, fig.11, 5, 6) were presented to the museum. Allen Grove was a scholar and antiquary, in the best sense of the term, with a wide-ranging insight into archaeology, and sadly his kind has now vanished. Shallow-minded 'collections managers' and similar functionaries, now reign supreme. One wishes that Allen had written more pertaining to Kentish prehistory but, nonetheless, during his quarter-century and more at Maidstone's Museum he encouraged and advised many.

Besides the assistance given to visiting scholars to the museum, notable among the enterprises that Allen Grove advised during the earlier post-war years, were J.H. Money's (1963; 1970) Iron Age hillfort work in the Tonbridge area and that by N. Piercy Fox (1969; 1970) at Caesar's Camp at Keston and Squerryes at Westerham. There was also D.B. Kelly's assessment of the Quarry Wood, Loose, *oppidum*, its linear boundaries and associated earthworks (1971). David Kelly, who had been at the University of London's Institute of Archaeology, was initially Allen Grove's assistant and thereafter his successor at Maidstone's museum.

Beginning with a round barrow in Wales, a system for the excavation of prehistoric and other ancient monuments was brought into being by the Ancient Monuments Inspectorate of the Office (later Ministry) of Works. This scheme of excavation of threatened sites was piloted throughout the war and the critical post-war years, by B.H. St J. O'Neil, Inspector for Wales and later Chief Inspector of Ancient Monuments from 1945 to his untimely death in 1954, championed by the Assistant Secretary of the Ministry, Dr F.T.E. Raby, who returned to Jesus College, Cambridge, in 1948. The only excavation carried out in Kent during these troubled times was at Manston, where Iron Age pits and hollows yielded a sequence of Iron Age pottery in quantity. (O'Neil, 1948, 29). The remains of a ring-ditch were recorded at the same time.

Despite the considerable resources of the post-war Ministry of Works, there were dimensions of what is today termed 'rescue archaeology' that evaded it. Since the 1950s, beginning with a sea-encroachment situation at Reculver, Kentish rescue archaeology has been synonymous with Brian Philp (2002). By 1960 he had brought into being the Bromley and West Kent Group, followed by the Council for Kentish Archaeology in 1964, and in 1971 the Kent Archaeological Rescue Unit. Initially supported financially by English Heritage, the examination of ancient sites when development is envisaged is now paid for by the developers. During the past half-century something in the order of 600 sites within the county have been excavated and published, while a number have been subject to preservation and presentation. Some 50 sites of substance are summarised in Brian Philp's lucid, and often entertaining, book *Archaeology in the Front Line* (2002, Dover), and this includes some which have significantly extended the perceived nature of Kent's prehistory. There are, briefly, the later Neolithic site, with flints and pottery, at Baston Manor, Hayes, encountered in 1964, and the Neolithic Lake at Darenth which yielded palaeobotanical material in profusion. Of particular note is the later Bronze Age occupation site at Sheerness, which has unique qualities and the Iron Age farm on Farningham Hill. Rescue Archaeology is now a vital component of the archaeological establishment. In Kent, Brian Philp's endeavours have served us well, and in the land at large these have been emulated in detail.

As new formations in archaeology emerged, the passing of the years saw the demise of some who, living in particular areas of Kent, had assiduously monitored local earth-moving enterprises and thus rescued and published a wealth of material pertaining to both antiquity at large and specific areas of prehistory. Pre-eminent among these were W.P.D. Stebbing of Deal and J.P.T. Burchell who lived near Sevenoaks. William Pinckard Delane Stebbing (1873-1961) came to live in Deal during 1920. He began life as an engineer and architect and turned to the Geological Association in 1895, becoming its President from 1940 to 1942. In 1925 he joined the Kent Archaeological Society and was elected an FSA in 1926. Besides his antiquarian interests he pursued prehistory, isolating and recording Neolithic pottery sites, Bronze Age remains and Iron Age material, particularly within the loam terrain inland from Deal. James Perry Tufnal Burchell M.C. (1898-1979) served in the Welsh Guards in both wars and was awarded the Military Cross in the first, at much the same time as he joined the Prehistoric Society of East Anglia which became the Prehistoric Society without qualification in 1935. His interests were often in the interface between prehistory and its environmental concerns. Of particular note was his isolation of the Mesolithic site on the edge of an extinct channel of the Medway (Clark, 1932, 63-5, fig.33). Indeed, when Grahame Clark viewed *The Mesolithic Settlement of Northern Europe* (1936), he was acknowledged in the preface and his work to date in this dimension, notably a series of papers in the *Proceedings of the Prehistoric Society of East Anglia* was a major inclusion in the bibliography. In 1946, when at Broadstairs, a shaft, thought of initially as a dene-hole, was revealed by a chalk-pit at Hammill, near Woodnesborough (Ogilvie, 1982), Burchell examined it and excavated, at some risk, within it, for about two years. It proved to be more than 70ft (22m) in depth and a broken Romano-Belgic pot was at the bottom. He thought of it as a ritual shaft, of which a few examples were known on the European mainland, and his paper at Burlington House, to the Society of Antiquaries of London, had a mixed reception. Subsequent research in Germany (Schwarz, 1962) and on Salisbury Plain (Ashbee *et al*, 1989) have shown the cogency of his observations and he emerges, clearly, as a pioneer in this dimension.

Apart from small-scale digging into the Kit's Coty House and Addington long barrows (Ashbee, 1983, 73, 91) and F.J. Bennett's investigations at Coldrum (Bennett, 1913; Ashbee, 1998) there was little known in detail regarding either their nature or the reason for their comprehensive ruination. However, during 1957 because of the impending construction of a house and the sequestration of the land for horticulture, the group of large sarsen stones, known as the Chestnuts, at no great distance from Addington's long barrow, was subjected to excavation. There was financial support from Richard Boyle Esqre, the landowner, buttressed by the resources of the Ancient Monuments Inspectorate of the Ministry of Works. The undertaking was directed by John Alexander (1961), now a Fellow of St John's College, Cambridge, supported by Laurence Barfield and Paul Ozamie also from Cambridge. It emerged that there were stoneholes and it was possible to pull their appropriate stones back to the vertical. There emerged a rectangular chamber remnant flanked by façade stones. Pits with pottery, at stone-bases, depicted a planned mode of demolition during the thirteenth century AD. The removal of barrows and systematic stone-chamber felling was a fate that befell the entire group.

Publications rather than personalities are the pattern of much of prehistory because writers were far-removed from the county. In 1912, there appeared from the Oxford University Press the two considerable volumes of the Hon. John Abercromby's *Study of the Bronze Age Pottery of Great Britain and Ireland*, which depicted four Kentish beakers (Nos. 34-37). It was a basic work of reference until 1970, in which year there appeared David Clarke's *Beaker Pottery of Great Britain and Ireland* (Cambridge) which detailed 1087 of these distinctive vessels and included 37 (Nos. 384-414) from Kent, with details of location and publication. This was followed, in 1980 by Joan J. Taylor's *Bronze Age Goldwork of the British Isles* (Cambridge). Almost 40 Kentish discoveries are considered which include the torcs and bracelets from the Medway at Aylesford. This Gulbenkian trio was completed by Ian Longworth's *Collared Urns of the Bronze Age* (Cambridge) in 1984. Curiously, only 10 Kentish sites have yielded these significant, and sometimes spectacular, vessels.

Although the study of art, mostly flamboyant metalwork, of the pre-Roman Iron Age peoples, termed 'Celtic', was introduced early in the twentieth century by J. Romilly Allen's (1904) *Celtic Art in Pagan and Christian Times*, a work which considered the exotic objects from the Aylesford cemetery, besides pieces from Canterbury and Folkestone, it was the publication by the Oxford University Press, in 1944 (2nd ed. 1969), of Paul Jacobsthal's volumes of text and illustrations that made English prehistorians conscious of this heritage. Jacobsthal was a refugee from Nazi Germany who, in 1935, was given a haven in Oxford. The work, begun in 1933, is essentially an examination of the Celtic art phenomenon across the European mainland. Domicile in England allowed the incorporation of English material, notably the Aylesford bucket and a brooch from Deal. Gaps in the narrative were explained by war and mention was made of a work on Celtic Art in the British Isles in preparation. Sadly Paul Jacobsthal died in 1957 but, happily, his work was continued by Martyn Jope, who had known him in Oxford and was at that time Professor of Archaeology in Belfast. Although much of Martyn Jope's *Early Celtic Art in the British Isles* (Oxford, 2000) was written during the 1960s, he concluded it in 1996, shortly before his demise. Although the textual volume is analytical and geared to the volume of illustrations, a wealth of Kentish material is detailed and depicted. As in Jacobstahl's volumes, the exotic objects, salvaged by Sir Arthur Evans at Aylesford (1890), take pride of place with eight revealing illustrations. Thereafter there is the famous Bapchild terret, followed by pieces from Canterbury, Deal, Faversham, Minster and Richborough. Each is accorded a description, with provenance and primary sources.

One has moved from Kentish antiquaries to their activities and publications, and in the present time we are faced with various discoveries that are products of our much-debated rescue archaeology (Jones, 1984), which is now a significant dimension of prehistoric archaeology at large. At Dover a Bronze Age sewn-plank boat was found, in waterlogged conditions, deep beneath Townwall Street (Parfitt, 1993), while at Deal, Iron Age burials, associated with the remains of a large Bronze Age round barrow, yielded a warrior burial and the remains of an individual adorned with a diadem (Parfitt, 1991, 1995). Work by the Canterbury Archaeological Trust (1991), preliminary to the Channel Tunnel Terminal, described an integrated pattern of Neolithic, Bronze Age and Iron Age occupation and land-use, together with a wealth of environmental material, while on Blue Bell Hill the remains of an apparent Neolithic long house were found, beneath hillwash, by excavations on the line of the projected Channel Tunnel railway (Glass, 1999, 192). Metal detection at Chilham led to the excavation of an Iron Age burial, furnished with a mirror and brooch by an inurned cremation (Parfitt, 1998), the first of its kind in Kent. An unexpectedly dramatic addition to the knowledge of the territory that is Kent has been the revelations regarding the emergence of what was to become Romney Marsh and occupation there in earlier Bronze Age and Iron Age times (Eddison, 2000, 30-41). Even more recently, metal detection upon the site of a razed round barrow, came upon a crushed advanced Early Bronze Age gold cup, comparable with that found at Rillaton, in Cornwall early in the nineteenth century. Excavation subsequent to the cup's discovery revealed the magnitude of the barrow (Parfitt, 2002). Those who conducted the excavations relevant to these discoveries have, despite the exigencies of rescue archaeology, worked with precision and insight, while all that has been published regarding them is a cardinal addition to our perspectives and has changed, and is changing, our knowledge of Kent's prehistory.

Kent, perhaps more than any of the regions of England which have within their bounds patent evidence of our prehistoric past, is a microcosm of the development of its pursuit and study. The Ancient British and later Druidical notions from the seventeenth and eighteenth centuries passed away (Piggott, 1989), to be replaced by the revelations of the antiquity of man which marked the nineteenth century (Casson, 1940, 155-201), besides the emergence of a pattern of prehistory (Lubbock, 1865). Between the wars of the twentieth century prehistory came of age and in great measure, we are building up the notions and activities of those who have been termed 'The Pastmasters' (Daniel and Chippindale, 1989). During the 1920s, outstanding figures such as O.G.S. Crawford (1955) and R.E.M. Wheeler (Hawkes, 1982) were concerned with Kent, as were during the 1930s, Grahame Clark (Fagan, 2001), Glyn Daniel (1986), Christopher Hawkes (Webster, 1991), Charles Phillips (1987), Stuart Piggott (1983) and Gordon Childe (Trigger, 1980; Green, 1981), the generation that largely created British prehistory. The post-war years, because of totalitarian agriculture, were remembered by the unprecedented destruction of barrows and other earthworks (Ashbee, 1960, 196-8). This led, in the 1970s, to the emergence of rescue archaeology as a signal dimension of our endeavours (Jones, 1984), a process brought about by the inertia and ineffectiveness of those charged with the care of our countryside and its ancient monuments. At the present time, British prehistory, from the exercise of archaeology, is served by numerous professional groups and units. Kent has been well served by Brian Philp's (2002) outstanding accomplishments, while the archaeological groups of East Kent, led by Keith Parfitt's pursuit of prehistory, have dramatically changed many long-cherished concepts. Since 1857, *Archaeologia Cantiana,* the journal of Kent's remarkable and well-supported Archaeological Society, based in Maidstone, has had a record of prehistory in its pages, and volume CXXII has appeared this year (2005). As Collingwood (1939; 1946) emphasised, any record of the past is from the exercise of the historian's (archaeologist's) mind. In this dimension – prehistory – Kent has, when scrutinised, an enviable record.

TWO

ENVIRONMENTAL CONSIDERATIONS

A pioneer assessment of Kent's environmental background was, back in 1982, written by Joan Sheldon at that time in the University of London's Institute of Archaeology. Presciently, she said that much work remains to be done before a detailed delineation of the county's early environment can emerge. Now, more than two decades later, certain issues can be seen with, perhaps, a greater measure of clarity but many elements are still opaque. Happily, few present-day excavations are conducted without thought to environmental issues (Cant. Arch. Trust, 1991, 7).

Today's Kent is a territory bounded upon three sides by the sea and of a form determined by the Holocene rise of mean sea-level. Its geological structure, a part of the Wealden system (Gallois, 1965, 1), is a series of strata, running from west to east and the sea. Their soil-determining characteristics are likely to have been the basis of differing environments which were settled by mankind after the climatic amelioration following upon the last, Devensian, glaciation. The county's south-western land boundary, the Weald (Rackham, 1986, 11, fig.2, 13) and its forest lands, have for long been thought of as unfavourable for settlement (Jessup, 1930, 59), but, nonetheless, there is evidence of movement therein from Mesolithic times onwards (Jessup, 1950, 127, Evans, 1975, 103, fig.42) The linear geological strata are cut through by north-flowing rivers, the Darent, Medway and Stour. It can be thought of as a topography that imposes certain behavioural patterns upon human communities.

Kent assumed a near-recognisable form during the later Holocene, this being the time since the last retreat of the Polar ice in the northern hemisphere until the present day. A glaciation, that is an expansion of the Polar ice, resulted in an enormous quantity of the world's water being locked up as ice, and therefore low sea-levels. Conversely, climatic amelioration brings about the melting and retreat of the ice and a corresponding rise of sea-level. Such sea-level movements are termed eustatic and are accompanied by isostatic movements of the earth's crust when relieved of the enormous weight of the ice. Britain's present-day coasts and islands can be seen as resulting from interrelated eustasy and isostasy. Our rivers have deep sunken channels brought about by erosion when sea-levels were low, while higher levels, particularly in Kent, deposited the gravel terraces in which Palaeolithic implements are frequently found (Drewett *et al*, 1988, 3, fig. 1)

As during the earlier cold stages of the British Quaternary Period (Wymer, 1982, 15, tab. 2) Kent, during the last Devensian glaciation, when sea-level was 100m, that is more than 900ft, below that of today, would have been no more than a tract of land within a considerable westward extension of what is today the European mainland. The ice advanced southwards to what is now Norfolk's northern coasts, as attested by the great moraine. Despite claims to the contrary there is nothing to suggest that Kent was subjected to the exactions of glaciation. Rather, the area would have been largely barren and in the grip of of harsh periglacial climatic conditions such as would have fostered the deposit of aeolian loess as in Pegwell Bay (Kerney, 1965), while permafrost, with seasonal freezing and thawing, was coupled with solifluction, particularly on the fore and backsbopes of the North Downs, However during the warmer Holocene the sea-levels rose and by about 7-8000 years before the present Britain was an island and Kent an entity (Coles, 1998, 68, fig. 11). Nonetheless, the English Channel would have been narrower and, in what is now the southern North Sea, an archipelago of islands, akin to those of Denmark which impede the outflow of the Baltic, would have moderated the meeting of the waters. Their remnants are the shoals, such as the Kentish Knock, while the famed Goodwin sands testify to a former land extension. The area would have been a contact zone, for boat crossings of such waters would have presented few problems (Clark, 1975, 124; Jacobi, 1982, 14; Christensen, 1999).

From later Mesolithic times onwards the terrain that is now Kent, although separated from the European mainland, would have been much greater in area than it is today, although it would have progressively diminished because of the inexorable rises of sea-level, together with coastal denudation and lowland inundation (Coles, 1998). Lower Halstow (Clark, 1936, 158) would have been on dry land, far from the river. Sheppey in Neolithic times, as illustrated by its causewayed enclosure (Dyson *et al*, 2000, 471-2), would have been a part of a considerably northwards-extending lowland, while coastal sites known at Tankerton and Herne Bay would have been inland. The later Bronze Age site at Minnis Bay (Worsfold, 1943) also indicates land to northwards, while Thanet's chalklands may have been almost twice their present area. The loamy land-loss in the Deal region would have been considerable while the white cliffs of Dover have truncated the hillfort (Colvin, 1959) occupied by the medieval castle (Chalkley Gould, 1908, 414). Indeed, when initially sited and constructed it could have been almost a mile from the sea-cliffs. Considerable areas of land to seawards survived in north-eastern Kent into historic times (So, 1971).

Kent has a variety of landscape brought about by its solid geology (7), which has determined contrasting regions. Indeed, it is a northern, considerable part of the Weald (Wooldridge & Goldring, 1962; Gallois, 1965), an eroded chalk anticline. The Higher Weald consists of the Hastings Beds, dominated by the Tunbridge Wells Sands, with exposures of the Wadhurst Clays and some Ashdown Sands. Northward there is the Lower Weald which is the obdurate, impermeable, Wealden Clay. This is followed by the Lower Greensand ridge and its localised members. One of these, the Hythe Beds, is the source of the Kentish Ragstone, a hard blueish-grey rock. These merge into yellow or white sands with, sometimes, beds of clay. To move from the Lower Weald up onto the Lower Greensand, one is confronted by a dramatic, massive escarpment in the early days of ubiquitous bicycles and early motor-cars the descent, or ascent, of such hills as Linton, Sutton

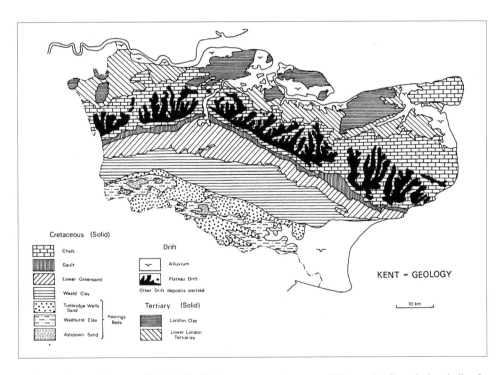

7 The geology of Kent: unlike the South Downs, extensive areas of Plateau Drift mask the chalk of much of the North Downs. The erstwhile Wantsum Channel is now alluvium, as are the areas of the North Kent Marshes. *After P. Burnham and S. Mcrae, 1978*

Valence or Hythe, could be hazardous. Between the Greensand ridge and the considerable chalk escarpment of the North Downs one encounters the Gault, a dark blueish-grey clay which could expand when wet in winter and contract and harden in summer. With exceptions, it has been avoided by all but ephemeral settlement. The chalk of the North Downs, East Kent and the Isle of Thanet presents to southwards, for the great part, escarpments which are, in places, 200m (600ft) in height. Here and there the Lower Chalk extrudes at the foot-slopes where it is masked by solifluction deposits and more recent hillwash (Glass, 1999, 192; 2000, 453, pl.1). The Middle Chalk, whiter than the Lower Chalk's yellow tinge and with few flints, makes up most of the escarpment, and the trackway, popularly called the Pilgrim's Way, follows the interface. Most of the dipslope of the North Downs is the soft, white Upper Chalk, with its bands of flint, which also underlies the Isle of Thanet. To what extent this flint was exploited is not known, for nothing comparable with the Sussex flint mines (Curwen, 1954, 96-141) has as yet been encountered. Clay with flints caps the North Downs, with some sands, gravels and an admixture of loess. A well-developed system of dry valleys characterises the dipslope and in some winters waters appear. To the north of the chalky North Downs, Grain, Sheppey and a considerable area north of Canterbury and the chalk region are of London Clay, largely bracketed by alluvium and seated upon the Lower London Tertiaries.

In North Kent, marshes are associated with the estuaries of the Thames and Medway and also fringe the Swale, which gives Sheppey the status of an island. The marshy outlet of the Stour merges with the erstwhile Wantsum which, until Roman or later times, was sea-serviced, making Thanet a separate island domain. Romney Marsh, an area of about 100 square miles, is the infill of a broad bay, bounded to landward by fossil cliffs cut into the Wealden series, and, seaward, stretching from Fairlight to Hythe. Whereas prehistoric accumulations and surfaces must exist at depths yet to be determined beneath most of our marshland, traces of Bronze Age, and later Iron Age, activities have emerged from the shingle spits of Dungeness (Eddison, 2000, 37-41).

Pioneer palaeobotanical investigation was undertaken during the 1920s when a late Mesolithic series of flint-surrounded hearths was investigated at Lower Halstow on the edge of the marsh-sealed sunken channel of the Medway (Burchell, 1925; 1927; 1928; Clark 1932, 63-65; 1936, 158-60). Samples of clay, from beneath the flint working floors, and from the peat mantle pollen (analysed by G. Erdtman), showed oak as the dominant tree and that pine had given way to lime. Although geared to Roman and post-Roman considerations the paper 'Archaeological horizons in the North Kent Marshes' (Evans, 1953) provided a searching insight into their characteristics and later development which could be an effective basis for, particularly, the Medway's buried channel exploration and assessment. An aspect is the cyclic nature of the depositions of alluvial clays and peat formation recorded in a Chatham Dockyard installation excavation in 1923. Nonetheless, there were irregularities, as at Hoo Fort, although work on the Isle of Grain showed a degree of harmony between the Thames and Medway succession of alluvial deposits. It should be observed that the process of new channel formation and redeposition of peats could have taken place even in prehistory. More recently there has been work regarding the Thames estuary (Devoy, 1979; 1980) which has shown that Fagus (Beech) was established even before the allegedly anthropogenic elm (Ulmus) decline of about 5000-6000 years BP. At a later juncture there is evidence of woodland recession associated with agriculture, which includes a Tilia (Lime) decline (Turner, 1962), but, notwithstanding, changing soil regimes could well have been unpropitious for a particular species. Five marine transgressions have been traced in the Thames estuarine region, the earliest some 8000 years BP and the most recent about 1800 years BP (Devoy, 1980). There are, nonetheless, difficulties brought about by such factors as differential sediment shrinkage and tidal position (Ackeroyd, 1972). However, down the years, salt-marsh, sedge-fen and reed-swamps, and the wider woodlands of the estuarine areas, would have been, because of their hunting, catching and gathering potential, a prime source of sustenance from Mesolithic times onwards (Devoy, 1980).

Alluvial marshlands mark the erstwhile Wantsum Channel which separated Thanet from Kent, making it an island, and flank the lower reaches of the Great and Little Stour and other north-flowing streams (Coleman & Lukehurst, 1967, 16; Hawkes, 1968) During the Pleistocene the Stour had a northwards course and flowed into the Thames, and remnants of its gravel terraces can still be traced near Reculver. Climatic amelioration, leading to the post-Devensian rise of sea-level, drowned a shallow syncline in the chalk, capturing the Great Stour, which was tidal to Fordwich. The alluvial silting process is likely to have been advanced by Roman times, although it is alleged that the last vessel used the sea channel during the seventeenth century. Much, however, must have been marshlands. Yet it is likely that there is some 50ft of alluvial mud mantling the surface of the syncline. Thus it could be examined by boring and palaeobotanical study which could yield information for a basis for the assessment of East Kent's environmental changes in prehistory.

The lighthouse and power station surmounted promontory of Dungeness is the apex of a series of shingle ridges, many at near right angles to the present coastline (Gallois, 1965, 81, fig.20, pl.XIII, A). Romney Marsh, as the general area is known, together with Denge and Welland Marshes, are the areas behind the shingle which once barred Dymchurch Bay. They also include the Levels of Broomhill, East Guildeford, New Romney and Pett. It is a series of sediments, in places as much as 33m (100ft) in depth, occupying a bay cut into the Wealden Clay and Hastings Beds, enclosed to landward by fossil cliffs. For more than a century its nature has been controversial but, recently, a series of seminal studies have outlined the work, discussing its problems and indicating the investigations of the Geological Survey (Cunliffe, 1980; Eddison *et al*, 1998; Eddison, 2000). Isolated radiocarbon dates (Cunliffe, 1980, 42) suggest forest conditions at about 3000 years BP while Bronze Age axes have been found near Lydd (Eddison, 2000, 37-41, fig.12). An apparent timber corduroy causeway has come to light close by. While as yet little is known of the shingle ridges and the marsh in prehistory, various inherent possibilities present themselves. First of all it is possible to fish with lines from the shingle shoreline, while a system termed 'kiddle fishing' (Eddison, 2002, 150), a form of trapping, could have been effective. To complement this, the extensive evolving marshlands, as for example in the vicinity of the Medway estuary, would have been a fertile field for fowling and freshwater fish (Clark, 1989, *passim*).

Kent, even today, is one of the most extensively wooded parts of England. Areas such as the back-slopes of the North Downs or the great arc of woodland north of Canterbury, parts of the Greensand Ridge, such as Kingswood or Mereworth Woods and areas of the Weald, High and Low, are densely mantled. Some of the wooded land is deemed to be of poor quality, to the extent that Kentish woodlands, and the nature of their geology, need detailed study. Much of the woodland, during the present writer's lifetime, was regularly coppiced, fencing and hop-poles being a principal product. There is in England at large a considerable body of evidence, from Neolithic times onwards, for coppicing (Rackham, 1986, 737) and there is every reason to suppose that this practice obtained in our Kentish woodlands, where giant coppice-stools can be of considerable antiquity (Rackham, 1976, 29).

It has for long been claimed that our deciduous forests were cleared to facilitate Neolithic agriculture, often by burning. Massive trees are not easy to burn *in situ* and it is more likely that they were ring-barked and left to die. The forging of breaks in the forest canopy, which could eventually lead to heathland, began in the Mesolithic when fire was used upon flammable secondary growths. Thus such clearances are likely to have been the areas for agricultural development which, in time, brought about progressive deforestation and soil impoverishment in various environmentally sensitive areas.

From the earliest times, humankind used wood as fuel for cooking, heating and ritual purposes. Presumably the various regions of proffered sources which were preferred and were used, perhaps, for specific tasks. Timbers of some substance, and in quantity, would have been needed for the construction of megalithic long barrows in the Medway Valley (Ashbee, 2000) and the ostensible long house (Glass, 1999, 192, fig.2). The logboats such as have been found at Erith, Woolwich and Murston (Fox, 1928, 148; Jessup, 1930, 96), and such as the Dover boat (Parfitt, 1993), would have demanded trees only used after a careful, wide-ranging, selective process. Certain long barrows used structural timbers on a lavish scale (Ashbee, 1966) although such situations have not as yet been encountered in Kent. In marshy areas timber causeways, often of considerable length, were regularly constructed (Coles & Coles, 1986). Furthermore, there would, in Kent, as elsewhere, be ample opportunities provided by the deciduous woodlands for the creation of wooden bowls, tubs, troughs, bows, axe and adze hafts, ladles, disc-wheels and carts. Wedge-splitting, axe-shaping and smoothing by abrasion were the techniques of production. Wood-turning was apparently an Iron Age introduction and the hubs of chariots, for example, were a product of this process. Considerable numbers, some 4000 chariots, were fielded by the Kentish tribes who opposed Caesar (Webster & Dudley, 1965, 334). These betoken a considerable fighting vehicle industry not to mention the breeding, maintenance and sustenance of the ponies. Wooden artifacts regularly come to light when wetland sites are excavated (Coles & Lawson, 1987). Nonetheless anerobic conditions can obtain in the most unexpected situations, for example the Bronze Age chalkland pond-barrow shaft at Wilsford, less than a mile from Stonehenge (Ashbee et al, 1939, 51-67).

Environmental prehistory is today an established endeavour, although from time to time it is far from easy to correlate the results with various emergent views of the wider archaeological issues. Nonetheless, such matters as the early history of cultivated crops and man's influence upon his immediate environment have been illumined by, particularly, palaeobotany. Charcoal identifications give insights into the nature of our woodlands while the exercise of dendrochronology in given localities can have valuable chronological implications. During the past half-century the bones and other animal remains recovered from archaeological sites, as at Deal (Legge, 1995), have given some remarkable insights into the nature of prehistoric communities and their environments (Davis, 1987). Many problems pertinent to animals in prehistory remain to be resolved, one of these being the factors involved in the process of domestication (8). For some early Mesolithic groups, for example those who had been dependant upon reindeer (Clark, 1980, 44-45), the nature of the Weald could have fostered the process of protecting and nurturing certain of principal food animals, such as cattle and ovicaprids, and thus beginning the process. Also to be taken into account is the development of palaeopathology, for much pertaining to the activities of early men has left its mark upon their bones. A pioneer endeavour in this dimension was Sir Arthur Keith's (1913; 1925, 1-22) examination of the bones disinterred from Coldrum's chamber remnant (9) in 1910 (Bennett, 1913) which, among other things, allowed him to aver that they were from a family or family

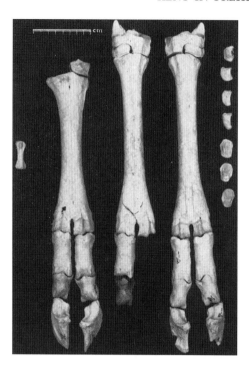

8 Ox feet from the collapsed timber mortuary house of the Fussell's Lodge long barrow. Traces of ox bones were found in the acid soils of the Addington, Chestnuts, stone-built long barrow. *After Caroline Grigson, 1966*

groups (Ashbee, 1998, 27). By contrast the burned bones from the Chestnuts at Addington (Barfield, 1961) allowed no more than the assertion that the remains of nine individuals were present, plus one or two infants.

The molluscan analysis of samples from two sections of hillwash in a coombe at Brook, near Ashford, indicated a woodland environment, with initial clearance during the third millenium BC (Kerney *et al*, 1964). This is complemented by the molluscan evidence from the ancient soil beneath the Julliberrie's Grave long barrow where an open environment preceding the building is indicated (Evans, 1975, 120). Pollen analyses, from a stream valley at Frogholt, near Folkestone, and Wingham, at the northern side of the chalky area, published in a Swiss journal by Sir Harry Godwin, show woodland clearance by Early Bronze Age times. At Wingham, beech (Fagus sylvatica), still to be seen on the chalk today, appeared as a small part of the woodland canopy. Although some areas of downland appear as open from Neolithic and Bronze Age times, there is evidence from the western part of the county which suggests that it was forested to a much later time. Thus wooded conditions obtained in the vicinity of the High Rocks Iron Age hillfort, near Tunbridge Wells (Dimbleby, 1968). Oak, a wood that when burnt produces a considerable heat, was preponderant among the charcoals. Investigation of the ancient surface beneath the initial stage of the inner rampart at Caesar's Camp, Keston (Dimbleby, 1970) showed, from soil pollen, that when it was constructed

9 Coldrum's bones, from a chalky context, are a remnant of a considerable deposit in a longer chamber. The bones illustrated are from a similar chalky context having been interred in a timber mortuary house. Fussell's Lodge Long barrow. *Photograph P. Ashbee, 1957*

the site was mantled by dense oak forest. However, at the Squerryes hillfort, near Westerham (Dimbleby, 1970), there were high forest remnants within cultivation clearances with scrub woodland close by, indicated by podsol pollen beneath the gravel of, again, an inner bank. The podsol is likely to have been of secondary origin, brought about by Bronze Age agriculture.

Kent's environmental prehistory, however, needs further exploration and assessment because of the information harvested when, in 1975, Brian Philp and his colleagues investigated what emerged as a Neolithic body of water, perhaps a small lake, at Darenth (Philp, 2002, 120-4). It had formed in the Darenth valley and peat, sealed by silt and soil-wash, survived. Hazel nuts, elder and raspberry seeds, a cherry stone, beech nuts with bracken, lime, hazel and elder pollen are evidence of gathering. Ox, sheep and pig bones point to stock farming while roe and red deer were hunted or trapped. Radiocarbon dates of 6000-2960 BC encompass the Mesolithic activity, attested by flintwork, which preceded the Neolithic farming. Indeed, these juxtapositions could suggest a Mesolithic-Neolithic transition, a situation comparable with that recently examined in Belgium (Crombé *et al*, 2002) the Neolithic struck flints reflecting changed circumstances.

The recent excavation at Bigberry (*sic*), Harbledown (Thompson, 1983) brought about the examination of what was termed a waterhole. A sample from the infill had in it 60 cereal grains and 27 weed seeds (Jones, 1983). Bread wheat

10 The silted ditch of the Fussell's Lodge long barrow, 1957. Similar ditches attend upon the Kentish chalkland long barrows. Such an accumulation could come about within some three decades. This ditch was some 3.75m (almost 12ft) in depth. *Photograph P. Ashbee, 1957*

(Triticum aestivo-compactum) took precedence, while spelt wheat and six-rowed hulled barley were also present. Among the weeds were vetches (Vici sp.), sheep's sorrel (Rumex acitocella), wild oats (Avena sp.) and Brome grass (Bromus sp.) Such a record of cereals and weeds of cultivation suggest well-organised sources from farmsteads either in the vicinity or, for example, on the Downs at a distance. Sickles were present among the series of iron implements and tools from Bigbury (Thompson, 1983, 265).

Kent's prehistoric earthworks, the barrows, enclosures, hillforts and the like are, for the most part, earthen, in that their material sources were engirdling ditches. A number are upon the chalklands which, as in Wessex, have largely cradled present-day prehistory. It was only during the last part of the nineteenth century that attention was given to the fact that such earthworks as they appear today are the product of complex natural processes, change and decay, in other words weathering and denudation. Mounds and banks have been smoothed and rounded while their attendant ditches and pits, beneath their mantle of turf and mould, were infilled with materials from their reduction and erosion (*10*). Appraisals of the timescales involved in these processes were, despite enlightened incidental observations, inexact, although it was tacitly agreed that initially they would have been speedy. Thus experimental controls or contrived replication, that would give precision to interpretation, were clearly a necessity. To this end two experimental earthworks were planned and built by a committee of the

11 The Overton Down Experimental Earthwork: a three-year accumulation in the ditch. *Photograph P. Ashbee, 1963*

British Association for the Advancement of Science (Ashbee & Jewell, 1998), the first on chalk downland (*11*) (Jewell (ed.), 1963) and the second on gravelly heathland (Evans & Limbrey, 1974). These have already shown that dramatic changes take place in a lifetime and, for example, that a barrow with a raw, chalk-cut, encircling ditch and chalk rubble mound, could have attained much the same form as is seen today within that span (Bell *et al*, 1996, 234-5, 14.1, 14.2). Since the establishment of the earthworks there have been emulations which are either simple forms or, here and there, barrow-like structures. In Kent a small experimental round barrow was built, with central mound, a wide berm, a ditch and internal and external banks. This, in the Monkton Nature Reserve, on the Isle of Thanet, has made particular provision for prevailing weather patterns besides fauna and flora. There has already been colonisation by land molluscs (Jay, 1993). It is now a matter of history that one of the original Experimental Earthworks Committee, as it became known, suggested that an experimental earthwork, conforming to the established pattern, be built upon the Kentish greensands. (Ashbee & Jewell, 1998, 502). Sadly it was impossible to find a suitable site which could proffer an appropriate security of tenure.

An archaeological experiment of particular relevance to Kent is the Ancient Farm Project at Butser, in Hampshire (Reynolds, 1979). There, using the excavated evidence from sites such as Little Woodbury (Bersu, 1940), in Wiltshire, and Gussage All Saints (Wainwright, 1979), in Dorset, the reconstruction of Iron

Age houses was undertaken. Such a farmstead has been found on Farningham Hill, where it was excavated by Brian Philp (2002, 125-7). Much was gleaned from house construction such as materials, manipulation, and necessary tools. Thereafter, the farming experiments, with crops and animal maintenance in appropriate enclosures, continued until the sad demise of Peter Reynolds who had devised the experiment back in 1972.

As Joan Sheldon (1982) so succinctly said, at the outset of her seminal essay regarding the environmental background of Kent's prehistory, 'Much work remains to be done before a detailed picture can be drawn of the changing landscape of this corner of Britain.' All too often environmental concerns are an appendage to archaeological endeavours and are thus incidental. However, in Kent, two environmental enterprises are eminent in so much as they set out what must be the basis of an undertaking in its own right. During the 1950s Sir Harry Godwin sought out the deposits – peat at Frogholt, near Folkestone, and peaty mud at Wingham, near Canterbury – which allowed unambiguous pollen analysis, and radiocarbon dates, which disclosed that clearance had taken place on the downs (Simmons & Tooley, 1981, 232). A more comprehensive project was Brian Philps (2002, 120) excavation of the lake at Darenth where evidence from primarily environmental sources was applied to archaeological considerations. Sir Harry Godwin and Brian Philp's work illustrates the deliberate selection of sites which could yield significant environmental evidence. Further sites of this kind should be sought out and a positive programme for Kent's environments in past times devised. Such work would be of considerable importance, for Kent's varied geology has determined a measure of differing environmental circumstances within a relatively small area. Thus movement could have demanded continual adaptation.

THREE

THE LONG PALAEOLITHIC LINEAGE

The Palaeolithic is the two million years from the first appearance of an early form of human, in Africa, until the last retreat of the Devensian glacial ice, about 10,000 years ago, by which time Homo sapiens, ourselves, was about and abroad. Neither the terrain that became Kent nor, for that matter, Britain, existed in a form that we would recognise today. Palaeolithic archaeology is coincident with the geological Pleistocene period of alternating glaciations, interstadials and interglacials. It studies the stone tools of humankind in collaboration with those who pursue Quaternary Studies: the geology and biology of the period. Any correlation of the global glacial and interglacial periods is fraught with uncertainties. For long they were considered as simultaneous by F.K. Zeuner (1950; 1964), who devised a terminology of general application. However, deviations led to a local nomenclature, which for us in Kent is based upon East Anglian stratigraphical evidence and phenomena, and is used in the present context. Thus:

Glacials	*Interglacials*
DEVENSIAN	
	Ipswichian
WOLSTONIAN	
	Hoxnian
ANGLIAN	
	Cromerian
BEESTONIAN	
	Pastonian

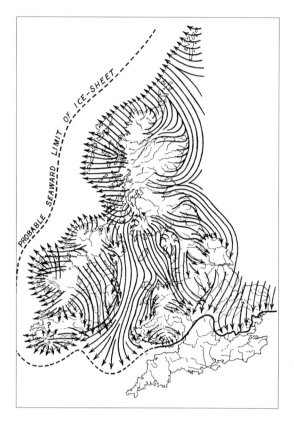

12 The limits of glaciation in the British Isles and the lines of ice-flow. Kent, and southern England, would have been periglacial terrain from which the huge ice-fronts would have been visible. *P. Ashbee, 1937*

BAVENTIAN

Antian

THURNIAN

Ludhamian

WALTONIAN

PLIOCENE

In relation to the land that is now Kent, the glacial ice (*12*), likely to have been 1km in height, advanced in Anglian times to just north of the Thames. The Wolstonian glaciation reached mid-East Anglia while the last, Devensian, glaciation reached northern Norfolk. Here, even today, the landscape has in it fossilised glacial and periglacial features, the great moraine, eskers and pingoes. Such phenomena are likely to have been features of the terrain that is now Kent, particularly after the Anglian glaciation, but have been eradicated by subsequent weathering. Nonetheless, Kentish Quaternary geology repeatedly encounters Coombe Rock, fossilised chalky solifluction sludge. During the glaciations there were low sea-levels, at times as much as 100m (more than 300ft), because sea waters were locked up in the enormous ice-sheets. Thus such rivers as were active cut deeply to adjust to these low levels, which accounts for their deep channels. The other extreme was during the warm interglacials when sea-levels were 30-40m (more than 100ft) higher than today. Which areas were inundated is far from clear, but rivers laid down their high terrace gravels, former flood plains, and alluvia, and pursued, sometimes, different courses. Dating the Pleistocene period is not without problems. The now well-known techniques of radiocarbon assay cannot be applied beyond the Advanced Palaeolithic. Thus other specialised techniques such as the oxygen isotope analysis of deep-sea cores, measuring the earth's magnetic field, or Potassium argon methodologies based upon the decay of the isotope potassium 40 in relation to argon gas have been developed. There is also a system which measures the gradual decay of uranium. Other ways for dating the distant past are highly specialised and involve interdisciplinary collaboration.

With minor exceptions the evidence for Palaeolithic hominid activity is their flint implements, found for the most part in riverine gravel deposits. Up to the late 1930s gravel extraction was largely by hand and artifacts were recognised by workmen and put aside for collectors and others. Indeed, the present writer has memories of being given some handaxes by kindly workmen when a schoolboy. At the present time mechanical gravel extraction discoveries are rare, unless the machine operators are unusually observant, as for example recently in Norfolk (Eastern Daily Press, 4 September 2002).

Besides their immense duration in time, the Palaeolithic stone tool traditions have a vast spatial distribution. Implements from southern England, the region that is now Kent and beyond, have identical modes of manufacture and form as their fellows from Africa, India and beyond. Moreover, much the same sequences evolve. For those who are concerned with the Palaeolithic must operate within a transcontinental dimension, for what can be seen in our western world seems simultaneous with that to be found in far eastern places. Indeed, the slow tool-making changes, measured in multi-millennia, may result from the communal, that is collective, consciousness of small groups of humans isolated within the vast habitable, food-providing regions. The stimuli promoting change, that is the technological progress that can be observed by present-day prehistorians, are evasive, although economic and environmental factors are not infrequently invoked.

As has been said, Palaeolithic progress is marked by the changes in the techniques of flint and stone tool-making. In Kent, any consideration of this must be prefaced by Benjamin Harrison's eoliths, the 'dawn stones' seemingly humankind's first essays in flint working, found in the Brown Flint Drift which cloaks parts of the North Downs, in the vicinity of Ash and Yoke (13). It may once have been a continuous and considerable deposit, but today only isolated scraps remain. It was thought to be the residue of still higher gravels on the Wealden

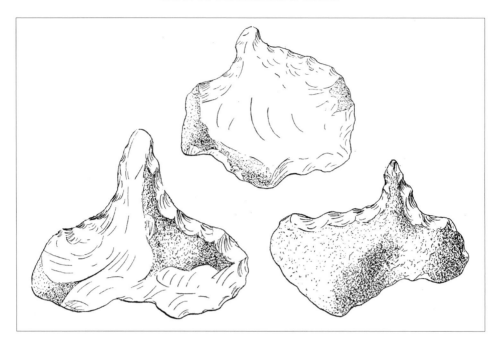

13 Benjamin Harrison's eoliths dug from the Brown Flint Drift which mantles the chalk, high on the North Downs, at Ash and Yoke. *After Benjamin Harrison*

anticline, which rose to the height of some 1000m (3000ft) and connected the North and South Downs. From the first the eoliths excited controversy. Ronald Jessup (1930, 1-11) discussed their problems in detail and, although sympathetic to the notions of earlier investigators (Macalister, 1921, 154-8), pointed out how flints in deep deposits could have been fractured by strata movements. T.D Kendrick (1932, 1-12) when writing his parts of 'Archaeology in England & Wales, 1914-1931' devoted a chapter to 'Pre-Palaeolithic Man' which began 'We begin with "eoliths" and not very happily'. He discussed them with cordial impartiality, saying that they were a problem beyond archaeology and that one should await further discoveries. Since then opinion (Roe, 1981, 27) considers that their simple, mostly unidirectional, edge chipping is likely to have been brought about by the pressures of soil movement. In passing, it should be remembered that the developing ideas of Benjamin Harrison's day were the application of Darwin's evolutionary notions to human artifacts. He was a skilled, observant fieldworker who collected hundreds of palaeoliths and made painstaking notes of their contexts.

Our British Palaeolithic industries are named after type-sites, thus the initial heavy flake, core and chopper industry is termed the Clactonian after a considerable assemblage recovered from gravels at Clacton-on-Sea, in Essex. Handaxes (made and used over a longer time than any other artifact in human history), the Acheulian type-fossil, received this appellation from St Acheul, near Amiens in France, where numbers were found during the very early days of Palaeolithic archaeology. Handaxes are an old world tool, having been found in, besides Europe, Africa, the Near East, southern Russia and India. The earliest, roughly chipped handaxes from the 45m (*c.*140ft) terrace of the River Somme, at Abbeville, are often termed Abbevillian. Their Old World distribution supports Darwin's notion of a diaspora from Africa. The Levalloisian is typified by regular flakes struck from carefully prepared cores. Levallois-Perret, where the nature of these assemblages was initially recognised during the later nineteenth century, in a suburb of Paris. Traces of this technique are found by themselves or, from time to time, together with later Acheulian handaxe industries. The Mousterian, so named from the rock shelter at Le Moustier 16km (10 miles) from Les Eyzies, in the Dordogne, is primarily a European mainland phenomenon characterised by fine, cordiform, flat-butted handaxes. It appears in the Middle Palaeolithic, associated with Neanderthal man. On the European mainland formal burials and the remains of houses have been encountered. The Upper or Advanced Palaeolithic is typified by flint, or fine stone, blades struck from prepared prismatic cores, and appliances such as spear-throwers (Garrod, 1955) and bows, while in France there are painted and engraved caves, adorned burials and elaborate houses. Four clear traditions are recognised, the Perigordian, named after a former French province, recently termed the Gravettian, after La Gravette in the Dordogne, which extends into eastern Europe, and the Aurignacian, after Aurignac, a cave near Toulouse, which also appears in the Balkans. They are thought to have had a mutually exclusive existence. There follows the Solutrean after Solutré, near Macon, characterised by finely flaked projectile points, and the Magdalenian after the site of La Madeleine, in the Dordogne, notable for bone and antler harpoons, plus the cave art (Sieveking, 1962). These distinct artifact traditions are likely to have been produced by disparate peoples. Only the Aurignacians, as far as can be seen, ventured onto the terrain that was to become Kent.

Although lithic artifacts are the criteria for the progress of the Palaeolithic, hominids from an early stage built dwellings (Wymer, 1982a, 126–37), perhaps temporary, the evidence for which is no more than stone settings and, in a rare instance, timber. A stone setting or floor was encountered at Hoxne, in Suffolk (Wymer, 1962, 132), and it would not be beyond the bounds of possibility for such a feature to be encountered beneath appropriate deposits in Kent. The use of fire should have been associated with these structures. Fire-hardened yew-wood spears, a point from Clacton-on-Sea (Oakley *et al*, 1977) and a long Levalloisian spear found at Lehringen, in Germany (Movius, 1950) attest to wood's early use. Direct evidence of the use of fire is difficult to isolate (Oakley, 1955). Nonetheless, at Hoxne (West, 1956, 135) fire was used for woodland clearance at the point at which Acheulian handaxes appeared. In Kent, the Middle Gravels at Swanscombe (Wymer, 1955) yielded small lumps of carbonised vegetable matter. This horizon also contained animal bones, likely to have been broken for marrow, besides reddened and crazed pieces of flint. Fires can occur naturally and incidental surface flints and stones can be calcined. Any excavation at, for example, the Oldbury Rock Shelters, or potentially comparable sites, should make the detection of traces of fire a priority.

Lower and Middle Palaeolithic industries, the Clactonian, Acheulian, Levalloisian and Mousterian, have all been found in Kent. Indeed, certain manifestations are fundamental to the English scene. Nonetheless, only the Advanced Palaeolithic series evade us, although open sites might still be found, such as Cranwich in Norfolk (Wymer, 1971). These should be sought whenever brickearths and river sediments are dug into Kent's rock shelters, Oldbury and the Chiddingfold-Penshurst series, from which Mesolithic material has been obtained, might prove to have been occupied, as were Creswell Crags (Morrison, 1980, 90, *passim*) and other comparable sites, in Advanced Palaeolithic times.

Fossil hominid remains are known from broadly the areas where handaxes were in use (Oakley, 1964; Wymer, 1982, 135-41) and, in Britain, the skull, minus its frontal, found at Swanscombe is of considerable significance. Its discovery, referred to in the initial chapter, was an historic event and its nature will be discussed later. From the outset of Palaeolithic studies, claims have been made for human bones found in the gravels of north-western Kent as deriving from that time. Human remains from Galley Hill, Swanscombe, have attracted considerable attention (Keith, 1925, 250-66), as have skulls from Dartford (Keith, 1925, 158, fig.57) and in the Coombe Rock at Baker's Hole, Northfleet (Keith, 1925, 158,161-2). There were for long rumours of a skull found in the great gravel pit adjacent to Aylesford's church (Jessup, 1970, 41) but it has never been traced. There is also the question of the apparent Advanced Palaeolithic flexed burial encountered at Halling (Garrod, 1926, 164; Jessup, 1930, 33-4).

The remains from Galley Hill, found in 1886, were ostensibly in gravels in which handaxes had been found, and they were thought of as illustrating that Homo sapiens was already current in Middle Palaeolithic times. However, in 1948, Kenneth Oakley's fluorine researches showed that by comparison of their fluorine content with that of fossil mammalia from the Swanscombe gravels they were an intrusive later burial (Oakley & Montagu, 1949), while radiocarbon dating (Barker & Mackay, 1961) confirmed this fluorine comparison. The other early discoveries which, a century ago, were considered as Palaeolithic have been similarly discounted.

Ronald Jessup (1930, 13) observed that about 60,000 implements have been recovered from Swanscombe alone. Derek Roe (1968) listed 492 sites which had yielded 7673 handaxes and John Wymer (1982, 9) stressed how this great number would have been incorporated into gravels by riverine action, observing also that they indicate occupation by rivers and bodies of water. Something of the magnitude of Palaeolithic problems is illustrated by the more than 100,000 artifacts and 3000 find-spots of implements recorded in Britain (Roe, 1968, 1, 9).

The Clactonian in Kent is best represented in the Lower Gravel at Swanscombe where, in the famous Barnfield Pit sequence, it precedes the Middle Gravel with its handaxes and the renowned hominid cranium. This Lower Gravel some 3m (10ft) in depth, is clearly a river gravel resting upon the Thanet Sand. The faunal remains from it suggest an interglacial episode, possibly even pre-Anglian rather than Hoxnian (Waechter 1969), and thus a much higher sea-level than today. The base of the Lower Loam, perhaps a soil, may also have been briefly occupied by those who made and used these distinctive Clactonian assemblages. The artifacts are usually crude, robust flakes, some of which have been retouched, and the cores from which they have been struck. These cores appear to have been waste products but, notwithstanding, they could have served as heavy choppers for smashing the bones of large food animals. Indeed, elephant, rhinocerous, horse and deer were hunted. A block of flakes in fresh, unworn condition, from the Lower Loam, which were rejoined provide an insight into the effective, not unselective, Clactonian technique. The associated faunal remains, bone, antler and mammoth tusks, would also have been a source of raw materials for tools and appliances, as was wood at Clacton. Indeed, careful observation during extraction, were that possible, might yield fashioned pieces. In view of the small number of clear Clactonian assemblages that have been encountered, it is likely that during the days of manual gravel extraction, the flakes, cores and choppers were not recognised by those eager to find handaxes. It must be stressed that the clear edges of Northern Kent's Thames-side Clactonian material points to it having, when initially embodied into the gravels, been transported for short distances only.

Twydall, near Gillingham (14), where between 1906-15 George Payne (1915) collected handaxes, some in mint condition, could well be considered as Kent's other Clactonian site. Gravel, at about 30m (100ft) OD, had been stripped from the chalk, which was quarried, and used to construct a causeway, thus the great number of artifacts found were not *in situ* (Roe, 1968, 21-22). This causeway has been found (Roe, 1981, 231) and among the many artifacts recovered therefrom were flakes and cores 'in the Clactonian manner'. It seems likely that a modest sequence was destroyed by the gravel's removal.

Apart from the Thames Terrace and Twydall, sites which have yielded Clactonian material are seemingly non-existent in Kent. During 1938 the present writer found, in Milner Pit, Sturry, the 30m (100ft) terrace of the Stour,

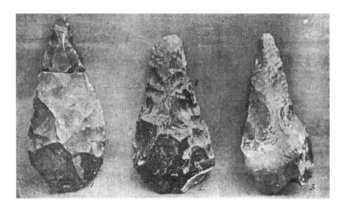

14 Handaxes from Twydall, near Gillingham. No.1 is ocherous and 23cm (9in) in length. No.2 is black-brown and no.3 light brown, with the original cortex of the nodule forming the butt. *After G. Payne, 1915*

a massive flake of Clactonian character, associated with what was taken to have been a handaxe roughout. These pieces are now in the teaching collections of the School of Environmental Sciences of the University of East Anglia and have been listed by John Wymer.

The distribution maps (*15*) of Lower and Middle Palaeolithic find-spots show that Kent's north-flowing rivers' gravel terraces and, for that matter, the summits of the chalklands and even the greensands, depict sites where implements, mostly handaxes, have been found (Roe, 1981, 132-33, 5.4; Drewett, *et al*, 1988, 3, 1.1). Indeed, the density of discoveries is only exceeded by the Thames Valley and inner East Anglia. When assessing such sites, one should remember that, because workmen were paid by collectors, particularly well-finished handaxes might not be from the areas, depths and even pits that were their alleged places of origin.

In general, handaxes have been found in great numbers in the 30m (100ft) terrace gravels of the Thames, where numerous pits, large and small, were dug, mostly close by Dartford and Swanscombe. In the Medway's gravels they emerged at Chatham, Cuxton, Gillingham, New Hythe and allegedly at Aylesford. The Stour's gravels were extracted intensively in the vicinity of Canterbury, notably at Fordwich, Sturry and close by Reculver. Handaxes have been found associated with the gravels of streams such as the Shode, near Ightham, and in minor gravel accumulations at such places as West Wickham and Wilmington.

Acheulian handaxes in Kent, as elsewhere in southern England and beyond, are normally pear-shaped or oval and have been carefully worked, bifacially from a core or sometimes a substantial flake. Indeed, it has been observed, following experiment, that a handaxe's manufacture would have required the removal of, initially, more than 50 major flakes; while finishing, to the standardised form, at times, more than 4000 minor flakes, chips, spalls and splinters. They have been considered as all-purpose tools, for cutting and hacking, and have for long been thought of as having been held in the hand. This would have often demanded an

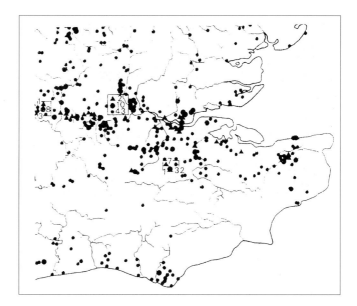

15 Places in Kent and south-eastern England where Palaeolithic implements, mostly handaxes, have been found

adherent protective substance, for many have, or have had, uniformly acute edges. For many tasks the primary flakes, initially disregarded by collectors, would have been more effective than handaxes. In view of their vast numbers and Old World distribution, their conventional uniformity hints at a standardised emblem or token, used in specific circumstances, which could have looked to the past, defined the present and indicated a future.

In Barnfield Ware, at Swanscombe (*16*), Middle Acheulian handaxes, and the famous cranial pieces, in the Middle Gravel, are manifestly later than the Clactonian of the Lower Gravel and Loam, which yielded handaxes considered Late Middle Acheulian. This sequence is to some extent mirrored by the stratigraphy of Rickson's Pit (Roe, 1981, 67, 3.2), and Baker's Hole. Its Coombe Rock infills the incut Ebbsfleet Channel and in this a Levalloisian industry with evolved handaxes was encountered. Indeed, it should be borne in mind that the sequence wrested from the numerous Northern Kentish gravel sites is the yardstick for Britain. Seemingly coeval with the Barnfield Pit Upper Loam material is the Bowman's Lodge, Dartford Heath, site, where handaxes, chopper tools and Levalloisian flakes, were found on the surface of a gravel at 30m (100ft) OD mantled by a loam.

Consideration of the Acheulian from the various deposits marking the terrain that is now Kent must be preceded by an examination of the general sequence which has been established by the observation and recording of the gravels flanking the southern side of the Thames. It is the basis for illustrating the place of the Acheulian handaxes in our Palaeolithic and their affinity with the other

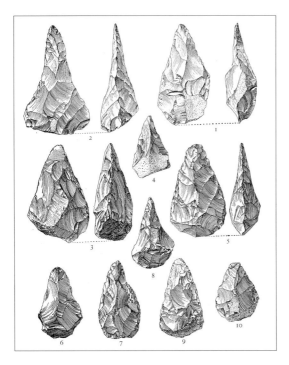

16 Acheulian handaxes from Barnfield Pit, Swanscombe. Nos.1-10 from the lower Middle Gravel; No.11 from the Middle Gravel. All were found *in situ* by archaeological excavation except No.9 which was recovered from a fallen accumulation. No. 1 is 12cm (5in) in length. *After RAI Swanscombe Report, 1938*

artifact traditions, the preceding Clactonian, Levalloisian, and Mousterian usages which appear to have have had, at times, a supportive role.

This sequence, thought of as basic, begins with the Clactonian (*17*) assemblages from the Lower Gravels of Barnfield and Rickson's pits, at Swanscombe, and is followed by similar material from the Lower Loam. They are succeeded by the often rough-butted handaxe industry from Barnfield Pit's Middle Gravels. An Acheulian industry employing well-made ovate handaxes, together with occasional incidences of a Levalloisian technique, distinguishes Barnfield Pit's Upper Loam. This is echoed in Rickson's Pit, and commensurate deposits have been identified in the Bowman's Lodge, Pearson's and Wannint pits at Dartford. It is followed by the spectacular Levalloisian flakes and cores found in Baker's Hole, at Northfleet, on naked, eroded, chalk covered and deranged by Coombe Rock, the chalky sludge of a periglacial summer. Handaxes have been reported as from this site but association is uncertain. Thereafter, in the gravels overlying the Coombe Rock of the Ebbsfleet Channel is a series of industries employing an advanced Levalloisian technique (*18*) for the production of flakes and near blades. Handaxes have been reported as from this site but association, as elsewhere, is uncertain. Similar assemblages have been encountered on the ancient surface at the base of the Lower Brickearth, besides incidences within the body of the deposit at Crayford.

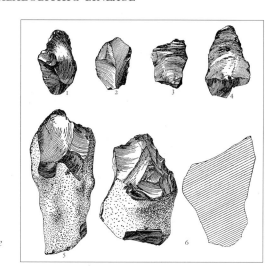

17 Barnfield Pit, Swanscombe. Nos.1–4, small Clactonian flake implements from the base of the Lower Gravel; Nos.5 and 6, core implements from the Lower Gravel. No.1 is 7cm (2.75in) in length. *After RAI Swanscombe Report, 1938*

Barnfield Pit's Lower Gravel is likely to be of the Hoxnian interglacial period, despite the claims for earlier origins, as are the Middle Gravels. At the lower levels, in the Ebbsfleet valley, cold conditions obtained which would have been the Wolstonian glaciation, followed by the warmer conditions of the Ipswichian interglacial period. This should be followed by the Devensian glaciation, the last, but sadly positive indications are evasive. This sequence, detailed from these Northern Kentish sites is, as far as can be seen, the best to be found in Britain, as it embraces the whole of the Lower and touches upon the Middle Palaeolithic. Given this sequence, there is the need for the identification of what are likely to be the remains of these sites, if they still exist. Further consideration of the nature of the deposits could be backed by fresh faunal and palaeobotanical investigation. The Hoxnian interglacial period was about 250,000 years BP, the Wolstonian glaciation some 190,000 years BP, the Ipswichian interglacial period 130,000 BP and the Devensian glaciation beginning at about 90,000 BP and waning by 25,000 BP. The post-glacial Holocene Flandrian stage was one of climatic amelioration, the genesis of afforestation and colonisation by our Mesolithic forbears, who developed, in response to this environment, especial techniques. Had hominids penetrated into the extreme periglacial conditions of the terrain that is now Kent, the ice of the Anglian glaciation, perhaps as in Greenland today, more than a mile in height, could have been awesomely visible from numerous vantage points. The Wolstonian ice stood in the vicinity of Bedfordshire and could have been visible in certain conditions, while the Devensian ice, reaching northern Norfolk, would have maintained periglacial conditions that would have allowed summer-time penetration and temporary habitations, although fire and smoke would have been necessary as protection from swarming mosquitos. A

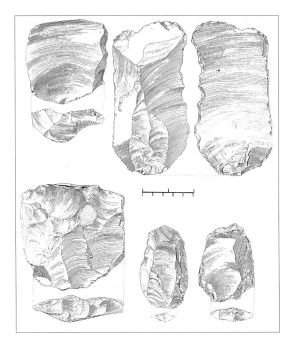

18 Levalloisian core and flakes from the lower loam of the Ebbsfleet Channel. The core, showing its flake facet, is top left. The remaining pieces are flakes. *After J.P.T. Burchell, 1933, 1936*

puzzling aspect of the Kentish landscape, in the light of its successive proximities to glacial ice and periglacial conditions, is the absence of fossil periglacial phenomena such as eskers and pingos.

Handaxes are known from a series of sites other than the Thames gravels and require comment because so many need further investigation. A case in point is the status of the Medway's gravels at Aylesford, notably Silas Wagon's Pit, north-west of the church. Benjamin Harrison (Harrison, 1928, 34, *passim*) had known of this 'River Drift' exposure from his schooldays and wrote, in 1880, 'I flatter myself that it was owing to the workmen at Aylesford examining the stones I had deposited in the museum (at Maidstone) that they first recognised the treasures of that place.' He later made many visits to the area, including the pit where gravel was bedded upon the Gault. It was observed that many handaxes were deeply stained, rolled, and apparently from the base of the gravel. Sir John Evans visited Aylesford to look for and obtain handaxes (Evans, 1890, 317) and included a notice of the site in *Ancient Stone Implements* (1897, 610). The handaxes that found their way to the Museum at Maidstone were large, some 22cm (8-9in) in length, heavy butted and pointed (Smith, 1931, 68). In 1930 Ronald Jessup was puzzled by the nature of the faunal remains, which included straight-tusked elephant, mammoth, cave-lion and red deer. He concluded that the associations of this gravel, which is no more than 15m (about 50ft) OD, were brought about by redeposition. Visits to the main gravel pit, adjacent to the church, by the present writer, Norman Cook and others, found neither implements nor flakes. A worn piece, about 23cm (9in) in length from a massive long bone was the only discovery in a decade. Moreover, patinations comparable with those of the handaxes, allegedly from this pit, could not be matched among the piles of substantial flints in the huge expanse that existed at that time. Derek Roe (1981, 204) records that some '350 handaxes and some other artifacts' are in the museums at Cambridge, Dartford, Maidstone, Manchester and Rochester. He also mentioned that a site at Snodland had produced handaxes similar to those alleged to be from Aylesford. Recently the present writer has thought the unthinkable and has wondered whether this well-known Aylesford pit, because there were so many seeking handaxes, and even faunal remains, who sometimes munificently rewarded workmen for specimens, led to material from other pits being brought in to augment their meagre wages. Handaxes may, hopefully, still exist in a number of the museums and some of the faunal remains may still be in store at Maidstone. Thus, despite Silas Wagon's great pit now being a lake, a critical survey and assessment of the circumstances of Aylesford's anomalous handaxes and fauna could still be undertaken.

Another problem, although of a different kind, surrounds the massive, archaic, handaxes from the high-level, some 45m (156ft), gravels of the Stour, at Fordwich. In assessing this series (Dewey & Smith, 1924, 134; Smith, 1933; Roe, 1965, 7, 14) it could be borne in mind that the earliest European handaxes, the Abbevillian, are possibly a product, in Alpine terms, of the high sea-level of the Mindel-Riss interglacial. This gravel at Fordwich is considerably higher than the series of nearby Sturry but, apart from its altitude, no clear indication of its age has been forthcoming. The handaxes were unworn and could not have been carried far in the high sea-level fluviatile conditions that determined the deposit's nature and altitude.

At Sturry the bench of the terrace is some 16-17m (50ft) lower than that of Fordwich, yet, over the years, Dr A.G. Ince, whose collections were seen by the present writer, assembled numbers of Chellean handaxes, comparable with those from the higher level at Fordwich. These were from West Pit, and were said to be from the top of the main gravels, below the brickearth overlay, and they have been thought of as derived. Milner's Pit, exploiting the same gravel terrace, however, produced a series of well-finished Acheulian ovates. Between Reculver and Bishopstone, now a part of Beltinge, the sea-cliff Stour gravel exposure, bedded upon Thanet Sand, which is little more than 5m (15ft) OD, has produced, for the most part, pointed handaxes, some well-finished, as were the ovates. It is likely that these deposits extend inland and that there has been a degree of planation. Nonetheless, the relationship of these gravels with those of the Thames, into which the early Stour debouched, is difficult to define

(Jessup, 1930, 27). Numbers of artifacts have been found, some, it is said, having fallen from the sea-cliff while others may be from agricultural land. There are numbers in the British Museum, at Canterbury and in the Ashmolean Museum at Oxford. The British Museum holds the large, weathered, white-patinated bout coupé handaxe from Bishopstone, an inland hamlet in 1866, found by John Brent (Evans, 1897, 613).

Handaxes, of which there are few details of provenance, have been found at Herne Bay, Whitstable and even Faversham (Evans, 1897, 617; Smith, 1915,37, fig.14). They may reflect the nineteenth-century exploitation of small, localised, deposits in areas that have now been built over. An example is the excavation of pits on the outskirts of Canterbury (Evans, 1897, 619, fig.464) at Wincheap, where it was said that the gravel was about 10m (30ft) above the River Stour. It is recorded that 'from this spot Mr. Brent has produced several well-wrought implements of various forms'. An ovate and a rolled, pointed, handaxe are illustrated. The gravel, a little more than 3m (10ft) in thickness, was bedded upon the chalk and was a mixture of angular pieces and pebbles in a loamy matrix. A mammoth molar was also found. Drainage works exposed gravels the length of Wincheap where Sir John Evans found flakes. Pointed handaxes were found on the surface of a gravel exposure by the southern side of the Stour at Thanington-Without, about a mile south-west of Wincheap (Evans, 1897, 619). It is recorded that 'The gravel beds near Thanington, out of which the implements appear to have come, must be from 80 to 100 feet above the river.' It is also recorded (Evans, 1897, 618) that '… at Rowton Chapel, near Lenham, Mrs G. Bunyard of Maidstone, found in 1885 a good ovate Palaeolithic implement of flint.' This site, close by the source of the Stour, was on the Greensand, at a distance from the foot of the chalk Downs.

Also in eastern Kent, handaxes have been recovered, as surface finds, from the chalk at Elham (Tester, 1952). Seven were collected from a ploughed field at about 120m (350-70ft) OD, which were worn and stained, their patina being buff or brown. For long it was thought that these handaxes from the chalk downlands had been deposited by some form of fluviatile activity. Handaxes have been collected from elsewhere on the chalk summits and backslopes of the Downs, notably at Ash (Smith, 1936, 70) and elsewhere west of the Medway. Surface implements have also been collected at Wilmington and their exposure may result from planation. Ovates were the dominant form. Although Benjamin Harrison (Harrison, 1928,46,87) found his first handaxe in a small gravel pit, dug in a field, many more were surface discoveries. It should not be overlooked that handaxes are known from a considerable elevation, some 185m (550ft) on the high chalk of the South Downs (Todd, 1936; Curwen, 1954, 43). Because of erosion, solifluction and chemical weathering, the original surfaces upon which the handaxe makers and users went their ways have long since vanished.

To revert to the Medway, a pit on the west bank at New Hythe, opposite Aylesford and now a part of a vast water-filled complex, yielded numerous handaxes, some of considerable size. It is not known whether or not the Levalloisian material was associated with the handaxes, numbers of which are in the Dartford and Maidstone museums. Many are fresh but some had been rolled for some time and distance. Johnson's Pit in New Hythe Lane, could well have been one of the pits just within the 15m (75ft) contour, still visible, but denuded and overgrown by the 1950s. A great deal of extraction at New Hythe was from the floodplain gravels. The gravels at Snodland, considered to be from a buried channel of the Medway have also yielded a few handaxes, unpatinated and unworn. Woolly rhinocerous, late mammoth, horse and large red deer remains were also found. The buried channel has been shown as about 7m (approximately 25ft) in depth and has been thought of as belonging to an early Devensian interstadial. P.J Tester's (1965) excavation into the 15m (50ft) gravel terrace of the Medway is a site of importance to our studies in that sections of the deposits were recorded, and a considerable number of artifacts recovered under carefully controlled conditions. The five trenches produced 199 handaxes, 11 cleavers, 1 chopper, 54 flake tools, 20 cores, 366 waste flakes and 6 fragments which could not be classified. The handaxes, some pointed, have been thought of as similar to those of the Middle Gravel of the Barnfield Pit exposure at Swanscombe from which the hominid cranial fragments were recovered. Affinities with the Middle Acheulian Boyn Hill terrace of the Thames industry have also been invoked (Wymer, 1968, 217-9). Sadly neither bones, nor shells, nor pollen were found and thus we are left with the character of the implements and their affiliations. Some of the artifacts were fresh and others rolled, both being intermingled. They were thought to be from a stream-side dwelling place, presumably temporary, periodically invaded by water.

Kent has, at Swanscombe, within its boundaries, the most important Acheulian handaxe site in Western Europe, for here a hominid, if not human, cranium was clearly associated with these artifacts. As was said in the historical introduction (Chapter 1), it was in Barnfield Pit in 1935 that part of an occipital bone was found in the Upper Middle Gravel, with well-finished handaxes, by A.T.Marston, who visited the pit, now and again, in search of implements. These cranial pieces were just over 7m (24ft) from the surface. A preliminary notice of the discovery appeared in *Nature* (19 October 1935, 637). He kept a look-out for further pieces and on 15 March 1936 found a left parietal bone which articulated with the occipital. It was again reported in *Nature* (1 August 1936).

Marston gave an account of his discoveries to the Royal Anthropological Institute on 12 January 1937. An outcome, which he suggested, was the formation of a research committee charged witil a further examination of the site, and a scrutiny of the skull pieces, together with the associated artifacts. The committee included Dr K.P. Oakley from the British Museum (Natural History), C.F.C. Hawkes, also from the British Museum, Dr M. (Molly) Alwyn Cotton, from the University of London's Institute of Archaeology and W.E. le Gros Clark. Notable features of the work were the careful sections, in the vicinity of the place of discovery of the skull fragments, which yielded flakes and handaxes, supervised by Molly Cotton. The Committee's comprehensive narrative, entitled *Report on the Swanscombe Skull, Prepared by the Swanscombe Committee of the Royal Anthropological Institute* appeared, with admirable promptitude, in 1938. Almost two decades later, the right parietal was found by Mr and Mrs B.O. Wymer during their 1955-6 excavations. It was about 15m (50ft) from the initial discoveries, presumably higher and upstream. The skull pieces are considered as those of a young man, perhaps in his twenties, with both sapiens and Neanderthal characteristics, recognisably human. He might have been an early sapiens form.

This Swanscombe hominid was not demonstrably the maker of the handaxes from the Middle Gravel and the fact of no more than association must be stressed. The find-spot was adjacent to a buried channel and thus the mechanics of deposition could have been complicated, and material from a variety of sources could have been brought together. This is shown by the section drawn by M.H.R. Cook (Roe, 1981, 67, 3.2). Swanscombe has recently been subjected to an intensive environmental study (Hubbard, 1982). The Lower Loam and Gravels point to grassy mud-flats, cut by channels and streams, bordered by hazel scrub. Flanking the Thames, the area could have been favourable for a hunting and gathering life and food animals could have been readily procured by the experienced hunters.

The site recently excavated at Boxgrove in Sussex (Pitts & Roberts, 1997) graphically illustrates an aspect of Palaeolithic hunting procedures, and, because of quantities and isolation, hints at a permanent station at no great remove. Boxgrove would appear to have been a carcass collecting and butchery area. It would have to have been at a considerable distance from the various places where animals were trapped and, perhaps, despatched, for the unfortunate creatures would not have readily approached a location which reeked of the blood of their kind. In 1996, over 250 slightly pointed oval Boxgrove handaxes, in sharp, fresh condition, were found (Pitts & Roberts, 1997, 228) and butchery experiments were undertaken. Limitations to the use of handaxes were experienced and it emerged that only the examples with a long cutting edged performed satisfactorily. Manipulation was also a problem as the handaxes became slippery when coated with grease and blood. These experiments, described in detail, and backed by macroscopic wear scrutiny, were valuable, but, nevertheless, they leave us with the functional problems of the handaxe, an artifact encountered in numbers at Boxgrove as elsewhere.

A site comparable with Boxgrove, where artifacts made by the Levalloisian technique were employed, was encountered, investigated, and dug away at Baker's Hole, Northfleet. It was on the naked chalk and had been smothered and disturbed by solifluctory chalk mud, soon after the deposit was left on the chalk. As the site has been completely destroyed one can do no more than view it via those who saw and recorded aspects of the considerable assemblage first recorded at the end of the nineteenth century. Mammoth, rhinocerous, horse and deer remains have also been recovered but, undoubtedly, much has been removed without record. The human skull found in the Coombe Rock attracted notice, but it emerged as of no great antiquity. The most important details have been chronicled by F.C.J. Spurrell (1883), R.A. Smith (1911; 1926), J.P.T. Burchell (1931) and H. Dewey (1932). The recent accounts by John Wymer (1968, 354-6) and Derek Roe (1981, *passim*) are valuable in that they bring together the scattered, sometimes diffuse, literature. By 1932, H. Dewey was of the view that some 100,000 flakes and implements had been taken from Baker's Hole.

The enormous Levalloisian assemblage from Baker's Hole is clearly a product of the extraction of flint, of good quality, from the naked chalk. The distinctive technique, employing the carefully prepared cores, was used to produce large, robust, oval and elongated flakes. Most of these would have had sturdy cutting edges and, for food animal dismemberment, would have been far superior to handaxes. Indeed, retouching could well have reduced the efficiency of the struck flakes for such tasks. However, retouching is unlikely to have been undertaken without reason and for such tasks as sawing sinews, and even small game bones, they would have had their uses. Large, thick flakes could also have been the basis of the manufacture of bifacial handaxes. Indeed, in certain assemblages, particularly those of, and resembling, the *bout coupé* variety, often a slight curvature indicates this basis. Whether or not handaxes were associated with this huge Levalloisian assemblage is unknown but, among the British Museum's (Natural History) Baker's Hole collection there is one made from a flake.

Associated Levalloisian artifacts, flakes and cores, are not uncommon in the gravel pits in the vicinity of Canterbury. A near-handaxe from the Riverside low-level gravels on the northern side of the Stour (Anon., 1939) illustrates the often ambiguous nature of the technique. At Ospringe elongated flakes have been reported from a pit close by the Old Union Workhouse (Garraway-Rice, 1911) but their precise provenance is obscure. However, at Bapchild (Dines, 1928), near Sittingbourne, Coombe Rock, beneath the brickearth of the area, several hundreds of artifacts were collected from two pits, about a quarter of a mile one from another. Large blades, flake implements and flakes were in abundance, while cores and what was considered as a boot-like anvil were encountered. Cores were often double, an effective flake having been struck from each face. The association with Coombe Rock occasioned comparison with Baker's Hole. Were appropriate deposits to be found remaining, the dating of this complex would be a significant addition to our appreciation of Kent's Levalloisian sites. Levalloisian material from beneath some 2m (6ft) of clay and flints, considered to be a solifluction deposit, was encountered at Stonecross, Luton, on the eastern side of the Medway's estuary (Turner, 1928). Were this deposit solifluction material an association with the Wolstonian glaciation would be a possibility.

West of the Medway, at New Hythe, quantities of Levalloisian material, particularly cores and flakes, appear as associated with handaxes. The flakes have led to it having been thought of as a working site, it being one of the New Hythe Lane pits. Some of the pieces are fresh and sharp while others have much the same degree of patina and abrasion as the handaxes. In Northfleet's Ebbsfleet Channel deposits there are flakes and cores from below the fluviatile gravel which is capped by a loam, deposits which have been assigned to a point during the cold of the Wolstonian glaciation. Crayford's artifacts have been collected since the 1880s (Spurrell, 1880; 1884) and were encountered beneath brickearths (Kennard, 1944). Spurrell found, and may have partially excavated, an area where Levalloisian flakes, cores, and various nodules lay as left by their makers, mingled with the bones of butchered animals. Indeed, a flake lay upon the jawbone of a woolly rhinocerous. He recovered the appropriate flakes from a nodule, with a broken core, and was able to fit them together. Another and similar site, also beneath the brickearth, was found at about half-a-mile distant in another pit, and, once again, a series of flakes were conjoined. A.S. Kennard knew the place and was able to detail the molluscs and mammalia (1944).

77 The last part of the Hoxnian interglacial and the early stages of the Devensian glaciation witnessed the manifestation of the Mousterian phenomenon (Cornwall, 1964, 57) and its European spread. Its characteristics are well-finished cordiform handaxes and allegedly those, termed as of *bout coupé* form, with, when fresh, circumferential sharp edges which would have made their use as a hand-tool almost impossible. In general, large numbers of scrapers were used and, from time to time, Levalloisian techniques were employed for their production. Within western Europe there are associations of Mousterian assemblages with Neanderthal man (*Homo sapiens neanderthalensis*), and it has been assumed that he traversed the territories that are now England (Shackley, 1980, for a general account). It must be stressed that the remains of Neanderthal man have so far not been encountered here and that association is far from proven. The Mousterian of Acheulian tradition is the only variant present in Britain. The artifacts from Oldbury's rock-shelters, near Ightham (Jessup, 1930, 30-2, pl.2; Collins, 1968-9), are clearly in that tradition.

Ian Cornwall (1958, 29), despite the association of 'a flake industry of Mousterian appearance' was sceptical regarding the rock-shelters on Oldbury Hill because of their north-facing location and the weathering propensities of their sandstone. However, he observed that the '… sandstone of the scarp of the hill is evidently being weathered back fairly rapidly, even in our time, so that the position of the face in Palaeolithic times must have been many yards north of this', a factor frequently forgotten. Sporadic quarrying of stone may account for the present position of the overhang (Harrison, 1933, 160-1). Nonetheless, recent research (Collins, 1968-9) has indicated the quantities of Mousterian material found on the hill and it is not impossible that even in periglacial conditions the rock-shelters would have afforded adequate shelter, for they could at that time have been inclined in a different direction, as suggested by one of the outcrops (Harrison, 1933, pl.II), while windbreaks could undoubtedly have been devised.

Benjamin Harrison found deeply weathered cordiform handaxes on Oldbury Hill initially in about 1870 (Harrison, 1928, 68) and 20 years later, on 4 August 1890, he undertook an excavation on its eastern slopes at a distance from what is today termed 'the shelters'. Forty-nine implements and more than 600 flakes were found. These are now housed in the British Museum, although selections are also at Maidstone and Manchester. The area excavated was said to have been 'a space no larger than an ordinary allotment' (Harrison, 1933, 150). The Basted fissures (Bennett, 1907, *passim*; Collins, 1968-9, 155, fns.6-9) at no great distance, produced faunal remains, as well as those of plants, insects, mollusca, amphibia, reptiles and birds, which are considered as early Devensian. In general terms the Oldbury flint implements and flakes could be considered as of this juncture.

Further *sondages* (Collins, 1968-9, 155-8), following those of Ian Cornwall (1958, 29) and Edward Pyddoke (1961, 21), revealed a stony deposit overlying the Greensand bedrock, and from this the artifacts were recovered. These were comparable with Benjamin Harrison's series and probably referable to the earlier Devensian. The excavations of 1965 unearthed 106 flakes, of which 72 are from the stony layer, and their patinas were not at variance with those found in 1890. It emerged that the numbers of handaxes from the enterprise, and from the vicinity, are difficult to account for. It was observed that there are cordiform handaxes from the immediate vicinity of Oldbury, and it was averred that a site at Stonepits, some two miles to the west of Ightham, should be accorded further investigation. Any excavation at Oldbury or Stonepits should have the possibility of Mousterian burials in mind. Following their assessment of the lithic material, their conclusions (Collins, 1968, 69, 174) reiterated the earlier assertion that the rock-shelters may never have been inhabited, a premise far from proven. Although the sandstone overhangs have been weathered back, a process prompting periodic collapses, and the fallen material removed by quarrying, it would seem unlikely that, as in the west country (Roe, 1981, 237,6.1) they were not used for shelter. Indeed, Oldbury could have been a convenient staging post for a modest Mousterian westward movement.

A matter involved with the Kentish Mousterian of Acheulian tradition, as exemplified by the Oldbury assemblage, is the nature and place of the *bout coupé* handaxes. It is considered as an intrusive form, from elsewhere in Europe, and one that signals a beginning, as it marks a late Ipswichian and early Devensian horizon. This distinctive form is numerous in northern Kent. They have been found in the Stour gravels, in the vicinity of Canterbury, at Herne Bay, Reculver, Faversham, and from the surface at Elham. West of the Medway they have emerged at New Hythe and Snodland (Roe, 1981, 247, 6.6). They appear as exceptional because of their regular form and all round acute edges. Unless they were used in a mode that evades us, it would have been near-impossible to hold them in the hand and exert pressure. We are towards the end of the long age of the handaxe and thus the possibility that they represent, at the end, a reassertion of the principles inherent in this long-lasting, distinctive tool form.

Dorothy Garrod's (1926) survey of the Advanced (or Upper) Palaeolithic in Britain is now more than 70 years in the past. In its pages, remarkable for their clarity and insights, three Kentish sites were described, North Cray, Halling and artifacts from Canterbury. These have been discounted; and we have been left with no more than an incursion by postglacial Hamburgian reindeer hunters, their distinctive implements having been found at Oare, near Faversham. Dorothy Garrod (Clark, 1989, 44-8) had seen and handled most of the Palaeolithic material of Western Europe and the Near East and thus her diagnoses should not necessarily be cast aside. Indeed, in each instance further investigation should, if possible, be undertaken as her selected material was well in keeping with the typologies of her time, which in good measure still obtain.

For general purposes, the Advanced Palaeolithic has been divided into an Earlier and a Later, a division separated by the Devensian maximum and differing techniques of artifact production. In general, blades are the basis of their manufacture. Struck mostly from prismatic cores, they appear as a development of, for example, the Levalloisian parallel-sided flakes, struck from prepared cores, such as were found at Crayford. For the most part Advanced Palaeolithic material has been found in caves, largely in the West Country and Wales while, in East Anglia there are what have been termed 'open sites'. At Ipswich (Moir, 1932; 1938) leaf-points, scrapers and a tanged point were found and leaf-points were also a feature of a site at White Colne, in Essex (Layard, 1932). Many so-called 'open sites' may have involved houses (Phillips, 1980, 83-7, fig.22, pl.3a and b; Wymer, 1982, 239, fig.67, 241, fig.68) and many more may remain in the vicinity of our rivers, whereas in Kent, estuarine and other low-lying tracts of land, have been buried beneath the sediments, soils and hill-washes brought about by the post-Devensian rise in sea-level, weathering and denudation. Radiocarbon dates (Wymer, 1982, 203) are available for the Advanced Palaeolithic, the Earlier centres upon about 28,000 years BP, the Later 12,000 years BP.

At North Cray flakes, considered Aurignacian, were beneath an alluvial deposit and upon gravel. Dorothy Garrod (1926, 160) accepted these as a core plus flakes, and the British Museum's collection supplemented them. At Halling a skeleton (Keith, 1925, 122) was unearthed from a depth of almost 2m (6ft) when a sewage-tank setting was dug into layered brickearth. Radiocarbon dating (Oakley *et al*, 1967) has shown that this interment is likely to have been a Late Neolithic grave. A cold fauna was present and the flint industry included, besides blades, some of which were obliquely retouched; a burin (Garrod, 1926, 165) also came to light. This modest assemblage was thought of as Aurignacian. A burin and some long flakes, noticed in the museum at Cambridge (Garrod, 1926, 167, fig.41), were from Canterbury and, again, were considered as Aurignacian. Ronald Jessup (1930, 35) records flakes from beneath the brickearth at Bapchild (Dines, 1928) and also a 'working floor' on peat, below brickearth bedded upon Coombe Rock. The site at Haywood, on the eastern side of a shallow dry valley, yielded, it was reported, some 200 implements, cores and a hammerstone. A number of the long flakes had battered backs, pale blue patination with white blotches obtained, besides some fine, near transparent, flakes. Again, this considerable assemblage was considered as Aurignacian. Indeed, this considerable industrial tradition, separate from the French Perigordian, might have emerged in the terrain that is now Britain. Technological developments in south-eastern England during the last stages of the Devensian are obscure and thus these sites and material, investigated and evaluated during the early twentieth century, need reassement and, where possible, reinvestigation.

The late Devensian climatic amelioration is marked by the Hamburgian reindeer hunters, a few of whose flint tools were found at Oare, near Faversham (Clark, 1938a; 1933b). These shouldered points and a long regular, flake, were acquired by the British Museum from the R. Garraway Rice collection but, sadly, nothing is known of their provenance. Shouldered points are not unknown in Britain and have been encountered in cave sites such as Creswell Crags and Mother Grundy's Parlour (Roe, 1981, 245). By about 12,000 years BP the ice had retreated to Scandinavia. Northern Germany was periglacial and afforestation had begun. The reindeer-hunting Hamburgians, at Meiendorf (Rust, 1937) and Stellmoor (Rust, 1943) were employing shouldered points and beaked boring tools, and had set up habitations by the glacial valley (*tunneltäler*) lakes, numerous in that area. They were active in what are now the Low Countries and thus evidence of their presence at Oare is not surprising, for they would have moved freely across the territory that has been termed Doggerland (Coles, 1998, 58-65, figs.8, 9, 10). They were the descendants of European mainland Advanced Palaeolithic groups who had adjusted themselves to changing environmental circumstances.

By Advanced Palaeolithic times and the retreat of the Devensian ice, *Homo sapiens* had emerged and established himself.

FOUR

THE MESOLITHIC PRELUDE

Remarkably, the territory that was to become Kent had, during the remote Palaeolithic handaxe regime, some claim to be a discrete entity, because of the many discoveries made in the gravels of the north-flowing rivers which ran into the early Thames. Thus, following the post-Devensian climatic amelioration, and its contingent afforestation, the Mesolithic communities gradually moved into the lands that would emerge as south-eastern England (Coles, 1998, 64, fig.10). As during earlier Pleistocene interglacials the vast waters locked into the glacial ice of the Devensian maximum were released, leading to eustatic rises in sea-level, while relief from ice brought about isostatic movements of land that had been depressed or, as fore-bulges elevated, by its weight. As the deciduous forests established themselves, the descendants of those who had hunted, devoured and made extinct the great animal herds of earlier times, had to become dependent upon different modes of sustenance. The Mesolithic (Middle Stone Age) interspersed between the Palaeolithic and Neolithic, involved a fresh formulation and redirection of the usages developed by the Advanced Palaeolithic hunters. Across considerable tracts of the Old World the presence of Mesolithic communities is attested by flint, and other suitable stone, microliths geometric shapes made from blades, which were affixed to arrows (19), lances, rasps and saws. This ingenious principle meant that the barbs and edges were easily replaceable. A microlithic waste product was the microburin which displayed a part of the technique of the notching and fracture of suitable blades. Microlithic does not always mean Mesolithic, for flint blade size-reduction was a feature of the Advanced Palaeolithic and some later industries.

In Britain, as across Northern Europe, the initial Mesolithic culture, or, perhaps, technocomplex (Phillips, 1980, 137), is the Maglemosian, a term from Danish signifying 'big bog'. Its nature was detailed by Grahame Clark in his *Mesolithic*

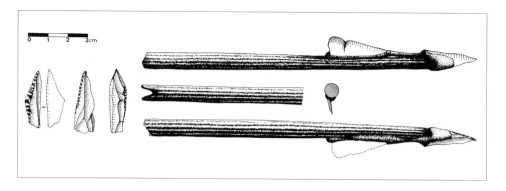

Settlement of Northern Europe (1936). This seminal work followed closely upon his *Mesolithic Age in Britain* (1932), a detailed distributional study, particularly valuable for its appreciation of sites on the various soils and geological solids of south-eastern England. At that time the English Maglemosian presence was shown by no more than a number of their characteristic bone and antler harpoons. Now several informative sites are known, the principal ones being Star Carr (Clark, 1954; 1989, 481-538), Thatcham (Wymer, 1962), Broxbourne (Warren *et al*, 1936), Deepcar (Radley & Mellars, 1964) and Kelling (Wymer, 1977).

Star Carr, near Scarborough, was recognised by Grahame Clark (Fagan, 2001, 146) as a place where Maglemosian material might be found in pollen-bearing peat. Excavation took place during 1949-51 and was an interdisciplinary undertaking with palaeobotanists present from the outset. A timber and stone platform emerged at the margin of an erstwhile late glacial lake. An early Maglemosian lithic industry was accompanied by a wealth of bone, antler and wooden artifacts, besides birch-bark containers. Animal remains were those of red deer, elk, cattle and pigs. Fish were absent and bird bones rare. Of note were the stag frontlets with carefully lightened antlers still attached. The parietal remnants had been carefully smoothed so that they might be worn as stalking-masks or cult headdresses. Mesolithic peoples, such as those of Star Carr, may have managed their herds. The skeleton of a Late Glacial Elk, found in peat at Poulton-le-Pylde, in Lancashire (Hallam *et al*, 1973) and associated with two barbed bone missile points, provides an insight into their meat obtainment methods. Already burning was carried out to create favourable animal habitats and the ecological changes thus wrought are shown by pollen spectra (Dimbleby, 1967, 143). The Maglemosian site at Thatcham (Wymer, 1962) was one of several by the Kennet, a tributary of the Thames. Besides flintwork, bone and antler artifacts were recovered, as were animal bones, from deep in the pollen-rich sediments. A run of radiocarbon dates, one more than 10,000 BP, show Thatcham to have been a pre-Boreal occupation.

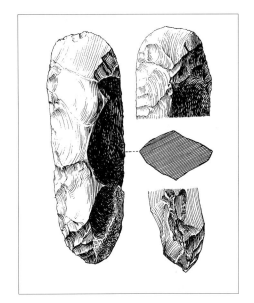

Opposite: 19 Microliths as arrow-points and barbs, secured with resin, from Loshult, Scania, Sweden. Such an arrow combined a cutting with a perforating function. *After M. Peterson, 1951*

Right: 20 A core-axe, or 'Thames Pick', of dark, mottled flint, from the Thames at Erith. Length 14.8cm (*c.*5.75in). *After R.F. Jessup, 1930*

The nature of these sites has been stressed because of Kentish estuarine systems and incidental riverine and other marshlands which could conceal such remains, and so positive fieldwork should be undertaken. Maglemosian harpoons have been found in the Thames (Clark, 1932, 1B, 123, fig.2) and thus, from that location, catchment areas and installations could have extended well into the lands that are now Kent. Log-boats are known from Mesolithic times (Clark, 1975, 124) and one thinks of those from the marshes near Maidstone, noticed by Stukeley (Ashbee, 2000, 71). A paddle has been found near Swanscombe, together with two transversely-sharpened flint axes (Jessup, 1970, 51). These core axes (*20*) found in Maglemosian contexts (Clark, 1954, 111, figs.9, 43; Wymer, 1962, 345, fig. 8; 346, fig.9), have been met with in considerable numbers in south-eastern England, and have been dubbed 'Thames Picks'. Suitable flint, as at Ash-cum-Ridley (Wymer, 1977, 144), was readily available in the area and, as in Kent, their distribution follows the principal river valleys. They have been thought of as tools for the construction of shelters and the making of log-boats. These axes were all too often isolated discoveries and thus a precise context cannot be established (Mellars & Reinhardt, 1978, 246). In the circumstances, Maglemosian occupation in south-eastern England awaits discovery and definition. The existence of a body of water frequented by Mesolithic people has been established at Darenth (Philp, 2002, 120-4). At Iping, near Midhurst, in Sussex, a distinctive Maglemosian installation, close by water and on the Greensand, has been examined (Keef *et al*,1965). Such situations are numerous at the foot of the North Downs in Kent.

The principal Mesolithic sites of south-eastern England fall into four categories. There are those of northern Kent, beneath marshlands and alluvium, a number, some long-known, strung along the Greensand country, a concentration clustered upon the many natural crags of the Lower Tunbridge Wells sand, and a southern, coastal line. Even before the establishment of full marine conditions around south-eastern England (Coles, 1998, figs.10, 11) salt-marsh resources could have attracted various groups to places now inundated. Nonetheless, from Maglemosian times onwards there are inland sites. Marine transgression may, from time to time, have been rapid and thus communities may have been impelled towards land-based resources. From what can be seen of the nature of Mesolithic sites, more than 250 have been recorded from Kent alone (Wymer, 1977, 143-617). The distributional patterning of such sites, and aberrant artifacts (Mellars & Reinhardt, 1978, 252, fig.3, 268, fig.4) suggests seasonal movement, presumably by small groups, with gatherings of larger numbers in specific places. Periodic assembly areas are not readily identified, as places of importance for present-day prehistorians were not necessarily prominent to prehistoric peoples. However at Addington, in Kent, several acres of the Greensand have yielded numerous Mesolithic flint artifacts. Indeed, a working area was located beneath, and material was incorporated into, the Chestnuts long barrow (Alexander, 1961, 29-36). It is thus not impossible that the long barrows at Addington (Ashbee, 2000, 337) were deliberately sited upon this Greensand area, because of its deep-rooted associations, and not on the chalk like their fellows.

It has been thought that post-holes detected at Addington might have held the principal supports for shelters (Jessup, 1970, 55), as traces of possible habitations, some associated with pits, have been encountered in southern England. At Downton in Wiltshire (Higgs, 1959) an assemblage of later Mesolithic flints was associated with a scatter of stake-holes, while in Hampshire near Havant (Bradley & Lewis, 1974) stake-holes were considered to have signified wind-breaks. However, on Broom Hill, above the Test valley, a large pit was surrounded by post- and stake-holes (O'Malley, 1978; O'Malley & Jacobi, 1978). Three elongated pits at Selmeston, in Sussex, (Clark, 1934) had a considerable associated flint industry, including axes. Four irregular, gravel-dug pits at Farnham, in Surrey, one of which had by it a substantial post-hole, were associated with a massive struck flint assemblage, of about 40,000 pieces, which included microliths, axes and scrapers (Clark & Rankine, 1939). At Abinger, also in Surrey, L.S.B. Leakey, while home from Africa, examined an elongated pit, dug into the Greensand, with two end-on post-holes, which had in and about it more than 6000 pieces of struck flint, mostly cores and utilised flakes, while traces of hearths were close by (Leakey, 1951). Although post-holes were noticed at Addington (Fisher, 1938, 147), infilled shallow declivities might not have been seen in the white sand.

Elongated pits could well have been formed by substantial trees falling and uprooting. Such a ready-made shelter could have been augmented by posts and stakes. Occupation sites in the vicinity of the rocky crags of the Tunbridge Wells sand have been investigated and radiocarbon dates obtained. A shelter at High Rocks (Money, 1962) appears to have been intermittently occupied. There was evidence of flint-working and a variety of artifacts, including microliths, were found. Patches of charcoal, and burned flints, remained from fires and from these a date of the order of 6500 BP was obtained. A similar site, in the lee of a great rock at High Hurstwood, near Uckfield, in Sussex (Jacobi & Tebbutt, 1981), yielded more than 4000 struck flints with a considerable number of microliths. Three radiocarbon dates indicated occupation some eight millennia BP. Similar sites have been found close by the stones of Chiddingstone, in western Kent (Wymer, 1977; Jacobi, 1982, 17). The question remains as to whether or not these various sites, some in the lee of considerable rocky outcrops, were, as in much earlier times, winter quarters or, as in the Eifel (Wegner, 1986, 24-41), eminences from which the movement of food animals might be monitored.

As has been observed thar the food animals of earlier, Pleistocene times may have been hunted to extinction and thus, in the post-Devensian age deer, wild boar and cattle were the principal quarries. Systematic woodland burning created open spaces where such creatures could congregate. This would, at appropriate times, have allowed selection and the use of the bow, which appears as a principal hunting weapon. Animal selection and management may have been aided by dogs who allied themselves with humankind at about this time (Degerbøl, 1937). Woodland food resources, such as hazel nuts, are likely to have been, in terms of nut-production, stimulated by burning and the breaking of forest canopies. Forests would also have been a considerable source of vegetable food, (Dimbleby, 1967, 37-8) demanding seasonal collection for winter storage. Water-plants (Clark, 1952, 48,600-), even the rhizomes of the common reed, were also exploited. At certain times, berries would have been of importance (Brothwell, 1969, 131). Indeed, it has been argued that tree and plant resources loomed larger in the Mesolithic domestic economy than is commonly thought and that composite equipment, employing easily replaceable flint microliths, was expressly designed for their harvesting (Clarke, 1976). Freshwater fish from rivers and bodies of water are likely to have been an important commodity. Basketwork traps, mounted in batteries, to obtain large quantities, may have been a favoured mode (Clark, 1952, pl.ii, a, b, c). Fowling by means of a series of snares and nets, besides the collection of, particularly, water-bird eggs would have been yet another seasonal dietary supplement. Forest and other fungi should also not be overlooked as their nitrogeneous qualities are greater than many vegetables. The taking of wild honey is known, albeit in Spain (Clark, 1952, 34, fig.12), from earlier times and for this bark or leather containers would have been necessary. Catching and gathering would have been an active life, punctuated by periods when particular commodities were unobtainable. Calorific needs vary but, nevertheless, an active Mesolithic male would have needed more than 3500 a day, a level which their efficient and comprehensive environmental exploitation would have been able to sustain.

Notionally, artifact assemblages should provide insights into economic and even social activities. For example, microliths, without axes or heavier tools, could point to hunting or collecting, while numbers of axes could remain from shelter construction or even log-boat fashioning. Thus, in Kent, one might expect particular tool combinations for the exploitation of estuarine marshland environments, for hunting and gathering on the chalklands, often distant from water supplies. Indeed, there may well have been an axe-production centre at Ash-cum-Ridley (Wymer, 1979, 144). The Greensand, beyond the Gault, appears to have been favoured and it is well-drained, warm, and has numerous watercourses emanating from the base of the chalk. It attracted activities as is shown by the many artifact concentrations along its length. Moreover, its generally dry conditions would have allowed environmental control employing fire. Movement down into the Wealden clay-lands would have left peoples, other than mobile task-force groups, at a distance from sources of flint, a factor that would have inhibited settlement. The rocky highlands of the Weald, the Tunbridge Wells sands, would have provided conditions analogous to those of the Greensand, but also distant from sources of flint. River valley occupation should reflect fishing and fowling, although the rivers would have been swifter, shallower streams, flowing to considerably lower sea-levels. Indeed, log-boat navigation might, for the most part, have been possible only in the lower, tidal reaches.

Of the more than 250 Mesolithic sites now known from Kent (Wymer, 1977, 143-61) few have been excavated or even closely examined. Less than half a dozen have been accorded a notice in print. The remainder are from various collections, made down the years, located in often distant obscure museums, which have been recorded by the exercise of much patience, perspicacity and erudition. The best known of this series is Lower Halstow (21) where, during the later 1920s, J.P.T Burchell (1925; 1927; 1928) excavated what were considered as occupation sites, a northern and a southern. Situated on the right bank of a one-time channel of the Medway, upon 'Marsh' Clay, above London Clay, and covered by some 6ft of rainwash, peats and marsh clays, there were patches of blackened earth with calcined flints. Subsequently, the southern site was examined and hearths, on the London Clay, isolated. These Lower Halstow sites have often been thought of as wetland and near-coastal. Pollen analysis of northern site samples indicated their appreciable antiquity, already apparent from the many flint artifacts. Although

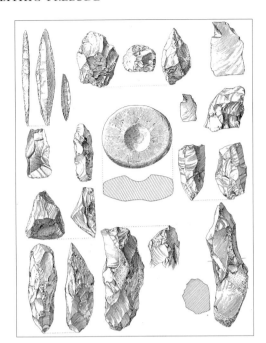

21 Flake and core implements from Lower Halstow. The counter-sunk circular sarsen stone pebble is 7.5cm (3in) in diameter. *After J.P.T. Burchell, 1927*

upon an alluvium, mean sea-level is likely to have been 60ft (18m) lower than today and distant from the coast (Coles, 1998, 66-9). Numbers of axes, adzes, sharpening flakes, scrapers, awls, plus a quartzite pebble with counter-sunk hollows, were recovered and heavy tools appeared to be in the majority, for microliths were few in number. It has been observed, however, that many might have been overlooked in the sticky marsh clay. Writing in 1932 (63-5), Grahame Clark considered Lower Halstow as contemporary with the Danish 'Kitchen Midden' culture and to belong to the later Mesolithic. In 1936 (158) he considered it as the British equivalent of the Ertebølle culture of Denmark (Clark, 1975, 180-98, *passim*), while observing that the 'southern' assemblage was patently earlier than a Neolithic flint scatter which included leaf-shaped arrowheads. Jacobi (1982, 16) considers that the Lower Halstow artifact assemblages are, because of selectivity, survival and wide dispersal, difficult to assess, although he includes them in his artifact analyses (Jacobi, 1982, 18, tab.4). A not dissimilar site may have been encountered at Swalecliffe (Worsfold, 1927). More than half-a-century ago it was said of Lower Halstow that much more needed to be known of it (CBA, 1948, 84), a sentiment expressed by many recent writers.

Other than Lower Halstow and Money's work at Chiddingstone (Wymer, 1977, 146), on Castle Hill, at Tonbridge (Money, 1975, 81) and the High Rocks at Tunbridge Wells (1960; 1962) the investigation of the Mesolithic in Kent has, for the most part, been confined to collection, preservation of material and brief,

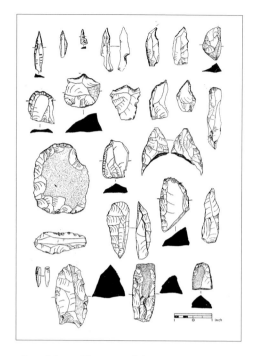 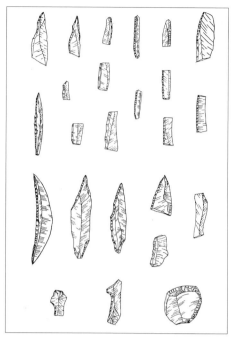

Above left: 22 Elements of the Mesolithic industry associated with the Chestnuts megalithic barrow at Addington. *After J. Alexander, 1960*

Above right: 23 Microliths from Shottenden (¼), on the west bank of the Stour, about a mile from Chilham. *After A.G. Woodcock, 1975*

note-form, publications. To supplement John Wymer's (1977) *Gazetteer*, there are summary notes, mostly from Maidsotne's Museum, in the Kent Archaeological Society's journal, *Archaeologia Cantiana*. In a paper which describes Mesolithic material from Perry Woods, Selling, near Canterbury (Woodcock, 1975, 169), members of the Kent Mesolithic Research Group are mentioned. Sadly, the present writer has been unable to find further details of what must have been a laudable, forward-looking, enterprise.

At Addington numerous artifacts (*22*), burins, flakes, cores, axes, microliths and part of a sarsen stone mace-head, have been collected. There have, however, since the initial notice of the the site (Fisher, 1938), been no more than a series of notes, one by the present writer (Ashbee, 1950) together with observations by W.F. Rankine (1956, 29, 61), J.P.T. Burchell (see Dimbleby, 1963) and G.W. Dimbleby (1963), who extracted pollen grains from the sandy soil, as had been done at an earlier juncture (Burchell & Erdtman 1950). Dense alder, birch and oak forest were detected and the assemblages have been assigned to the Atlantic Zone VII stage. A by-product of the Chestnuts long barrow excavation (Alexander,

1961, 5) was a considerable, more than 2000 pieces, Mesolithic flint assemblage in and beneath the long barrow remnant (Alexander, 1961, 29-36). Notice was also made of the flint collection made by the then landowner, M.R. Boyle. Sadly most of the material has been dispersed and can no longer be seen (Jacobi, 1982, 16-17). Mesolithic flints from Ditton, at no great distance, have been located in Cambridge (Wymer, 1977, 147), while Grahame Clark (1932, 70-1, 85) recorded material from East Malling, Ivy Hatch and Sevenoaks. At Orpington flints were collected with earlier work in mind (Jones, 1952).

Mesolithic implements and flakes were collected by the present writer from the site of the Whiteheath round barrows, at Hollingbourne (Grove, 1952). A well-worn pebble of a fine-grained rock was also found. Recently (Glass, 2000, 452) the Essex Archaeological Unit has examined a considerable site between Sandway and Harrietsham, on a slope by a tributary to the River Len. Two large scatters and two pits were found besides numerous microliths plus more than 7500 pieces of worked flint. A site just to the north of Ellis Barn, Kenardington, at no great distance from the fossil cliffs fringing inland Romney Marsh, produced axes, cores and. microliths. Some had been struck from small Tertiary pebbles (Harrison, 1943, xxxii; Bradshaw, 1968).

With Northern German reindeer hunters in mind J.P.T. Burchell (1938) investigated two Mesolithic 'floors' in the Ebbsfleet valley, west of Northfleet. During 1960 this site was reinvestigated (Sieveking, 1960) and microliths, flint waste, Neolithic leaf-shaped arrowheads and pottery were found. It was adjacent to the type-site of Ebbsfleet's later Neolithic pottery (Piggott, 1954, 309, fig.49, 1-3).

The excavation of two sites on a patch of the Thanet beds in Perry woods, Selling (Woodcock, 1975) yielded more than 3500 flakes and artifacts, which included axes, cores and microliths (23). Soil-pollen samples pointed to the Boreal/Atlantic stage. Flint-bearing chalk is at no great distance. At Shorne, near Gravesend (Allen, 1971, 164), a fire on Randall Heath revealed a concentration of Mesolithic flintwork comparable, presumably, with the Fenn Wood assemblage from that parish (Wymer, 1977, 157). At Grovehurst a tranchet axe was among the well-known 'hut-site' material (Payne, 1880), while J.P.T. Burchell has collected Mesolithic flints from the area. A broken transversely-sharpened axe from Ulcombe was brought into the museum at Maidstone during 1960 and it is likely that associations would be found were fieldwalking undertaken (Kelly, 1961, 202).

These comments on sites and discoveries emphasise more than anything the necessity of discovering and selecting sites, inland, perhaps riverine or adjacent to a body of water, where bone, antler and wooden artifacts might be found, and palaeobotany plus radiocarbon dating undertaken. A further consideration is the nature of and reasons for the location of specific sites upon particular geological formations. It seems likely that in immediate post-Devensian times when the lands that are now Kent were still joined to the continental landmass (Coles, 1998, 65-9) or at least readily accessible to the Maglemosians, and those that came after them, the population of the area may not have been great but, aside from this, we are looking at an ingenious and efficient mode of life that persisted for more than three millennia.

As has been observed, vegetables and forest foods are likely to have loomed large in the Mesolithic domestic economy. This would have entailed the evolution of an enquiring environmental husbandry which would have involved an intimate knowledge of the qualities of the essential staples. Mesolithic control and direction of vegetation by burning has already been alluded to but it should not be thought of as an isolated process. There would also have been an awareness of the implications of seeding and growth, besides root production. Thus appropriate clearances could have been seed-beds and the modification of bodies of water could have stimulated the desired aquatic roots. In short, systems of almost arable agriculture could have been practised. In like manner the relationships with animals, presumably dog-assisted, is likely to have been more intimate than is commonly thought, for taming, controlling reproduction and culling also had clear, desired consequences. In later Mesolithic times, particularly in Kent (Ashbee, 1999) there is the possibility that cereals were obtained from LBK (*Linearbandkeramik*) sources, on the European mainland, and cultivated. There could have been a millennium of traffic, for the lands that are now Kent are a contact zone, before the first early recognisable Neolithic modes and usages developed upon the Kentish chalklands and their surround. Mesolithic food animals within the territories of specific groups are likely to have been conserved and controlled, with all the advantages that such practices brought in their train, although such premises are difficult to prove. Within a pollen spectrum the first appearance of plantain (*Plantago lanceolata*), a principal weed of cultivation, could be significant. Behavioural prerequisites for animal domestication (Clutton-Brock, 1981, 15-6) have been defined and whereas deer can be herded, wild cattle – creatures that moved in the Mesolithic forests – were ultimately subjected to man on a global basis, with remarkable and unexpected consequences (Jewell, 1993, 114-5). However, at some point, the husbandry of a considerable spectrum of vegetable resources became systematised food production with cereals as a primary consideration. Yet these changes, which are likely to have come about from close contact with LBK farmers, were not without ideological, and, ultimately, monumental baggage (Ashbee, 1982).

FIVE

NEOLITHIC HUSBANDMEN AND THEIR MONUMENTS

At the outset of the twentieth century, the Neolithic was seen as a lengthy polished axe period, during which agriculture emerged and the British buried their dead in long barrows (Kendrick & Hawkes, 1932, 56). Ronald Jessup (1930) adroitly separated his New Stone Age from the megaliths, our spectacular Kentish stone-built long barrows. Stuart Piggott (1931) detailed the *Neolithic Pottery of the British Isles* and Gordon Childe (1931) its affinities with the European mainland. A decade later (Childe, 1940) he was able to envisage a *Neolithic Revolution* from food-gathering to food-production, supported by the long barrows, earthen and stone-built seen as the monuments of a megalithic religion. Thereafter, in 1954, Stuart Piggott's *Neolithic Cultures of the British Isles* brought together an amassment of material, frequently fragmentary, to which it gave clarity, direction, and purpose, within, as far as possible, a European context. He saw the Neolithic, as in 1931, occupying no more than about 500 years, before 1500 BC. However, the radiocarbon revolution has progressively lengthened our notions of the Neolithic and, today, a body of dates that indicates changes as early as 7000 BP exists, the chronological view that T.D. Kendrick and others had moved away from.

The term Neolithic literally 'New Stone' was coined by Sir John Lubbock for the first (1865) edition of his *Prehistoric Times,* and his intention was that this later stage, defined largely by polished stone axes, should be separated from the handaxes of the Palaeolithic, the Old Stone Age. Down the years, it came to be thought of in economic terms, the cultivation of cereal crops and the herding of domestic animals for meat and milk. Neolithic societies in this mould appeared in south-eastern Europe as early as 9000 years BP and these farmers, dubbed the LBK (*Linearbandkeramik*) people, distinguished by their groups of long timber houses and adherence to the loess, were eventually established by the English Channel. As a result of contacts, the peoples of what has emerged as the British Isles, in common with other parts of Northern and Western Europe, ultimately became farming communities. The process was gradual, although sometimes accelerated by local conditions, and in no region has the outcome been quite the same. Often, substantial settlements following the LBK pattern have been sought, but the most that has emerged has been flimsy, isolated, mostly rectilinear post and stake structures.

The integral parts of the earlier Neolithic are earthworks, causewayed enclosures, pits, long barrows, and distinctive artifacts, pottery, polished axes of flint and fine-grained rock, and leaf-shaped arrowheads (24). Wooden artifacts, such as axe-hafts, have been found in anaerobic deposits while traces of isolated, more or less rectangular, houses are known. The later Neolithic saw the emergence of earthwork henge monuments, enclosing stone circles or massive circular, timber houses, cursûs, parallel banks and ditches, often of considerable length, while long barrows continued in use, their numbers possibly augmented. Distinctive, impress-decorated pottery styles, Ebbsfleet, Mortlake (Peterborough) and Fengate wares emerged and were accompanied by the well-made and unmistakable Grooved wares, termed by some 'Rinyo-Clacton'. Earlier Neolithic modes were

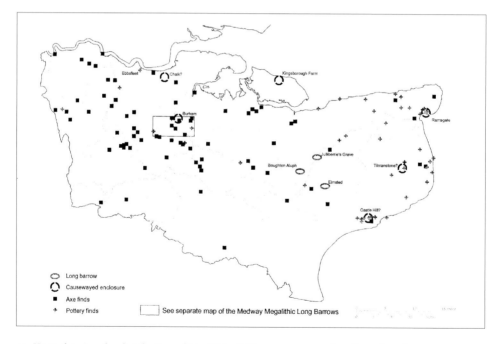

24 Kent: showing the distribution of Neolithic field monuments and artifacts. See also separate map of the Medway megalithic long barrows (31). *After T.G. Lawson and D. Killingray, 2004*

established by about 6000 BP and the Later became apparent a millennium-and-a-half thereafter. For the most part the basic radiocarbon dates, the foundation of chronological evaluation, are from earthwork sites and they may not always embrace the fundamental environmental and economic changes.

Causewayed enclosures, exemplified by Windmill Hill, in Wiltshire (Smith, 1965; 1971; Palmer, 1976), are circular or near-oval areas on hilltops and low-lying ground, enclosed by from one to four ditches, distinguished by undug causeways at mostly irregular intervals, with, for the most part, corresponding internal banks (25). Since their initial identification and excavation, notions of their functions have changed from settlement to centres for congregation, cattle-slaying, rituals, feasting – as shown by the Coneybury pit (Whittle, 1996, 234, fig.7.97) – and even burial (Drewett, 1977, 222; Mercer, 1980). The reburied material, largely cattle bones and occupational debris, in the Windmill Hill ditches could support the notion of periodic gatherings of small, dispersed groups. In about 1970 only about 16-18 causewayed enclosures were known, today, more than 70 from Wessex to Scotland have been identified. With such a number, few have been extensively excavated, a variety of functions is not impossible. Pits, hollows, and spreads of pottery have been encountered in south-eastern England, including Kent (Field *et al*, 1964). Following the excavation of the Hurst Fen site in Suffolk,

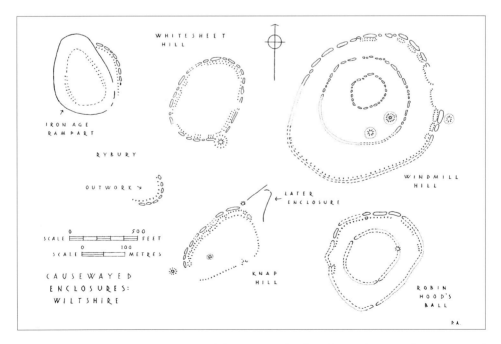

25 Neolithic causewayed enclosures in Wiltshire. Traces of such enclosures have now been recognised in Kent, at Burham, on Sheppey and at Ramsgate. *After P. Ashbee, 1978*

26 The Fussell's Lodge earthen long barrow excavations, 1957. With a timber façade and kerbing it would have resembled the sarsen stone-built long barrows of the Medway Valley. *Photograph P. Ashbee, 1957*

(Clark *et al*, 1960), an operation which included a search for traces of timber houses and where some 200 pits and hollows were exposed, such complexes have been accorded a functional explanation. It was thought that most of the Hurst Fen pits had been used for the storage of grain and other foodstuffs. At Hazard Hill, in Devon (Houlder, 1963), an attempt was made to assign functions to pits on the basis of dimensions, content and relative positions. A good number of causewayed enclosures are within the region of maximum pit density and such pits occur in at least five of them.

Earthen long barrows (Ashbee, 1984; Kinnes, 1992), which sometimes conceal timber chambers and surrounds (Ashbee, 1966) (*26*) are known in southern and eastern England, besides Scotland. Excavation has revealed regional variations (Kinnes, 1992). Stone-built, sometimes megalithic, long barrows (Daniel, 1950; Powell, 1969; Lynch, 1997) also display territorial variations in middle and western England, Wales, Ireland and Scotland.

Neolithic axes have been found in great numbers. It has been claimed that the flint mines, as in Sussex (Curwen, 1954, 96-141 and at Grime's Graves, in Norfolk, Mercer, 1981) were primarily for their production. Sadly the use of trace-element analyses to determine the sources of such axes have yet to be fully developed (Craddock *et al*, 1983). They were supplemented by axes made from fine-grained rocks from distant sources. Their origins have been determined by petrological thin-sectioning (Clough & Cummins, 1988). Here and there suitable erratic pieces may have been utilised. Leaf-shaped arrowheads which have a considerable European distribution in areas adjacent to south-eastern England (Childe, 1931, 43), are known in the area from particular sites and as stray discoveries. Scatters of such arrowheads in the vicinity of enclosure sites (Mercer, 1981; Dixon, 1985) point to internecine conflict, as does their association with human remains (Kinnes, 1992, 109-10).

The appearance of pottery in quantity (Piggott, 1931; 1954; Smith, 1965; 1974; Cleal, 1992) is an innovation in that, by the use of fire, raw clay is converted into a durable, leathery container of a kind that can be readily replaced. Regional styles, sometimes intermixed, have been identified. The interment of pots in pits, the quantities of pottery found in the ditches of certain causewayed enclosures, and the related vessels accompanying the human bone deposits in certain long barrows (Ashbee, 1984, 71) may betoken more than daily domestic use. Wooden artifacts and appliances have for long been known from Neolithic contexts (Piggott, 1954, 295-9), although wooden bowls, which some ceramic containers resemble, have not been found in English wetland contexts, despite the skills for their production being present (Coles, & Coles 1986; Coles & Lawson, 1987).

Henge monuments, earthwork enclosures (sometimes of great size), characterised by an outer bank and inner ditch, emerged in later Neolithic times (Wainwright & Longworth, 1971; Wainwright, 1979; 1989). Certain of these, as at Avebury (Smith, 1965) surrounded stone circles, often had within them enormous timber buildings, periodically occupied, while others enclosed pits and shafts (Bradley, 1976), and were clearly the focus of arcane rituals. One must observe in passing that Stonehenge is likely to have been a massive, composite, timber and stone structure in the mould of those detected in neighbouring henges (Ashbee, 1978, *passim*). Henges, once a southern English rarity, like the causewayed enclosures, are now a considerable category (Harding & Lee, 1987). Cursus monuments (Stone, 1948; Bradley, 1993, 99-106), the long parallel banked and ditched enclosures, as by Stonehenge and crossing Cranborne Chase, emerge by about 5500 BP but, despite their numbers and associations their function eludes us.

The flint and stone artifacts developed in earlier times continue in use but the distinctive, impress-decorated ceramic styles emerge. These, coarse in fabric, but nonetheless robust, and named after type sites, are the Ebbsfleet, Mortlake (Peterborough) and Fengate forms (Smith, 1965), accompanied by the appearance of the Grooved ware (Rinyo-Clacton) series (Wainwright & Longworth, 1971; MacSween, 1992). Whereas the impressed decoration, and also the grooving, is likely to have had significance for its makers and users, it also facilitated handling (Ashbee, 1983, 34), particularly if the contents were wet and greasy.

As was stressed in the preceding chapter, the Mesolithic peoples brought about environmental changes as particular areas of forest were cleared to facilitate plant growth and animal management. Thus molluscan analyses (Evans, 1972, 67-8) and pollen sequences (Godwin, 1962,83) probably record established situations rather than new Neolithic incursions. Although far from obvious from the limited environmental investigations that have taken place within the area that is now Kent, it is likely that, with the effluxion of time demands for timber, progressive forest clearance took place. On the other hand there is molluscan evidence from Sussex (Thomas, 1977, 234) which shows that Neolithic activities, even the establishment of a causewayed enclosure, could have taken place within a wooded environment.

As long ago as 1937 an ostensible causewayed enclosure was claimed for West Wickham (Hogg & O'Neil, 1937; Hogg et al, 1941; Hogg, 1981). Its antiquity was indicated by two superimposed round barrows but, notwithstanding, it was never included in the series. Recent investigation makes a Neolithic origin for this earthwork unlikely. Ronald Jessup (1970, 73) recounted that a causewayed enclosure, now destroyed, may have existed at Chalk, near Gravesend, on the south bank of the Thames, where it might have balanced the substantial enclosure excavated at Orsett, in Essex (Hedges & Buckley, 1978). This destroyed enclosure has received many mentions but, as has been shown (Barber, 1997, 81), they all emanate from Ronald Jessup's brief statement. Rescue archaeology (Shand, 1998), near Ramsgate, revealed ditches, seemingly part of a causewayed enclosure, which the present writer considered as supplementary to the pits and scatters which characterised eastern Kent (Ashbee, 1999, 276). It was also observed that such enclosures are evocative of the systems surrounding some LBK villages and that they could also serve as an ordered, concentrated expression of the pit principles. Deposits of animal bones, which included two cattle skulls, with marine shells and pottery sherds, as well as indications of episodic flint knapping, repeated what is now a recognised formula, while parts of human skulls may denote traffic with long barrows (Ashbee, 1999, 276-7). Further work (Dyson, Shand & Stevens, 2000) has shown that this chalkland causewayed enclosure was more than 150m (480ft) in diameter and consisted of three concentric ditches which had been recut, the outer ditch being the deepest and widest. It emerged that the ditch deposits differed significantly. The inner ditch had the most cremated bone, the middle ditch flints, notably scrapers and leaf-shaped arrowheads, noticeably at ditch ends, while the outer ditch had deposits of animal bones, seashells and broken pottery, besides parts of two human skulls. One of these, it was said, was associated with the ditches' recutting. Linear causewayed ditches, with pottery and flint implements in them, were close by while, as at Maiden Castle (Ashbee, 1984, 18, fig.7), a bank-barrow or cursus superseded the primary enclosure. A round barrow was at no great distance, as was a later Bronze Age installation.

Another and not dissimilar triple-ditched causewayed enclosure has been located and partially excavated on Kingsborough Farm, Eastchurch, on the Isle of Sheppey (Dyson, Shand & Stevens, 2000, 471). It was towards the top of what is now a low hill within the 50m (200ft) contour. In earlier Neolithic times, with mean sea-level some 18m (60ft) lower than that of today, this low hill would have been a considerable eminence. On a slope, a siting not unlike that of Windmill Hill (Smith, 1965), it was more than 150m (500ft) in diameter. It was reported that the inner and middle ditches had in them considerable quantities of broken pottery and flintwork. To the north, and at the top of the hill, a substantial later Bronze Age, or perhaps Iron Age, ditch was encountered. Lower Halstow, where a Neolithic flint industry included leaf-shaped arrowheads (Burchell, 1927, pl.1; Clark, 1936, 158), and Grovehurst (Payne, 1880; 1893, 1-6) are sites that would have been within this causewayed enclosure's catchment area.

It is possible that a Neolithic earthwork, perhaps a causewayed enclosure, lies beneath the medieval earthworks on the summit of Castle Hill, Folkestone. Trenching has detected ditches with later Neolithic pottery in the upper layers of their infill (Bennett et al, 1991, 8-9). The Creteway Down assemblage of Neolithic pottery was found at no great distance from this site (Dunning, 1966, 11-12).

Intensive fieldwork, aided by aerial photography, has identified two more causewayed enclosures in Kent. One is at Burham, on the lower slopes of the North Downs and east of the Medway, which is adjacent to the eastern series of the megalithic long barrows of the Maidstone Gap (Ashbee, 2000, 320, fig.1). This discovery brings the Medway's long barrows into line with the distributional patterns observed elsewhere in southern England (Ashbee, 1978, 83, fig.22). There is also the inherent possibility that another such enclosure might be found in the vicinity of the western long barrow group, perhaps on a corresponding foreslope of the Downs, at a remove from Coldrum. The second is close by Tilmanstone, to the south-west of Sandwich. Neither is, as in Wessex, sited upon a hilltop, but occupies a slope.

Pits, often accidentally encountered, singly or in groups are often indicative of settlement somewhere in their vicinity, although, as at Hurst Fen, Mildenhall, in Suffolk, they do not neccesarily indicate houses (Clark et al, 1960). In Kent, one such site, Grovehurst, has been known since the later nineteenth century (Payne, 1880; 1893, 1-6), and at that time was thought of as a series of sunken huts. Payne (1880, 123) wrote:

> On the 21st January, 1871, intelligence was received of the discovery of Flint weapons and flakes, together with pottery and animal remains. An examination of the ground from whence they were taken, showed that originally a hole had been dug out to a depth of from three to four feet, and about ten feet in diameter, the bottom of the cavity, which was in the form of a bowl, being covered with a layer of burnt vegetable matter about a foot thick. From the year 1871 to 1878 discoveries have been

frequently made of a precisely similar nature. During that time the writer on several occasions personally conducted the excavations, and was thus enabled to determine with certainty, that the layers of burnt and decayed material represented the floors of primitive dwellings.

Regarding the 'flint weapons and flakes', which he listed and illustrated, he wrote:

> A closer inspection, however, of the debris upon the so-called 'floors' revealed quantities of flint weapons and tools, evidently made on the spot, as innumerable chips and flakes were found which had been splintered off in the process of their manufacture. Blocks of sandstone were occasionally met with for grinding and polishing purposes, some of the smaller pieces being conveniently fashioned for use in the hand. One large block was much hollowed, and worn quite smooth from friction. Several bones, skulls and horns of Bos were likewise found, doubtless the remnants of daily meals, also fragments of rude urns made of clay mingled with minute particles of flint. The urns appeared to have been, when whole, in the shape of a flat-bottomed basin, some specimens being pierced with holes round the rim, about an inch apart.

The flint artifacts included a Mesolithic transversely sharpened axe, polished flint axes, mostly broken or reworked, a single-piece sickle (Clark, 1932, 70, pl.IX) and various leaf-shaped arrowheads, while the sandstone block was a grain-rubber, such as were found on Windmill Hill (Smith, 1965, 122, fig. 52), and pieces of others were present. Commodities other than cereals can be ground on such rubbers and they were, presumably, broken and discarded when they became foul. Stuart Piggott (1931, 138, fig.21) considered the blackish flint-gritted ware fragments as all of one pot, with an original diameter of about 30cm (12in) and a thick-ended rim, in some places lightly turned over, below which, at intervals, were perforations. At a later juncture he indicated its possible TRB (*Trichterbecherkultur*), northern European affinities (Piggott, 1954, 314) Although it was thought of as of the Ebbsfleet series, its earlier Neolithic affinities can be accepted (Smith, 1954, 228).

At Wingham (Greenfield, 1960, 60, fig.3) a pit in chalky soil yielded pottery fragments, flint flakes, ox, sheep (or goat?), pig and red deer bones, an antler comb, a bone point and a sandstone rubber, with its rider. Seven pots were represented by rim sherds and other pieces were present. They had been buried as sherds, not complete vessels. All were of round-bottomed bowls, sloping in from from rim to base with simple, beaded, turned-over, out-turned or flared rims. The assemblage was notable for its high burnish and hard fabric. Antler combs, a dozen of which where found on Windmill Hill (Smith, 1965, 125), have been encountered on

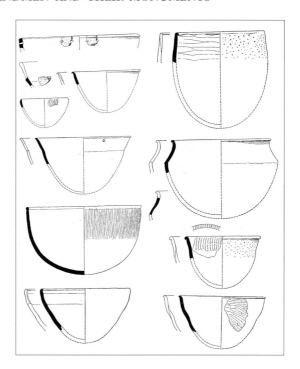

27 Early Neolithic pottery from
Deal and Ramsgate (1/4). *After G.C.
Dunning, 1966*

the European mainland in Belgium (Childe, 1940, 41) and at Heikendorf, near
Kiel, in Schleswig-Holstein (Piggott, 1956, 99). The flint flakes were from a single
nodule and, as at Fussell's Lodge (Ashbee, 1966, 23), could be fitted together. It
is noteworthy that rims of open bowls, comparable with those from Wingham,
were present among the sherds from the Chestnuts long barrow at Addington
(Alexander, 1961, 36-42, fig. 11).

Pottery from East Kent, the Deal area, Preston, Ramsgate and Folkestone,
collated by G.C. Dunning (1966) (*27*) was for the greater part open bowls. It was
mostly from pits and probable pits, circumstances comparable with Grovehurst
and Wingham. Of particular note was a pit at Mill Road, Upper Deal, where
parts of some six open bowls were at the bottom of a flint-packed pit, which
also had in it flint flakes and a grain rubber. Similar pottery has been found
in an area of flint implements, which included a leaf-shaped arrowhead and
parts of polished axes, on an ancient clay surface beneath peat, at Birchington
(Macpherson-Grant, 1969). The sites at Deal were upon a spread of brickearth
from which was obtained a considerable, similar, flint assemblage (Dunning, 1966,
18-24). At Preston, near Wingham, a hearth 1.7m (5ft) in diameter, comprised of
black ash and charcoal 22cm (9in) in depth, had in it some 60 small plain sherds
as well as flint flakes, cores and a piece of a polished axe. One rim was that of a
carinated open bowl (Ogilvie, 1977, 97).

Mindful of the wider English scene, G.C.Dunning (1966, 17) considered the Kentish pottery as comprising a discrete derivative group, which had links with other regions, a situation which could be considered in reverse. Open bowls (Clarke, 1982, 27, fig.9) characteristic of eastern England, are not out of keeping with those of the earliest TRB series despite the virtual absence of flat bases (Midgley, 1992, 193) except perhaps at Grovehurst. These Kentish sites provide little evidence of agriculture. As has already been stressed, the sandstone rubber and fragments of rubbers found at Grovehurst do not necessarily betoken cereal cultivation. At Wingham, however, the animal bones indicate selective breeding, the creatures having been artifacts. In general, these isolated, accidentally encountered, pits and deposits could well have been elements of larger concentrations, as, for example, at Hurst Fen, in Suffolk (Clark *et al*, 1960) In the absence of groups of houses, the causewayed enclosures, presumably places of intermittent resort, the scattered pits, hearths, occasional posts, with pottery, flints, stones and other apparent rubbish, might be more indicative of Mesolithic modes than has hitherto been supposed. It should not be overlooked that some of the earlier TRB settlement sites, for Kent is at no great distance from that vast territory, were similarly shifting and ephemeral. At its margins there were profound changes within Mesolithic societies which gave rise to long barrows surrogate LBK houses, and, in the fullness of time, positive agricultural usages (Sherrat, 1997, 333-71; Midgley, 1992, 355-405).

The pits and scatters which have been found in eastern Kent are only about 30km (25 miles) from the LBK installations of the Pas-de-Calais (Ilett, 1984). Thus some of them may be the initial, clear, manifestations of Neolithic activity on what is now English soil. As has been stressed, they have a pronounced Mesolithic character.

Ostensible houses, many ephemeral, have been encountered, always single and scattered, in England and Wales (Ashbee, 1982, 137; Darvill, 1996), a circumstance that may point to a shifting lifestyle, as in earlier Mesolithic times. It has been suggested that a scattered croft economy might have obtained (Kinnes, 1994, 95). In spite of this, these structures have also been considered as pertaining to cult usages (Pryor, 1974; 1988).

At no great distance from the Medway's eastern bank megalithic long barrows, rescue excavation has disclosed a not unconvincing, slightly irregular, long house (Denison, 1999; Glass, 2000). A pattern of post-holes and bedding trenches indicated a timber structure some 20m (65ft) in length and 7m (22ft) in breadth. In the absence of flanking pits or ditches, rendering for the panels between the vertical members was presumably dug from the Gault, at no great distance. Of the number of seemingly Neolithic houses encountered in England and Wales, this example, on Blue Bell Hill, is the first to be reasonably comparable with the

LBK series. The associated pits do not, however, necessarily connote a domestic function. Unless the remains of further houses are found it could be thought that the erstwhile structure was an exemplar for the long barrows. It is perhaps significant that indications of a structure similar to that of an LBK house (Ilett, 1984, 28, fig.2.12) has appeared in Kent, no more than about 50 miles from the European mainland. However, a not dissimilar long house has been found in close association with a developed, stone-built long barrow in Co. Mayo, on the western coast of distant Ireland (Waddell, 1998, 80, fig.39, 1.2).

Arrows, with leaf-shaped points and long shafts, propelled by long bows, examples of which have been recovered from English wetland sites (Clark, 1963), were a feature of our Neolithic. Numbers of such arrowheads have been collected, largely from the Kentish Greensand, while examples are known from such sites as Lower Halstow (Clark, 1936, 158), Grovehurst (Payne, 1880) and the brickearth at Deal (Dunning, 1966, 22, fig.11, 1, 2). They appear as a reversion to an earlier form (Champion et al, 1984, 44, fig.2, 21). Although, when used by a practiced bowman, they would have allowed the selection, stalking and despatch of such creatures as deer and cattle, they appear to have had a role as weapons (Darvill, 1987, 73, 76). Sir John Evans (1897, 378) records how he found a leaf-shaped arrowhead 'near Kit's Coty House' while Ronald Jessup (1930, 55-6) records examples found in the vicinity of Ightham, presumably by Benjamin Harrison, at Platt, East Malling and Linton, besides a number found on Drow Hill, Luton, associated with what may have been a hoard of thin-butted flint axes. Leaf-shaped arrowheads (Smith, 1927; Whittle, 1977, 75) are few in Kent as compared with the numbers from particular sites and other areas. This may change with causewayed enclosure and long barrow investigation.

The British Museum holds a magnificent polished jadeite axe, allegedly found at Canterbury (Smith, 1926, 100, fig.94; Jessup, 1930, 51). It is more than 21cm (8.5in) in length and bears no signs of use, and with Breton discoveries in mind (Patten, 1993, 19.28) they could be considered as pertaining to an axe cult. An abraded fragment of a large axe of pyroxene jadeite, with a high glossy polish, was found on the paving of the antechamber of Cairnholy, a developed stone-built long barrow, in Galloway, south-western Scotland (Piggott & Powell, 1949, 137-9). Some 50 such axes have been found in Britain and this piece is the only occurrence in an archaeological context, the remainder being incidental discoveries. This Canterbury axe could be an import from Brittany but, nonetheless, similar rocks are known from Italy and Germany (Piggott & Powell, 1949, 139).

An integral feature of our Neolithic is the incidence of polished flint and fine-grained rock axes, for long its type-fossils (Taylor, 1996). There are numerous Kentish flint examples, although flint mines, from which raw material of the appropriate quality would have been extracted, have not as yet been found in the county (Barber *et al*, 1999, 26, 72), while Spurrell's early claims have been reconsidered (Pitts, 1996, 364, 10). Flint suitable for axes could have been extracted from the chalk sea-cliffs of Thanet or Dover, while open-cast quarrying into parts of the escarpment of the North Downs could be envisaged. Axes made from fine-grained rocks (Clough & Wooley, 1985; Clough & Cummins, 1988; Pitts, 1996) have been found at Keston and Murston (Gp.I, Cornwall), Ashford, Bexley and Rolvenden (Gp.VI, Great Langdale), New Hythe (Gp.VII, Graig Lwyd), Gravesend and Sittingbourne (Gp.IX Tievebulliagh) and Downe (Gp.XVI, Cornwall). Of note is the flint axe (*28*) from the Julliberrie's Grave long barrow (Ashbee, 1996, 24, fig.6) and the adze from Bearsted (Cook, 1934), both of which are of forms current in Northern Germany and Scandinavia. Sadly many such axes and other artifacts may have been discarded from nineteenth-century collections (Piggott, 1938, 101). Although one was found deep in the clay at Cranbrook (Harrison, 1943, xxxiii), the greater number have been surface discoveries.

Flint and stone axes and adzes accompany everywhere the advent of Neolithic productive endeavours. They are notably effective for light timber felling and general working, although it must not be overlooked that timber, trimmed and rendered into useful sizes, could have been taken from beaver dams and lodges (Ashbee, 1984, 80; Coles & Orme, 1983). In England the more substantial timber

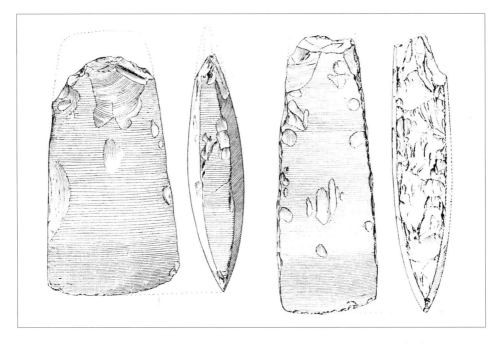

28 Julliberrie's Grave, Chilham, the damaged square-sided Northern flint axe from the loam core. Length 13.6cm (5.125in). *After R.F. Jessup, 1939*

structures were the long barrows (Ashbee, 1966; Kinnes, 1992), as groups of houses comparable with those of the LBK settlements (Whittle, 1994, 157), and the later TRB people were not, it seems, built. Sarsen stone moving, as by the Medway, would have involved a considerable use of appropriate timbers, all sized, cut and prepared.

Of note are the hoards or caches of flint axes from southern England, three of importance being from Kent. There is good reason for flint axes to be put into the earth in that their inherent moisture may be preserved, for when absolutely dry they become brittle (Pitts, 1996, 340). Within the TRB territory of the European mainland, axes were placed into chosen waterlogged places for presumably practical reasons, although votive considerations are not impossible (Midgley, 1992, 282). The Bexley Heath hoard, found in a celery trench, is of particular importance in that it could be a woodworker's selection of axes, heavy and light, including an adze. Seven pieces were found but only five reached the British Museum (Spurrell, 1891; Smith, 1926, 103, pl.VI; Jessup, 1930, 52; Pitts, 1996, 356, 12). Three flaked axes, cached perhaps, prior to polishing, have been found in sandy soil at Pembury (Tester, 1951) while three polished axes from Saltwood (Pitts, 1996, 367, 5) (possible caches) may have been in a pit with occupation debris.

Many polished axes have been for the most part polished well beyond the needs of functionality and there is the possibility that, in Kent and elsewhere, they could be a manifestation of an axe cult (Piggott, 1965, pl.VII; Bradley, 1990, 46, 50, fig.7). They have, from time to time, been found deep in the ground and thus they may have been buried in places where timber production and wood wokring were undertaken, All in all, more than 70 polished flint axes are known from the county. Functional flint axes would have had polished edges (Curwen, 1954, 124, fig.29) and their flaked butts would have made for firmer hafting. As they were of high quality flint many were recycled, when their use-life came to an end, by being reflaked into blades and scrapers.

A small group of earthen long barrows flanks the Stour (*29*), the principal river of eastern Kent (Holgate, 1981, 226, fig.3; Parfitt, 1993). Julliberrie's Grave, the subject of careful, comprehensive, excavations (Jessup, 1937; 1939; 1970, 81–6; Ashbee, 1996) has been known since the sixteenth century (*30*). Presciently, Ronald Jessup said that further mounds might be found in the vicinity were fieldwork undertaken and possible long barrows have been found at Boughton Aluph and Elmsted (Bradshaw 1970, 180). His excavations were carried out in July 1936 and for some eight weeks a year later in 1937. They showed that Julliberrie's Grave was, indeed, a long barrow, and not a pillow-mound, and also something of its erstwhile character, possible associations, later usages and vicissitudes. Its ditch, detected from thickened grass growth, proved to enclose

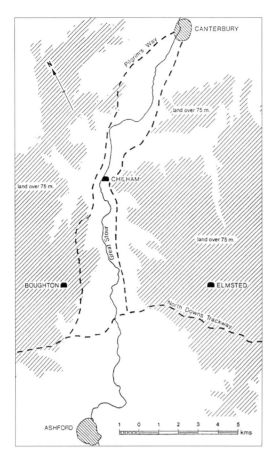

Left: 29 The earthen long barrows flanking the Stour. *After K. Parfitt, 1998*

Below: 30 William Stukeley's prospect of Julliberrie's Grave, 11 October, 1724

Opposite: 31 Kent's megalithic long barrows flanking the Medway. The Burham causewayed enclosure is adjacent to the pronounced westward bow of the river. *After P. Ashbee, 2000*

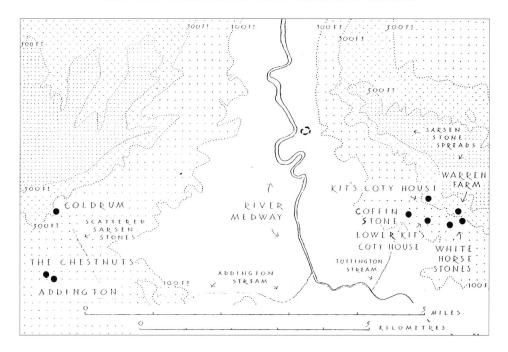

the southern end, in the manner of some long barrows in Dorset and Hampshire (Ashbee, 1984, 42, fig.30; Kinnes, 1992, 179, 181). The mound, scarred by earlier excavations, was a spine of soil and turf, mantled by chalk from the ditch. Flint flakes and the bones of oxen and sheep were found in the loamy spine. A possible post-hole was contemporary with the mound which had been truncated at its ends by chalk-digging and plough encroachment. The broken, polished flint axe, of Northern European mainland affinity, was recovered from the heart of the mound while coins and other objects, as well as pottery and burials, from the ditch at its southern end, testified to a more than casual Romano-British interest in the long barrow. Ronald Jessup's undertaking was one of a small series of long barrow excavations carried out during the 1930s which were the valued precedents for later, post-World War II, endeavours.

Kent's megalithic long barrows flank the Medway (*31*) where it cuts through the chalk of the North Downs to form the Maidstone Gap. On the eastern side there is Kit's Coty House, the best known, the Lower Kit's Coty House, the Coffin Stone and the Warren Farm chamber, as well as the White Horse Stones, uncertain sites. Coldrum, the Chestnuts and Addington lie to the west of the river, some 5 miles distant. Their chambers, façades and kerbs were built with sarsen stones, silicified sand from the Eocene, a dense, hard, heavy, durable rock, found close by (Bowen & Smith, 1977; Ashbee, 1993a, 109). The Kentish sarsen stones (*32*), mostly upon Blue Bell Hill, were, as they are now sorely

depleted, the largest southern English concentration of such stones, apart from northern Wiltshire (Piggott, 1962; Barker, 1984; Whittle, 1991). As has been observed, they have been visited and commented upon by antiquarian and archaeological writers since the sixteenth century (Ashbee, 1993a). Of particular note are William Stukeley's drawings made in the earlier eighteenth century (Ashbee, 1993a). Because of their ruined state, their nature has been recurrently misunderstood and misrepresented. Stone-built and earthen long barrows are of similar intent. Some may be timber translated into stone or vice-versa (Ashbee, 1984, 33-54; Clarke, 1982, 28). A long barrow's timber chamber preserved in the anerobic conditions of a Cambridgeshire fen (Hodder & Shand, 1988) was of fashioned timber-slab construction, a clear copy of a stone edifice.

Despite slighting of unexampled ferocity during the thirteenth century (Alexander, 1961, 7, plan 2; Ashbee, 1993a, 64), the characteristics of the Kentish sarsen stone-built long barrows are still discernible. The largest, with a chamber perhaps almost 3.75m (12ft) in height, from which the Coffin Stone remains, was, however, all but obliterated. At the eastern ends of stone-bounded trapezoidal barrows (33), sometimes more than 60m (200ft) in length, there were massive chambers, rectangular in plan, and almost 3m (10ft) in height. These were about 5-7m (14-21ft) in length and sometimes more than 2m (7ft) in breadth. They contained deposits of human bones, finally sealed by occupation debris, a

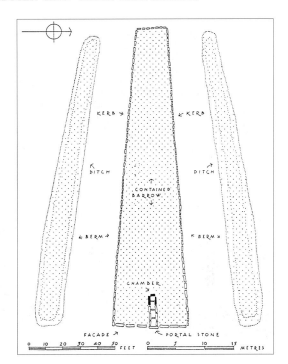

Opposite: 32 Substantial sarsen stones, some damaged, on Blue Bell Hill. *Photograph H. Elgar, c. 1908*

Right: 33 A plan of a Medway megalithic long barrow, based upon the Warren Farm chamber remnant. It illustrates the considerable number of stones required for the form common to the series. *After P. Ashbee, 2003*

formula encountered elsewhere in southern England (Piggott, 1962, 21-30, fig.9). The remnants of the contents of Coldrum's chamber (Keith, 1913; 1925; Filkins, 1928; Ashbee, 1998, 34) indicate that the erstwhile deposits of human bones may have been considerable. They are in close-knit groups conforming to Northern European mainland conventions.

Megalithic long barrows had a function which was the antithesis of the LBK long houses, the lineaments of which they portray. As is shown by the bones from Coldrum's chamber (Keith, 1913; 1925); they were the foci for usages involving human remains. There was deliberate selection, and skulls, arms, legs and hands were significant (Hodder, 1990, 246). At Coldrum skulls were well represented. Access to chambers was, presumably, controlled and from time to time, bones were taken away or added (Piggott, 1962, 66-7; Smith, 1965, 137, 251; Ashbee, 1966, 39; Woodward, 1993, 3). If, as seems likely, these practices involving bones took place over a long period, before they were covered and sealed by occupation debris (Piggott, 1962, 26, 68), we see only the final depositions. These may have signified a relationship with forbears, and causewayed enclosures, but could also be linked with agricultural efficiency, particularly when moves were made onto various, sometimes unsuitable, soil regimes (de Valera & Ó Nualláin, 1961; Ashbee, 1978, 89).

Animal bones have also been found associated with long barrows (Ashbee, 1984, 158-60; Hodder, 1990, 250), indeed, some unburned pieces were found at the Chestnuts (Alexander, 1961, 53) in ambiguous circumstances. Apart from the oxen heads and hoofed hides hung from chamber portals (Piggott, 1973, 309), ox bones have been found with such deposits and in mounds and ditches (Ashbee, 1966, pl.XV, a). In Yorkshire, Mortimer (1905, 102-5) encountered pig bones, including some 20 jaws, associated with the Hanging Grimston long barrow. Like oxen, pigs are meat animals and thus feasting as an element of the activities centred upon long barrows seems not unlikely.

There are three sites east of the Medway which are palpably long barrows, with traces of stone kerbs and ruined chambers. Kit's Coty House is a remaining chamber component standing at the end of a substantial ditched and, initially, kerbed trapezoidal long barrow remnant (34), while the Lower Kit's Coty House is an overthrown chamber (35) at the eastern end of a razed mound. Its present condition recalls the Chestnuts before restoration (Alexander, 1961) and they may have been thrown down by the same hands. Only the outline of the Coffin Stone's considerable long barrow can be seen. Recently, another substantial stone has been set upon it, while in times past, a number were pitched into the Tottington springhead (Coles Finch, 1927, 266, opp.). At Warren Farm (Ashbee, 1993a, 84) a smaller, not dissimilar, chamber-end was uncovered in 1823 (36). No barrow can be seen and hillwash mantles the area. Other sites on the eastern side

34 Kit's Coty House from the north-east. Photograph taken in 1946, showing the rectangular sidestones. The northern sidestone leans inwards, probably as a result of the erstwhile chamber's partial demolition. *Photograph P. Ashbee, 1946*

35 Lower Kit's Coty House, the slighted chamber as seen by William Stukeley in 1722. *After W. Stukeley, 1776*

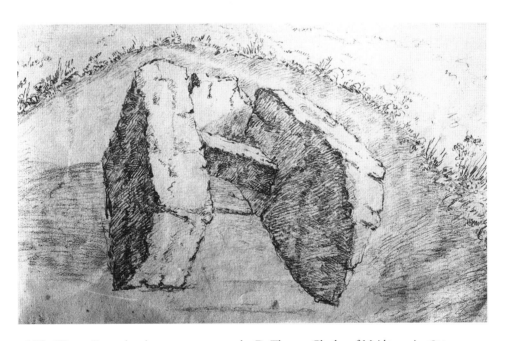

36 The Warren Farm chamber remnant as seen by Dr Thomas Charles of Maidstone in 1822

of the Medway must also be taken into consideration. The Upper White Horse Stone (Ashbee, 1993a, 87), which stands beside the Pilgrim's Way, may survive from an erstwhile long barrow. It is at no great distance from the Warren Farm chamber and pieces of sarsen stone, some substantial, have come to light in its vicinity. The Lower White Horse stone, recorded as a single standing stone, may also have remained from a dismantled chamber. These long barrows can, perhaps, be seen as two discrete groups, one headed by Kit's Coty House and the other by the Warren Farm remnant. It should not be forgotten that a causewayed enclosure has been found on the lower slopes of the North Downs, east of the Medway, at Burham, about a mile to the north-west of Kit's Coty House. This raises the possibility that traces of further long barrows, long since razed, might be detected further down the Medway's valley.

Two of the three long barrows west of the Medway, Addington and the Chestnuts on the Greensand, are close to each other, with Coldrum, on a chalky deposit at the foot of the Downs, the most intact, at a distance. It is possible that it may have had a companion, now denuded and apparently without sarsen stones, about half-a-mile to the north. Addington's chamber was wrecked almost beyond recognition but much of the massive, ditched, stone-bounded mound survives. It is likely that stones were taken to repair and extend the church during the nineteenth century. After careful excavation (Alexander, 1961) the surviving stones of the chestnuts' facade and chamber were pulled upright into their original stoneholes and thus these features were restored. It was here at the Chestnuts, that clear evidence of the mode of slighting of the Medway's megalithic long barrows, barrow removal and chamber felling, was obtained (Ashbee, 1993a, 63). The barrow's vestiges had been truncated and thus its original length could not be determined. The excavation trenches, designed to detect flanking ditches, may not have been pursued far enough. The remnant suggests an erstwhile structure larger than Addington.

At Kit's Coty House the kerbstones had been dragged away or buried in the ditches by the slighting party (McCrerie, 1956, 251). Those at Addington had been thrown down and, despite removals, sufficient remain to show the original trapezoidal nature of the barrow. At Coldrum the massive stones of the kerb largely remain, although thrown down onto the berm and partially buried when the mound was razed. They might be the surviving phase of a larger, longer structure. Stones unearthed close by the Lower Kit's Coty House and the Coffin Stone are clearly from their kerbs and others remain to be found. The larger stones in Tottington's western springhead are probably from the Coffin Stone's long barrow facade. Although only two positive trapezoidal kerbstone arrangements have survived, the general uniformity of barrow remains, and of chambers and facades, have survived, and the general uniformity of barrow remains, size and

37 William Stukeley's prospect of Kit Coty's House and record of the nature of its long barrow, 1722. This appears as about a metre (3ft and more) in height. *After W. Stukeley, 1776*

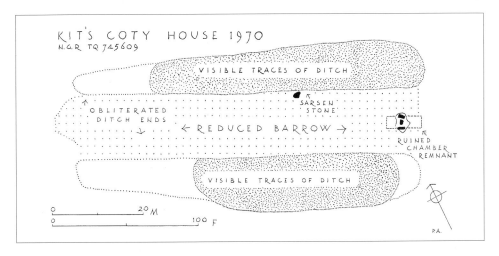

38 Kit's Coty House and its long barrow, the remains visible in 1970. *After P. Ashbee, 2000*

orientation, and of chambers and façades, makes for an homogeneous group.

Clear traces of ditches, now in danger of destruction by deep ploughing, and the reluctance of English Heritage and its forbears to protect them, have for long been visible flanking the ever diminishing long barrow remains at Kit's Coty House (Ashbee, 2000, 329, pl.II; 250-1, figs.2, 3) (*37* and *38*). Similarly, indications of ditches, clear in the nineteenth century (Petrie, 1880, 16), were until recently to be seen indicating a broad berm, on the southern side of the Addington long barrow. Traces of ditches appropriate to the Lower Kit's Coty House long barrow, deep beneath ploughsoil and hillwash, were seen in a pipe trench which, in 1994, had been cut across it. Similar ditches are likely to be found flanking the great razed barrow from which the Coffin Stone remains, also deep beneath ploughsoil, hillwash and dispersed barrow debris. At the Chestnuts, because of the broad berm, a characteristic of the series, the excavation trenches may not have been pursued to a sufficient length to locate the ditches. Coldrum's ditches, because of hillwash and agriculture, are likely to remain at a considerable depth (*39*). That on the northern side may have been impinged upon by the slighting incut and subsequent chalk removal. Before their slighting, overthrow and stone removal, the series in general appearance, would have been not unlike Wayland's Smithy II (Whittle, 1991, 65, fig.2), trapezoidal, stone-retained structures.

Human remains, those of some 22 people, have been excavated from Coldrum's chamber (*40*), besides a sherd of pottery and a serrated flint flake (Bennett, 1913; Keith, 1913; 1925; Filkins, 1924; 1928; Ashbee, 1998, 34). The sherds and bones found from 1804 onwards (Evans, 1950, 70) are likely to have been from the truncation and partial clearance when the monument was slighted, and it should not be overlooked that Kemble and Larking removed pottery (Way, 1856, 404), perhaps a remnant of settlement debris sealing. A recent study (Wysocki & Whittle, 2000, 595) of Coldrum's bones, such as have been preserved (Ashbee, 1998, 36), has revealed evidence of corpse dismemberment employing lithic instruments. A quantity of burned bones and potsherds, with various flint artifacts, come from the Chestnuts chamber (*41*), indeed, it seems likely that the

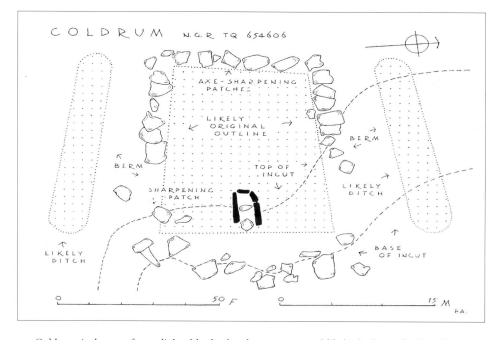

39 Coldrum, its barrow form, slighted kerb, chamber remnant and likely ditches. *After P. Ashbee 2000*

40 Coldrum, the chamber remnant from the east in April 1946. The surviving sidestones are more than 2.20m (7ft) in height. *Photograph P. Ashbee, 1946*

41 The collapsed Chestnuts chamber at Addington in about 1925, showing the northward toppled sidestones. *Photograph H. Elgar*

chamber deposit was sealed with occupation debris when Rusticated wares were current (Alexander, 1961, 36). The burned bones may be from its slighting rather than a Neolithic rite. Indeed, two unburned teeth were found. Cremation is no more than occasional in long barrows (Daniel, 1950, 98-100; Kinnes, 1992, 101) and would thus have an especial significance. Charcoal and human skulls have been found in close proximity to the Coffin Stone (Dunkin, 1871, 74). It is also possible that the medieval chapel close by attracted incidental burials, pieces of which may have surfaced during agricultural operations. Potsherds were found when the ruined chamber of the Addington long barrow was dug into (Wright, 1854, 180) and it has been said that human bones also came to light (Philp & Dutto, 1985, 3). The account of the disinterment of the Warren Farm chamber remains (Evans, 1948; Ashbee, 2003) allows the possibility of the bones and pottery having been beneath an infill. At Kit's Coty House, James Douglas (1795, 181) set a man to dig on the western side and recalled that '... the spot had been, by the appearance of the soil, previously explored'. Thomas Wright (1854, 175) observed that 'fragments of rude pottery have I believe been discovered under Kit's Coty House itself ...', while small worn sherds, some of a reddened fabric, have been picked up from the surface of the razed barrow (Cook, 1936, 234).

Apart from the accounts of the excavations at Coldrum and the Chestnuts, the evidence regarding the deposits in the chambers is meagre. Nonetheless, consideration should be given to the likelihood of their contents having been human bones, from dismemberment, disinterment, or an ossuary (Ashbee, 1966, 37-42), having been, as at West Kennet and elsewhere, beneath infills which contained settlement debris, much of which could have been broken pottery (Piggott, 1962, 68-71). Some chambers may have had in them no more than soil or settlement debris, a widespread phenomenon (Henshall; 1972, 87-90; Ashbee, 1976, 21). Thus the use-life of the Medway's massive stone-built long barrows is likely to have been considerable before they were finally sealed. We see only the conclusion of usages, which may have continued for centuries. The final sealing and portal-stone erection may, at the outset of the series, have determined further sitings and foregatherings.

When first built, the Medway's long barrows had high rectangular chambers. These, their entrances finally blocked by a focal portal stone, and with a façade, were at the eastern end of considerable, in surviving instances more than 60m (200ft) in length, long barrows. Flanked by quarry ditches or scoops, they were retained by sarsen stone kerbs, the surviving boulders being mostly of modest size. Kit's Coty House at the eastern end of the remains of its substantial long barrow, and the seemingly almost intact Coldrum long barrow's stones, have distracted attention from other, ruined and near-destroyed sites, which were at the outset even more grandiose and imposing. On the eastern side of the Medway there is the Lower Kit's Coty House where, when scrutinised from the east, it can be seen that the chamber's side-stones have fallen to the north. Were they, as were those of the Chestnuts (Alexander, 1961, 8), merely pulled back into a vertical position, there would be a chamber almost 7m (18-22ft) long and 3.5m (8-9ft) wide (a recent estimate), with an astonishing internal height, at least at the entrance, of almost 2.8m (9ft). At the Chestnuts this procedure showed that its stones demarcated a chamber 4m (12-13ft) long, 2m (7.5ft) wide and 3m (10ft) high. The Coffin Stone's chamber could have been at least 3.5m (12ft) in height and of commensurate length. The chamber of which Kit's Coty House is a remnant would have been for the most part more than 2m (6ft 6in) high, while for the Warren Farm chamber remainder an internal height of 1.6m (5ft) is possible.

On account of their largely ruined state it is difficult to tabulate, even approximately, the chamber heights of our stone-built long barrows (Daniel, 1950, *passim*). In southern England only West Kennet, with a barrow more than 100m (330ft) long, and an elaborate transepted chamber, the passage of which is 2.5m (8ft) high (Piggott, 1962, 17) is comparable. The internal height of the chamber of Wayland's Smithy II (Whittle, 1991, 83) was no more than 1.5m (5ft). Further afield in Wales, Pentre Ifan (Grimes, 1948; Lynch *et al*, 2000, 72, fig.2, 12) was 2.3m (7ft 6in) high at the entrance while in Scotland, Carn Ban, on Arran, has a long rectangular chamber with a roof 2.8m (9ft) above its floor (Henshall, 1972, 382). Such chamber heights are exceptional and thus the Medway's megalithic long barrows were undisputedly a unique group of the largest and most grandiose of their kind.

Sarsen stones eminently suitable for the enduring examples of the earth and timber surrogate long houses, seen as integral to the changes in train, are a prominent feature of the Medway valley (Ashbee, 1993a, 58). Although the distances are not great, the workforces had to manipulate blocks of Stonehenge calibre (Cleal *et al*, 1995, 566). Indeed, their size, with high chambers, reflects their erstwhile cogency. Because of their proximity to LBK territory and culture, only some 50 miles away, an expression of qualities transcending the earthen mounds by the use of stone may have been intended, for their close-knit siting recalls the more modest LBK village patterns (Whittle, 1996, 160-7).

The Coffin Stone and Coldrum long barrows were built upon positive lynchets, the size of which denote fields of many years cultivation. We do not know, however, in which order the Medway's long barrows were constructed, although embryo agricultural activities may have determined their locations. It is possible that the clusters upon Blue Bell Hill were completed, and complemented, by the Burham causewayed enclosure, while the group west of the Medway, a pair on the Greensand an area with Mesolithic associations, and a pair close by the chalk, may not have developed beyond their present pattern.

As has been shown, megalithic long barrows with commodious chambers are not unknown elsewhere in Britain, but nowhere, except by the Medway, is there such an adherence to grandiose dimensions, especially for chambers and façades. As they are likely to have been the first of their kind there can be no question of emulation or constructional competition (Tilley, 1996, 160). The Medway formula, long barrows of trapezoidal plan, flowered in Wessex, in timber and chalk at Fussell's Lodge (Ashbee, 1966) and in megalithic form in northern Wiltshire (Piggott, 1962, 57-65; Barker, 1984). Indeed, Wayland's Smithy II, apart from its transepted chamber (Whittle, 1991, 65, fig.2), would have closely resembled a Medway stone-bounded long barrow. Here, as by the Medway, the facade was integral to the kerbing. Thereafter came the Cotswolds (Darvill, 1982) and subsequently we enter a realm of complexities and usages that developed in areas distant from Kent and its proximity to LBK sources. Despite the development of regional diversity, which reflects the lengthy, piecemeal process which led to agricultural subsistence, it should not be forgotten that south-eastern England was, even more so, at the time of lower, Neolithic sea-levels (Coles, 1998, 64, fig.10, 68, fig.11), the western extremity of the Northern European Plain. As has for long been implied (Piggott, 1954, 269), the Medway's megalithic long barrows are a part of a fundamental European phenomenon which is manifest across its northern and south-western lands.

There are two Neolithic single graves (Piggott, 1954, 48; Whittle, 1977, 61) that have been encountered in eastern Kent which should be noticed. A round barrow on a spur of the chalk escarpment, Cherry Hill, Folkestone (Stebbing & Cave, 1943) had beneath it human bones that were unearthed by the workmen of the Waterworks Company. They appeared to have been accompanied by a small, rough piece of ironstone from the Hythe Beds, at no great distance. The bones, examined by A.J.E. Cave of the Royal College of Surgeons, because of the dolichocephalic skull, were considered 'ancient British' and it has been thought that they might have been Neolithic (Grinsell, 1992, 356). At Nethercourt Farm, Ramsgate, a grave contained the contracted burial of a male which had been covered by the sherds of a large bowl of Whitehawk affinity (Dunning, 1966, 9, fig.5; Curwen, 1954, 71-84), while above it were the disarticulated bones of an adolescent. An unfurnished contracted burial, found in 1942 at Acol, near Birchington, in Thanet (Harrison, 1943, xxxiii), the bones of which were removed by the police and destroyed, might also have been an example of a Neolithic single grave.

Apart from the recently unearthed ditches of a possible cursus monument on the chalk above Ramsgate, an abraded Ebbsfleet rim-sherd from Swalecliffe, from the F.H. Worsfold collection, the assemblage of pottery from Ebbsfleet, near Northfleet, and the Baston Manor material from a patent occupation site, which had pieces of all the later Neolithic wares, Ebbsfleet, Mortlake and Fengate are the bases of what is known of the later Neolithic in Kent. Henge monuments (Harding & Lee, 1937) are as yet unknown. Stukeley, however, depicts the Richborough ampitheatre as a henge (Ashbee, 2001, 86, fig.5) and it is possible that it might be an adaptation, as was Maumbury Rings, near Dorchester. There are also the pieces of a Grooved ware vessel from East Malling, plus some sherds from Snodland in Maidstone's Museum. There is also Grooved ware associated with the later Neolithic pottery from the 'long house' found beneath hillwash on the lower slopes of Blue Bell Hill. A good number of Grooved ware sherds have been reported from the various rescue excavations undertaken in eastern Kent, as have other later Neolithic pieces, notably from Folkestone and Thanet.

Until further investigation is undertaken, one can say little about the possible Ramsgate cursus, except that its character was seen upon some aerial photographs which came to the then Ancient Monuments Inspectorate of the Ministry of Works during the early 1950s and which were shown to the present writer by G.C. Dunning. The Swalecliffe sherd, although abraded, was recognised as Ebbsfleet ware after the discovery and publication of that site.

Ebbsfleet's pottery was encountered beneath some peaty alluvium, which proved to contain a high proportion of alder, with some hazel, lime and birch, and was recovered under controlled conditions (Burchell & Piggott, 1939; Sieveking, 1960). Presumably the pottery was from a settlement area, for flint-working debris was found at no great distance. The sherds indicate large, well-made, pots with thin walls, although some, with rounded bases, were thick and heavy, while the simple rims are thickened, flattened and everted. Any decoration is simple and, where present, consisted of cross-hatching or lattice-work incision, circular neck impressions, plus finger-nail and -tip imprints and occasional corded rims. The site has given its name to a distinctive pottery style and, after its initial definition, it emerged as widespread in southern and eastern England (Piggott, 1954, 308). There has, however, been a looseness of definition and many assemblages are distant from the positive characteristics of the type-site material (Kinnes, 1994, 93). There are within the series vessels which are close in style to those of northern, mainland Europe (Burchell & Piggott, 1939, 412, fig.4; Piggott, 1954, 314, fig.49, 1), and the Grovehurst sherd is likely to be in this category. These similarities have been the subject of critical consideration (Whittle, 1996, 202, fig.56) and, in the circumstances, with the nature of our Kentish long barrows in mind (Midgley, 1992, 29, fig.8), the likelihood of parallel development from intermingled common sources emerges.

One of the few later Neolithic sites to be the subject of a careful, controlled excavation was undertaken at Baston Manor, Hayes (42) during the 1960s, (Philp, 1973, 4-19; 2002, 38-9). An ancient surface was on a small, dry area of brickearth and flint-bearing Upper Chalk outcropped close by. Fire-marked

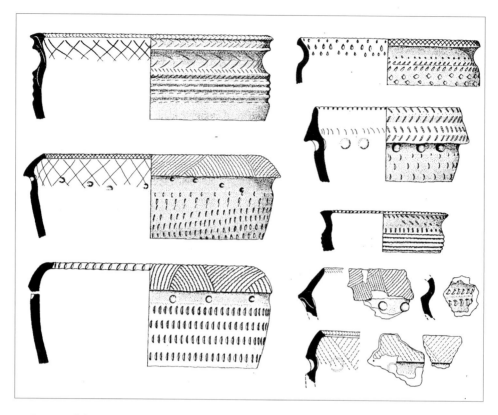

42 Late Neolithic Ebbsfleet pottery from Baston Manor, Hayes. *After Brian Philp, 1973*

stones and struck flints were found in their thousands and more than 200 pieces of pottery were associated with them. The flint industry was considered in detail (Broadfoot, 1975) and 93 implements, which included a partially polished flint axe, a leaf-shaped arrowhead, a polished knife, besides numerous blades and scrapers, were identified. The extent of the site is unknown and we may have seen no more than a small proportion of it. The pottery, the parts of some 50 vessels, was examined and reported upon by Isobel Smith (1973). They were mostly of Mortlake and Fengate styles, with some Beaker sherds, besides earlier Neolithic and Ebbsfleet pieces.

Isobel Smith isolated a decorated Ebbsfleet bowl (Philp, 1973, fig.6.3) which was indistinguishable from those of the type-site assemblage. The Mortlake bowls are at home in the Thames Valley while the Fengate vessels have a distinctly East Anglian flavour. There is also evidence of decorational interaction with Beaker ceramic traditions (Piggott, 1962, 38). A rare survival was the shallow dish (fig.7, 20) which could be an ancestor of the miniature vessels found in the later round barrows.

Archaeological endeavour, particularly that of the Thanet and Canterbury Archaeological Trusts, in East Kent, has added considerably to our knowledge of later Neolithic activities in that area in that their many and varied excavations, some on a large scale, have produced, for the most part, what are termed 'later' Neolithic sherds. Their precise identification is fraught with difficulties and may be imprecise. Indeed, some may be from rusticated beakers and even later urns. Of particular note are the remains of three bowls from Chalk Hill, Ramsgate (Cleal in Hearne *et al*, 1995). Their fragments indicated vessels which were thought to be Peterborough wares, or perhaps of the Ebbsfleet–Mortlake sub-styles, while a ditch yielded eight later Neolithic or earlier Bronze Age pieces. Work in 1989, by the Canterbury Archaeological Trust, on Castle Hill, Folkestone (Rady & Ouditt, 1989, 352) produced more than 40 Peterborough ware sherds, of the Mortlake style, which were in the upper register of a ditch, found below the rampart of the medieval earthworks. Indeed, such pottery may have been found by Pitt Rivers (Bowden, 1991, 86) in 1878, which he termed 'rough British pottery'. At no great distance excavation in Holywell Coombe (Bennet *et al*, 1980, 7-10), of a site beneath hillwash which was substantially a Beaker installation, produced later Neolithic pottery and struck flints. A Beaker burial at Manston (Perkins & Gibson, 1990, 19), probably from beneath the reduced barrow, had the impressed sherds of a small hemispherical bowl, while the Monkton Gas Pipeline (Perkins, 1985, 45, 55, figs.7, 26) impinged upon a pit deposit which was substantially charcoal traces, flint flakes, animal bones and later Neolithic pottery. Later Neolithic sherds, sometimes with beaker fragments, have also been unearthed at St Peter's (Perkins, 1997, 229), Cliffsend, Ramsgate (Perkins, 1998, 357) and Minster (Boast & Gibson, 2000, 361), while such sherds have also been found by field-walking (Parfitt, 1984, 333). In fact, it has been observed that the chalklands of Thanet have now produced nine sites which indicate Neolithic activities, more than a quarter of those known in the county.

Elsewhere in Kent there have been incidental discoveries of later Neolithic pottery at Ospringe (Higgenbotham, 1978), Castle Hill, Tonbridge (Money, 1975, 62, 30) and at High Rocks, Tunbridge Wells (Jessup, 1955, xlvi), in the vicinity of the Blue Bell Hill long house (Glass, 1999; Oxford Arch. Unit, 2000), at Holborough, Snodland (Evison, 1956, 89) and at Otford (Leach, 1977, 225; Pyke, 1980), from beneath a coombe deposit at the foot of the North Downs. Mention must also be made of a site, found by the present writer, at the foot of the North Downs at Detling, just to the east of East Court and above the Pilgrim's Way. Here, hillwash had been cut into by a lynchet, and rabbits, endemic during the 1930s, had thrown out a mass of scrapers, cores and flakes, all with a heavy white patination, together with the body-sherds of a shell-gritted, hard, reddish ware. Subsequent visits were made to the site but rim-sherds were never found. The crushed shell temper of the sherds had given, perhaps from their firing, a lime-like consistency. It may be that as at the foot of Blue Bell Hill or at Otford, the lower slopes of the North Downs were, perhaps because of their proximity to springs of water, a favoured location.

Long Grooved ware, sometimes labelled 'Rinyo-Clacton', was, in Kent, only represented by material from East Malling, possibly from a habitation site, unpublished and extant in the Sidney Thompson Collection (Piggott, 1954, 386). More details of its context (Field *et al*, 1964) revealed that it came from a pit, said to have been shallow, which also had in it a barbed-and-tanged arrowhead. East Malling was conflated with Snodland and it was stated that details would be forthcoming in *Archaeologia Cantiana*. The present writer, during the later 1950s and following Ernest Greenfield's work at Wingham, prepared a brief list of Kent's Neolithic pottery (Greenfield, 1960, 68) aided by Allen Grove who found Rinyo-Clacton sherds from Snodland in Maidstone's museum. Ian Longworth's definitive list (Wainwright & Longworth, 1971, 273-9) continued the conflation, and added that the sherds were from a single Grooved ware vessel. Grooved ware has since been found associated with a small enclosure in Thanet (Macpherson-Grant, 1980) at Buckland, Dover (Ashbee, 1987) and in the vicinity of the 'long house' on the lower slopes of Blue Bell Hill (Glass, 1999, 192; 2000, 451). In addition, there are now some 10 or more incidences of this distinctive ware now known, mostly from eastern Kent, which await definitive publication.

An unusual aspect of Neolithic, possibly later Neolithic, ceramics is the Ightham pottery spoon (Piggott, 1935). It had been found by a workman, who presented it to Sir Thomas Colyer-Fergusson, who had resided at Ightham Mote since 1899. It passed to his grandson, Gilbert Monckton, a member of the Kent Archaeological Society from 1933 onwards, who put it on loan in Maidstone's Museum. It is about 10cm (4in) in length and has a tapering, cigar-like, handle which expands into an hemispherical bowl. Of a sandy ware, which shows evidence of burnt-out organic fragments, it is grey at the handle which shades to a pale reddish-brown bowl. Two such spoons were found at Hassocks, Sussex, at the beginning of the twentieth century (Couchman, 1919). They were in a rabbit-chuck, at the edge of a disused sandpit, and could have been from a flat grave. Their finish is far from sophisticated and they appear to have been rapidly shaped before firing. One is a crude version of the not inelegant Ightham form while the other has a tapering ovate outline. Another pair of such spoons was found in the mound of the Netherswell long barrow (Leeds, 1927) while another came to light at Niton in the Isle of Wight (Piggott, 1935, 140). This small series has been compared with the ceramic spoons known from the later fourth millenium BC cultures of western and middle France (Piggott,1954,75). Ceramic spoons are not, however, unknown in TRB contexts (Midgley, 1992, 109, fig.34,

10). Few in number and fragile, they show no signs of wear and are likely to have been non-functional. They could well have been copies of wooden spoons which would have had a wide currency (Coles & Lawson, 1987, 107-9).

There is no direct evidence on the European mainland, Holland or Northern Germany, for the origins of the Medway's megalithic long barrows (Piggott, 1954, 269; Whittle, 1977, 61) although marked similarities and the notion of an early date for their construction has currency. There are various axes and flint daggers, copies of early bronze, hafted, blades (Piggott, 1938, 101), the axes and adzes comparable with the square-sided examples from the Julliberrie's Grave long barrow, from Canterbury and from deep in the ground at Sandy Mount, Bearsted (Ashbee, 1996, 24). Two such axes, plus a flint dagger, are said to have been found on White Cliff, Ramsgate (Hicks, 1878, 18) while there are daggers from the Thames at Erith and a gravel pit at Upchurch (Anon 1934). When compiling his list, Stuart Piggott (1936, 101) felt that while some were from questionable contexts, and could have been from nineteenth-century collections, the numbers from southern and eastern England allowed for some prehistoric imports. With this in mind, Norman Cook (1937) published and illustrated sherds of Nordic passage-grave pottery, allegedly found 'in a field near Orpington'. They were given to Maidstone's Museum by K.P. Oakley, then at the British Museum (Natural History) and had been in the collection of J. Rhodes, of the Geological Survey. Sherds similar to these were reported as from the Durham Coast (Childe, 1932) but C.T. Trechman (1936, 168) cast doubts upon this context, a midden, because of the Romano-British pottery present, although he had obtained 'chipped' flints therefrom. During the earlier 1960s it was seen that the Orpington passage-grave pottery was from Lord Avebury's collection (he lived at High Elms, Farnborough) for their exact counterparts from this source could be seen among material preserved in the Priory Museum, Church Hill, Orpington. Claims have also been made (Smith, 1925) for the pieces of a biconical vessel from Brantham, in Suffolk, but despite some general similarities among our south-eastern English ceramic assemblages, there is no clear connection. The long barrow tradition that evolved within the TRB usages as a whole (Midgley, 1985; 1992), however, found expression in the Medway's valley, but our Neolithic ceramics, early and later, display their own clear, local characteristics.

For long it has been thought that our Neolithic began when skin-boats, laden with eager immigrants, seed-corn and animals, landed upon our shores. The initial intruders, it was argued, may have brought only the background of their material culture when they left the LBK regions of the Rhineland or northern France. To sustain this contention, generalised similarities in pottery, flint and stone artifacts, possible antecedents for the causewayed enclosures and even the lineaments of our long barrows, have been regularly invoked. Nonetheless, these do not provide particularly satisfactory precursors for our insular Neolithic, and furthermore, the distinctive LBK houses are conspicuously absent. Archaeologically observable innovation is complemented by the palaeobotanical evidence of human interference with forest and plant cover, which, although contemporary, cannot be precisely related to it. Despite its disadvantages, the notion of an initial Neolithic colonisation is all-pervading and persistent. The alternative, which involved the concept of change brought about by processes which involved no immigrants has never been adequately explored. The notion that our Neolithic is the continuation of our Mesolithic communities has been dismissed because of overall dissimilarities, supported by the belief that the changes involved could only be the work of incomers. Moreover, the move from Mesolithic to Neolithic modes was not an inevitability, involving concepts of progress (Piggott, 1981, 23); people did not have to change. A clue to the nature of the changes may be our long barrows, particularly those adhering to the Medway formula. Their striking similarity to the LBK long houses (Ashbee, 1982) would have arisen from the interchange across shifting frontiers (Alexander, 1978) and they embodied form rather than substance. Furthermore, our causewayed enclosures may also have been conscious imitations of the earthworks surrounding LBK settlements. Together, these monuments, integral to our Neolithic, result from paraphrastic ritual and organisational behaviour arising from social intercourse with LBK farmers. It could be thought ironic that the bases of our Neolithic agriculture, a traditional preserve of materialistic archaeology, may have been stimulated by imitative structures, expressions of the mind.

The emergence of the economic, technological and social conditions that we term the Neolithic was a slow, piecemeal process. Kent, as has been observed, has a topography which imposes certain behavioural patterns upon human endeavour. Its terrain is at no great distance from the developed LBK societies of the adjacent European mainland and thus, because of this contiguity and social contact, it may have been one of the first English regions where, from Mesolithic selection and protection, their near-horticulture, the subsistance changes that we term agriculture, came about. These may have been no more than partial as it has for long been recognised that fundamental Mesolithic practices endured and are a part of the various manifestations of our diverse Neolithic (Piggott, 1954, 15; Whittle, 1977, 99-106). Plainly our Neolithic is a continuation and development of much that came to pass among those Mesolithic communities who assimilated aspects of economic endeavour and material culture from their close European mainland neighbours and developed them in their own distinctive modes. Once the advantages of a specific were clear, adaptation and development may have been, ultimately, rapid.

SIX

BRONZE AGE CHANGES AND INNOVATIONS

In 1839, Christian Jurgenson Thomsen set out the three prehistoric stages, stone, bronze and iron, a notion arising from his classification of the antiquities in Denmark's National Museum (Daniel & Renfrew, 1988, 22-4). Later in the nineteenth century this framework was the basis of Sir John Lubbock's grouping of prehistory. Writing in his study at High Elms, Farnborough, he set down the divisions of prehistory, the Palaeolithic, Neolithic, Bronze and Iron Ages in his *Prehistoric Times* (1865). He was concerned with the origins of northern Europe's Bronze Age, invoking influences from the Mediterranean lands and Indo-Europeans, while dismissing evolutionary considerations. In the event, the Bronze Age was given body and direction by John Evans' magisterial *The Ancient Bronze Implements, Weapons and Ornaments of Great Britain and Ireland* (1881). It included such bronzes as had been found in Kent, classified them, and considered their uses. A more recent landmark was Gordon Childe's *The Bronze Age* (1930). He stressed the plasticity of molten copper and the various changes involved. There was also concern with the social and economic mutations wrought by metalworking, the status of the artificers, and the changes brought about by metal tools and equipment, besides its place within the evolution of society, in Europe at large. Until the advent of radiocarbon dating (Renfrew, 1973, 47-68) the typologies of bronzes, particularly tools and weapons, were the fundamentals of the chronologies which linked Europe, and even Britain, to the timescales of the Mediterranean lands. In general terms, the Bronze Age can be thought of as the time from about 2500 BC to about 750 BC, some 1700 years, by historical standards a considerable span. Two seminal works now present the Bronze Age as a European phenomenon (Coles & Harding, 1979; Harding, 2000) and it is possible to see the territory that became Kent as a discrete dimension within their intricate systematisation.

An early aspect of Bronze Age studies, which preceded Thomsen's classification, was the mass opening of barrows, begun in about 1803 by Sir Richard Colt Hoare and William Cunnington in Wiltshire (Robinson, 2003). This process was emulated in other areas where numerous barrows had survived, throughout the nineteenth century (Marsden, 1974). Happily some of the considerable assemblages of grave furniture therefrom have now been published to clear contemporary standards (Annable & Simpson, 1964; Kinnes & Longworth 1985; Barrett & Collis, 1996), as have their particular classes of ceramics, beakers (Clarke, 1970), food-vessels (Simpson, 1968) and urns (Longworth, 1984). During the twentieth century orderly excavation techniques were applied to barrows, many being threatened by agriculture and land development, and they were seen as social structures, with ditches, mounds, internal dispositions and graves often emerging as more informative than grave furniture (Fox, 1959; Ashbee, 1960). The extant round barrows of southern England have been detailed by L. V. Grinsell (1936; 1953; Fowler (ed.), 1972). All in all, in 1961, some 18,000 barrows were thought to have been known in England, of which about 6000 were still to be seen in Wessex. The number carefully excavated and systematically published were at this time thought to be 2.5 per cent or even less. Recently, the Bronze Age round barrows of Kent, some 170, with flat graves which may have remained from razed barrows, have been enumerated (Grinsell, 1992). It should not be overlooked that artifacts from the barrows of eastern Kent, some exotic (Ashbee and Dunning, 1960), find common ground with those elements which are a constant feature of the barrows clustered around Stonehenge, on the geographically transinsular Salisbury Plain (Piggott, 1938; 1951).

Later Neolithic times had seen the establishment in Wessex of the great henges (Wainwright, 1989). The most important, supplanting Robin Hood's Ball, the causewayed enclosure, were Durrington Walls, with Woodhenge close by, and the early stages of Stonehenge, with its adjacent cursus. This area, because of the nature of Stonehenge (Ashbee, 1978, *passim*) became the focal domain of earlier Bronze Age England. To the north Windmill Hill is succeeded by Avebury (Smith, 1965) and all pertaining to it, a complex which may have been primarily concerned with ideological considerations. In the south there is the great Dorset cursus, with Knowlton near by and, by Dorchester, Mount Pleasant and Maumbury Rings. As during earlier times, society appears to have been largely mobile, periodically meeting at these great centres. Henge enclosures were constructed by communities distant from Wessex which, as far as can be seen, were within the limits that local conditions and resources allowed. Their regular form suggests a widely diffused basic formula. From about 2500 BC onwards the character of the later Neolithic communities was to be modulated and redirected, and thus changed, by the Beaker phenomenon. Their personified observances prevailed, namely the development of a stratified society, the principals being individually interred beneath round barrows, which often looked to an earlier past. The usages involving the human remains in the long barrows ceased and chamber deposits were sealed with occupation debris, which, as at the Chestnuts (Alexander, 1961; Holgate, 1981, 231), often contained beaker sherds.

Whether or not the appearances of the beakers which accompany the first intimations of metallurgy marked an incursion of peoples from the European mainland is a matter of debate. However, the recent discovery at Amesbury, in Wiltshire, of a richly furnished grave, is likely to be that of an individual from the Alpine region (Fitzpatrick, 2003). We know these from their encoffined burials beneath distinctive round barrows (Ashbee, 1960, 70; 1978, 142; Donaldson, 1977) and their readily recognisable beakers, sometimes accompanied by tools and weapons, copper knives, barbed-and-tanged arrowheads, likely to have been propelled by short composite bows (Piggott, 1971), stone wristguards, which protected the archer's wrist, besides personal ornaments of gold, such as discs and earrings, amber, jet and bone. The emergence and expansion of beaker usage was rapid. It is possible that the first beakers were imported, a matter that could be decided by thin sections, and thereafter the potters produced locally and regionally distinctive versions. It was thought by the present writer (Ashbee, 1978, 133) that beakers denoted an incursion of peoples, a notion that has been pursued down the years. Indeed, they have been associated with a distinctive physical type with a round head and a rugged physique (Ashbee, 1978, 136; Megaw & Simpson, 1979, 178). Nonetheless, it seems that these distinctive vessels may well have been accompanied by a small number of people rather than a mass immigration, and that their qualities and usages wrought the considerable changes which transformed later Neolithic society. Indeed, one might envisage the beakers as status symbols, used, perhaps, for an especial drink, all being bolstered by their metallic associations. Although beakers were the dynamic of profound changes in our prehistory, their development was no short-lived phenomenon but one that may have endured for half-a-millennium or more. They led, seemingly, to chiefdoms, reflected in the concentrations of funerary wealth which became apparent in Wessex, and to some extent in other regions of southern England. One can but speculate as to whether particular individuals from such areas as Kent, Cornwall or Gloucestershire, were given burial within sight of Stonehenge.

It should not be forgotten that beakers have for long attracted investigation and classification. Colt Hoare (1810) termed them 'drinking cups' as did Thurnam (1871, 388-400) while the term 'beaker' was introduced by Abercromby (1904; 1912) who thought it more scientific. He defined three principal forms, with sub-groups. David Clarke (1970) detected no fewer than seven influxes of beakers into Britain, which stimulated further indigenous forms. This scheme was promptly replaced by a simpler European mainland step-system (Lanting & van der Waals, 1972), although Clarke's style terminology survived. A further development has been a commendably simple system of early, middle and late forms (Case, 1977). Nonetheless, beakers are almost impossible to resolve into chronological order, despite their considerable currency, and, as was shown by the burials in the Amesbury 51 barrow (Ashbee, 1978), more styles may have been current at any one time than is commonly thought.

With the passage of time, beaker people became dominant in Wessex, where they were involved in the development of Stonehenge and the elaboration of Avebury. Burials became opulent and we see the emergence of what has been termed the Wessex culture (Piggott, 1938; Ashbee, 1960, 140-8; 1978, 160-80; Megaw & Simpson, 1979, 207-30); the grave furniture from distinctive barrows which, before their partial destruction, lined Stonehenge's supportive landscape. The aggrandised grave furniture displayed in various dimensions has clear beaker origins (Ashbee, 1960, 140; Case, 2003). Opulently furnished burials and dagger graves are more common than is supposed and are known from Cornwall, Sussex and even northern Wales. Links with Wessex were seen among the pieces, taken down the years, from particular barrows in eastern Kent (Ashbee & Dunning, 1960) and it was said that such material served to underline the connections between that region and what may have been a dominant society, that of Wessex.

Briefly, the Wessex culture's components come from about 100 richly furnished graves, beneath bowl, bell and disc barrows. Defined largely by the European mainland affinities and accompaniments of the daggers found in certain graves, there is the division between Wessex I and Wessex II (ApSimon, 1954). The first inhumation burials were superseded by cremations. Bronze pins from Germany, Baltic amber and Mediterranean faience beads were in some graves, and besides the funerary gold (Coles & Taylor, 1971), incense cups as from Tilmanstone (Ashbee & Dunning, 1960, 50) as well as the first collared urns (Longworth, 1984) were the principal accompaniments. Finely finished, geometric, barbed-and-tanged arrowheads, following the Beaker tradition, have been found in a few graves (Ashbee, 1960, 104-5). Those who interred this funerary wealth brought Stonehenge to its final form (Cleal *et al*, 1995), a grandiose timber and stone building.

Some 36 beakers (*43*) are known from Kent (Clarke, 1970, 484-5) but, notwithstanding, beaker accoutriments, with modest exceptions, are absent. Had a beaker (was it missed?) accompanied the flexed burial at Sittingbourne (*44*) (Payne, 1883; Clarke, 1970, 111.139; Gerloff, 1975, 30), furnished with a tanged copper dagger, wristguard and girdle-fastener, it would have been considered classic. The grave, presumably, at the outset, beneath a low barrow had been cut into the chalk, 5ft below ground level, and the skeleton was upon its left side. Corrosion products had

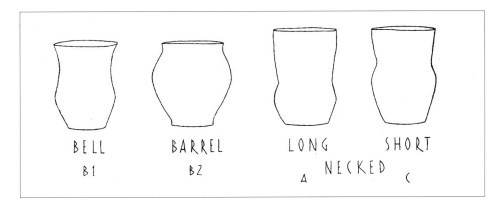

BELL
B1

BARREL
B2

LONG
NECKED
A

SHORT
NECKED
C

Above: 43 The basic beaker forms: Kent's beakers are for the most part bell and barrel types, although necked beakers are not unknown. After P. Ashbee, 1960

Right: 44 Left The tanged dagger, bracer and girdle-fastener from Sittingbourne; Right The tanged dagger and halberd from Faversham (¼). After S. Gerloff, 1975

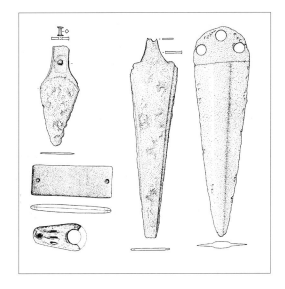

stained both humerus and radius. Another copper dagger, some 22cm (9in) in length, with its cutting edge emphasised by grooving, was allegedly found associated with a halberd (Ó Ríordáin, 1936, 312, fig. 56, 2, 3) in a pit encountered while digging for brickearth. Their condition suggests association. Another tanged dagger, from the Brent collection, likely to have been found locally, is in the prehistoric collections of Canterbury's Beaney Institute (Jessup, 1930, 96; Gerloff, 1975, 30). In terms of David Clarke's nomenclature (1970), the Kentish beakers are mostly of the European Bell, Barbed Wire and East Anglian forms, together with late northern British examples. These, in terms of the step-system (Lanting & van der Waals, 1997, 38-9) are signal components of the East Anglian–Kentish area, where many vessels are decoratively atypical. For example, beakers from Capel-le-Ferne, Chislet, Bromley, Dover and Maidstone bear motifs which are found upon the, mostly Irish, lunulae (Taylor,

1980, 41-4). Almost all of Kent's beakers are incidental discoveries and may have been accompanied by bones, daggers and ornaments that went unnoticed. Many are likely to have been beneath barrows, long since razed. Of particular note is the careful excavation of a Beaker burial at Manston, in Thanet (Perkins & Gibson, 1990). Here, in an oval grave, eccentric to the centre of the barrow, was a contracted burial accompanied by a long-necked beaker, a jet button and retouched flint blade. In Clarke's terms the beaker is of the primary southern British series and, in terms of the step-system of Lanting and van der Waals it is steps 4-6. A radiocarbon date, BM2642, 1680±50 bc (2132-1922 BC) was obtained from the skeleton. With this barrow and date in mind, it would seem likely that numbers of beakers from Kent are earlier than this patently stage 4-6 example.

Beaker graves with barbed-and-tanged arrowheads, singly, in twos and threes, and now and again in numbers, have, from time to time been found (Harrison, 1960, *passim*). Arrowheads have not as yet appeared with Kentish beakers although many have been picked up incidentally, particularly along the Greensand corridor flanking the southern face of the North Downs.

During recent years, various spreads of beaker sherds and an alleged enclosure have come to light. These additions to our records result from the many rescue excavations now undertaken within the county. It should also not be forgotten that R.F. Jessup (1933) was able to add beakers from Barham, Bromley, Dover, Ightham and Sturry to his initial (1930, 90-4) list, all of which can be accomomdated in the earlier stages of the East Anglian–Kentish grouping (Lanting & van der Waals, 1972, fig.2). A beaker of East Anglian form has come to light at Swalecliffe (Tatton-Brown, 1977), while yet another of this kind emerged at Cottingham Hill, Ebbsfleet, Ramsgate (Jay [Thanet Arch. Trust], 1990, 275). It should also be noted (Kelly, 1985) that the beaker from Brenley, Boughton-under-Blean, of primary southern British form, which is stage 6, has been returned from Taunton to Maidstone's Museum. As has been observed, beaker sherds are regularly found associated with Later Neolithic material; however, close by Folkestone (Bennett, 1988, 8; Macpherson-Grant, 1989, 355), substantial spreads of beaker sherds were found when, prior to the Channel Tunnel installations, areas were excavated into hillwash. Beaker pottery has also been found, although not in quantity, in similar circumstances at Otford (Pyke, 1980). Rescue excavation has also brought to light All-over-Corded beaker sherds from the ditch of a ploughed-out barrow at Northdown, Margate (Smith, 1987). A Wessex/Middle Rhine beaker, found at Cliff's End, Ramsgate, is preserved in the Public Library of that town (Perkins & Gibson, 1990, 17). A ditched enclosure of oval plan and about 75m (240ft) in length, at Minster-in-Thanet, has been thought of as of Beaker origin because of sherds found therein and in the infill of Anglo-Saxon graves, but, sadly, their incidence cannot be regarded as a direct association (Boast & Gibson, 2000, 367).

Later nineteenth-century gravel extraction from the Parish Field, just to the north-west of the church at Aylesford (Evans, 1890, 325-7; Jessup, 1930, 116; Ashbee, 1997), led to the discovery of three cists constructed from slabs of tufa and sandstone, which are likely to have each housed a skeleton in 'a contracted attitude' (Evans, 1890, 325). It is recorded that Bronze Age pottery had been found in the area but, as far as is known, the burials in the cists were without accompaniments, although one had in it the bones of a young woman (Ashbee, 1994, 149). As far as can be seen, two of these cist-graves, which may have been below low barrows in line, long since obliterated, were discovered prior to 1886 and their description by Arthur Evans is from details provided by the workmen, supplemented by scrutiny of the cist (No.1) taken to Maidstone's Museum, and that set up near the gravel pit's office (No.3). The cist slabs taken to Maidstone's Museum were available in the chapel during the later 1920s and early 1930s. They had vanished when a new museum inventory was compiled in 1960-1 and it was hazarded that they had been lost during the war years (Kelly, 1992, 404). The cist set up at the rear of the old gravel pit office was seen by L.V. Grinsell and the present writer during the earlier 1930s. It was still in position at the outset of the 1939-45 war but a visit in 1946 revealed that it had been removed. It emerged that it had been taken to Croydon and set up in a garden by a member of the Natural History & Scientific Society. Presented to Maidstone's Museum in 1983, it was reported upon by David Kelly (1992, 404). Meanwhile the whereabouts of the slabs of Cist No.1 remain a mystery. The absence of grave furniture from these cists leads one to think the unthinkable. There were, in 1886, collectors visiting the Aylesford pit and considerable rewards were paid for good Palaeolithic handaxes, and antiquities in general. Also, it should not be forgotten that details of the spectacular Iron Age burials and their associations (Evans, 1890) are also based upon information provided by workmen and the pieces obtained from them. Moreover, it is recorded that Iron Age gold coins were found close by the first tufa cist to be encountered. They were sold surreptitiously in Gravesend but were traced and eventually illustrated. In the circumstances it is not impossible that beakers, and perhaps even daggers and ornaments, were removed from the cists and sold. Unprovenanced Bronze Age pottery and other objects lurk in many museums and beakers such as might belong to the East Anglian–Kentish series may have been found at Aylesford. Spurious provenances for antiquities are far from an impossibility.

On 23 March 1899, Frederick James FSA, Curator of Maidstone Museum from 1891 to 1902, formerly secretary and principal archaeological assistant to General Pitt Rivers, in Cranborne Chase (Bowden, 1991, *passim*), read a paper to the Society of Antiquaries of London (James, 1899). While digging away the brown loam mantling the river gravels, during the opening out of the pit close by Aylesford's church, the workmen had encountered a skeleton some 1.6m

(5ft) below the surface (Ashbee, 1997, 150), which James was able to examine and detail. Nothing was found in the grave, although beneath the skeleton were burnt animal bones, pieces of wood which proved to be willow (*Salix L.*) and some grains of wheat. He enlisted his friends to examine the human bones and. the pieces from the large grave. All had been disturbed although he mentions a piece of bronze from the excavation. Another burial (Ashbee, 1997, 152) was found about 460m (500yds) to the east of the first and James said: 'No description of the human remains ... possible owing to the fragile state in which they were found the whole falling to pieces on exposure to the atmosphere'. These fragmentary bones were allegedly from the base of the gravel, almost 5m (16ft) from the surface and on top of the Folkstone Beds. Deep graves are not unknown (Grinsell, 1941, 102) in chalk but such a grave would have been impossible to dig in the friable river gravels at Aylesford. James, however, said:

> The bones had been taken out, or rather had fallen out of the side of the cliff before my arrival, so that I had to depend entirely upon the word of the workmen as to the depth below the surface.

He continued, saying:

> The bronze implements [two flat daggers and a flat axe (45)] were found with the bones, and sufficiently indicate without further comment the age and character of the interment. It will be noticed that three fragments of limb bones, the humerus, ulna and fibula, are stained green, through having been in close proximity to the implements.

These bones, displayed in Maidstone's Museum during the 1930s, appeared as robust and far from fragile. It may be that the daggers were close by the arms of the corpse and that the axe, hafted when deposited, was by the legs. It is likely that James, after the initial discovery he investigated, established a rapport with the workmen, who were paid upon a piece-work basis for gravel dug out and graded. It says much for his diplomacy that he was able to secure this important group of bronzes for his museum.

Ronald Jessup (1930, 97) included the axe and daggers in his study of Kent, saying:

> The Aylesford flat axe was found in an inhumation burial with two knife daggers ... One is but 5.25 inches long and has probably been ground down considerably; this dagger is plain, but the larger, length 6.7 inches, is decorated with incised lines.

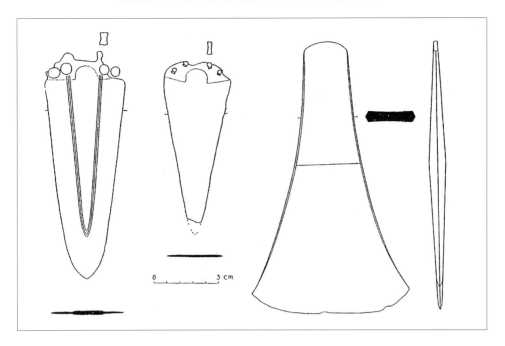

45 The daggers, one grooved and one flat, with the axe recovered from a grave at Aylesford. The axe has slight, hammered side flanges. After P. Ashbee, 1997

The daggers had been included in the *List of Flat Riveted Knife Daggers from England and Wales* (Fox & Grimes, 1928), marked upon a pioneer distribution map (Fox, 1933, 18), and were mentioned by Stuart Piggott in his seminal paper upon 'The Early Bronze Age in Wessex' (1938,59). Arthur ApSimon (1954) considered the Aylesford axe as notable for its narrow butt and expanded cutting edge, as an Hiberno-Scottish form. The daggers were thought of as derived from or related to Wessex six-rivetted daggers (ApSimon, 1954, 56). J.J. Butler (1963, 200-1, 242), in his study of Bronze Age connections across the North Sea, saw the flat dagger from Aylesford as a Middle European Unĕtice model and called attention to a virtually identical hafted blade from Bargeroosterfeld in Holland (Ashbee, 1997, 155, fig.2). The spectroscopic analysis of Wessex culture bronzes (Britten, 1961; 1963) included the Aylesford axe and daggers. Their tin and arsenical copper contents confirmed their place within the sequence. Peter Harbison called attention to Aylesford's grooved dagger when examining the material of his Frankford-Killaha-Ballyvalley period in Ireland (1969a, 23), while the axe was seen as similar to, but not identical to, those of his Type Killaha in the same period (1969b, 77). These groups are equated with A.M. Apsimon's Bush Barrow phase (Harbison, 1969b, 83, fig.6). Further broad, comprehensive, typological considerations led Sabine Gerloff (1975, 60-1) to see Aylesford's flat dagger as an element in her Type Masterton, while the grooved example was one of her modest Aylesford Group. They were seen as hybrids between flat and grooved Wesses blades. As her work was concerned with daggers, the nature of the axe was not pursued. More recently, Colin Burgess (1980, 76) has used the Aylesford axe as definitive of a Ballyvalley-Aylesford interlude within his Mount Pleasant period, of the later third millennium BC.

A fluted ogival dagger from Ashford is not unrelated to the later phase of the general Aylesford context. Found on Digg Farm, Potter's Corner, it may be from a reduced barrow grave (Gerloff, 1975, 109). A single rivet remains and the finely defined edges are battered, although its slightly atypical lineaments have sustained only a little damage. Within this advanced Early Bronze context there is the Buckland hoard Dover, (Megaw & Hardy, 1938, 283, fig.10), which was found in 1856 on the Union Brickfield. As far as was ascertained, it consisted of three flanged axes and a short-bladed, tanged spearhead. Two of the axes have decoration characteristic of the type, while two have an incipient stop-ridge. The blade of the spearhead is difficult to match among the extant examples of this form. The fluting of the blade suggests a distant affinity with certain Irish socketed examples (Coffey, 1913, 29, fig.24). A flanged axe in Liverpool Museum is reputed to have been found at Buckland in 1856 also (Evans, 1881; Jessup, 1930, 97, pl.V, 11). Whether or not it was associated with the hoard remains to be ascertained. A heavy flanged, wide-bladed, axe was found near Reculver (Jessup, 1930, 97) and is in the Ashmolean Museum at Oxford, while a flanged axe of atypical form from Wye Down is possibly an import from the European mainland (Ashbee, 1952, 182). A flanged axe from Ashford is in Glastonbury Museum (Grinsell, 1948, 185), while a fine decorated flanged axe has been in the collections of the Kent Archaeological Society for many years, having been received from 'Mr Battely, Medway Brass Works, Oct. 1883' (Ashbee, 1952).

Besides the bronzes appropriate to the advanced Early Bronze Age, there are positive links between Kentish and Wessex barrow burials. One of the Ringwould urns contained three small segmented faience beads of light green colour, and one oblate bead, also of faience and of the same colour. Four urns, each of which was inverted over a cremation, perhaps the burials of a specific social group, were in graves beneath the barrow. One urn contained, as well as the cremation, a miniature vessel, and another urn had in it two miniature vessels, one of which is said to have held a burned substance and the faience beads (Woodruff, 1874; 1877; Ashbee & Dunning, 1960, 53-4). Of considerable importance is the slotted incense cup from a small barrow apparently covering an inhumation burial, destroyed during an extension of Tilmanstone Colliery, early in the twentieth century (Jessup, 1930, 122). Another, similar, cup is known from Luddington (recorded as Lutinton) Wood (*46*), between Bekesbourne and Littlebourne (Jessup,

46 The slotted 'incense cup' from Lutinton Wood, near Littlebourne (⅘). *After P.Ashbee and G.C. Dunning, 1960*

1936). There is oblique cord-ornament below the rim and above the shoulder, and the vessel, although fragmentary, had been made from greyish-brown clay, presumably Gault, while the draught holes had been cut while the clay was damp. Indeed, such cups have now been classified upon the basis of form and perforation (Longworth, 1983). The significance of faience beads is well known and their integral role in Wessex society scarcely needs emphasis (Beck & Stone, 1936; Stone & Thomas, 1956). Less well known are the affinities of the slotted incense cups such as those from Tilmanstone and Luddington Wood, or even that dug from a destroyed Thanet barrow (Longworth, 1983, 86). Another was in a gold-furnished cremation grave beneath the great bell-barrow Wilsford 8, at no great distance from Stonehenge (Piggott, 1938, 105 (No.71), pl.11). Outside Wiltshire, four slotted cups are known from the central regions of Hampshire and Sussex. On Hengistbury Head, Barrow I had in it a cup of this kind, found with a cremation, in an urn, in association with small gold cones, amber beads and a halberd pendant (Bushe-Fox, 1915, 16, pl.III). Another slotted cup accompanied a gold-covered V-perforated button, with amber and shale beads, in a cremation grave, that may have remained from a destroyed barrow, on Portsdown, Portsmouth, excavated in 1948. (Ashbee, 1967). Two more cups are known from the South Downs, in Sussex, where they probably came from destroyed barrows; one from Lancing and the other from Clayton Hill (Curwen, 1954, 157, pl.LII, 5 & fig.44).

A metal-detectorist's quest on Ringlemere Farm, near Woodnesborough, late in 2001, in an area which proved to be that of a reduced round barrow of some size (Parfitt, 2002), discovered a crushed, corrugated, golden cup, comparable with that from the Rillaton barrow, in distant Cornwall (Ashbee, 1960, 117-18, pl.xxiv, a, b). The Ringlemere cup (Ashbee, 2002) is 15.2cm (6in) in height and 10cm (4in) in diameter at the rim and thus is the largest of its compeers. Beaten from a sheet of 20 carat gold, it is ribbed in a mode comparable with its Rillaton counterpart and has a closely similar handle. Unlike the Rillaton cup, considered to be a copy of a beaker (Taylor, 1980, 47), it has a plain ovoid rather than a flat base. Indeed, it is not impossible that the base of the Rillaton cup may have been ovoid but was flattened at some point in its chequered post-discovery history. In gold, the unambiguous counterpart of such a base is displayed by the plain, handled, gold cup from Fritzdorf, near Bonn, in the Rheinland (von Uslar, 1956; Ashbee, 1960, pl.XXIV, C; Piggott, 1965, 134, pl.XXIV). Until the discovery of this golden cup on Ringlemere Farm, the Fritzdorf cup, with its rounded base, was exceptional. Indeed the closest counterparts for the form of the Ringlemere cup are the series of amber and shale cups from Wessex. The amber cup from the Clandon barrow, in Dorset (Drew & Piggott, 1937), has an ovoid, almost pointed, base, and its handle is missing. It was accompanied by an atypical Wessex II dagger, a sheet-gold lozenge, a shale macehead with golden studs, a slotted incense cup and a collared urn. The shale cups (Newall, 1928), two from the 'Amesbury District' in Wiltshire, and two from Honiton in Devon (Ashbee, 1960, 118, fig.37), have line-ornamented handles similar to those of the Ringlemere, Rillaton and Fritzdorf golden cups, and ovoid bases. In general terms, apart from Fritzdorf, the form of our Kentish Ringlemere golden cup is that of the amber and shale series. An ogival Wessex II dagger, comparable with the example from Digg Farm, near Ashford, accompanied a round-bottomed, handled, amber bowl (Curwen, 1954, 152-4, pl.XIII) found in a timber coffin beneath a great barrow on the coastal plain at Hove, in Sussex. As with other funerary gold (Coles & Taylor, 1971), there is the inherent possibility that these handled golden cups from Ringlemere, Fritzdorf and Rillaton may be from the hands of a single craftsman, who practised a particular mode of handle attachment.

A list of round barrows, entitled *Barrows and Tumuli* concluded the account of Early Man in Kent by George Clinch (1908, 331), from Borden, who, early in the twentieth century, was Librarian of the Society of Antiquaries of London. It had been compiled by I.Chalkley Gould, who had listed Kentish earthworks, and was a feature of the initial volume of the Victoria County History published in 1908. Kent's barrows were listed by L.V. Grinsell and R.F. Jessup together, during the 1930s, but sadly the notes and details were lost during the 1939-45 war. However, after a lifetime of the pursuit and recording of barrows, Leslie Grinsell (Fowler (ed.) 1972; Grinsell, 1989) turned to Kent once again and has given us a comprehensive examination and listing of our Bronze Age round barrows (1992). He has detailed 170 recognisable round barrows and 15 flat graves, which may remain from razed barrows, almost all on the chalk, east of the Stour and in Thanet. To this total must be added some 30 beaker graves, likely to have been covered by low barrows, and the ring-ditches (Elworthy & Perkins, 1987), mostly remaining from reduced barrows, which he said were in number comparable with the extant barrows. Thus there could have been, at a conservative estimate, between 600 and 700 round barrows within the bounds of Kent, a density comparable with Cranborne Chase or even the Avebury area of northern Wiltshire. The barrows on the chalk of eastern Kent are in discrete groups, mostly linear, although there are several nuclear assemblages. It would seem likely that continued aerial photography will reveal henges, levelled and dispersed, which succeeded the earlier causewayed enclosures. The barrow overspill from the chalk in the Folkestone area, on to the Gault and Greensand, is notable and betokens, perhaps, improved agriculture and clearance. North-west of the middle Stour, the chalk carries few barrows, presumably because of its inhospitable capping of clay with flints. Dispersed barrows, still extant, follow the line of the Medway while, towards the Thames, barrow groups are at the boundaries of the Eocene bed formations. As far as is known the majority of the Kentish barrows are of the bowl variety, although three saucer barrows are known. The excavation of massively reduced barrows, such as that from which the Rnglemere cup was obtained, might reveal them to have been bell-barrows.

As has been stressed, Kent's round barrows were never 'opened' as in, for example, Wiltshire, Derbyshire and Yorkshire (Marsden, 1974), because, probably, of the attention given to Anglo-Saxon grave mounds (Meaney, 1964). Nonetheless, barrow excavations were undertaken and, in instances, details

47 J.Y. Akerman's presentation of the Iffin's Wood, Chartham, barrow excavation, 1842. *After J.Y. Akerman, 1844*

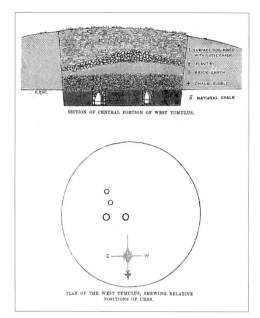

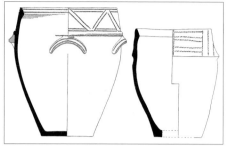

Left: 48 Section and plan of the western barrow excavated at Ringwould, near Deal, in 1872. *After C.H. Woodruff, 1874*

Above: 49 The urns, one horseshoe-handled and one collared, from the Ringwould barrow, excavated in 1872. *P. Ashbee and G.C. Dunning, 1960*

were recorded and urns and other things have survived to this day. Thus, at Iffin's Wood (*47*), Chartham (Akerman, 1844; Woodruff, 1874; 1877; Ashbee & Dunning, 1960, site 9) 'a tumulus 150 feet in circumference and nearly six feet high' was examined 'by causing a trench, four feet broad, to be cut through the centre of the barrow, north and south'. At the centre of the barrow, the excavation being illustrated by a proportionate plan and an isometric drawing, was a collared urn inverted over a cremation, with four others, also inverted over cremations, in satellite positions, two south of the centre and two more to the north-east. The largest urn was the most distant from that at the centre. A not dissimilar barrow, on Free Down, Ringwould (*48*) between Deal and Dover, was examined in 1872 (Woodruff, 1874, 21-6; Ashbee & Dunning, 1960, 56; Grinsell, 1992, 369), by methods, as far as can be seen, comparable with those employed in Iffin's Wood. The barrow was some 22m (70ft) in diameter and 1.35m (almost 5ft) in height. Woodruff drew a section and, above the natural chalk, there was chalk rubble, brickearth and flints, all capped by what he termed surface soil mixed with loose chalk. His plan, a counterpart of that depicting the Iffin's Wood barrow, shows the collared urns, which were inverted over their cremations and in precisely cut pits with one in a central position, another immediately to the east, with two lesser urns to the south-east. One of these urns (*49*) contained the slotted incense cup and the faience beads already mentioned. These groups of urn burials as assembled beneath the Iffin's Wood and Ringwould barrows could both have been other than simultaneous burials and thus it is possible that the inurned cremations were kept, in appropriate circumstances, until they were brought together and the barrows raised. Whether or not all of a particular region were accorded barrow burial is unknown, although population averages have argued from this source. There is evidence from Holland and Wiltshire of flat graves between and around barrows which are not normally found because it is usually only the barrow, and not its surround, which is examined. The barrows of Kent have a familial appearance and, with more than a millennium of barrow building, the earlier Bronze Age population could have been of the order of about 8000-10,000 souls.

An early excavation of note was undertaken at Shorne in 1899 (Payne, 1900). Here, just to the south of the Rochester–Gravesend road, in a field called 'Great Bargrave' a large circle had, for years, been seen in the corn, especially during seasons of drought, when it grew more luxuriantly upon the circle than elsewhere in the field. It was a ring-ditch which would have been readily visible from the air (Wilson, 1982, 88, 111.51) and, from time to time, from the ground (Harden, 1948, pl.1, b). When the barrow was reduced much of it was used to infill the ditch. The site was stripped and, in a grave just to the south-west of the central point there was, unfurnished, a contracted skeleton, the bones of which had partially decayed after the removal of the barrow. Five further inhumation burials were found in the ditch, wherein was also found a whetstone, a sarsen stone grain-rubber and pottery described as 'thick, rudely made, and liberally sprinkled with grains of flint'. One of the ditch burials had been covered with flint nodules. The report is notable for its lively plan and sections, and a depiction of the location of the erstwhile barrow. It is clear that some of the principles of Pitt Rivers had been assimilated.

The recent excavation of a barrow site, scraped to the chalk, at Wouldham (Cruse & Harrison, 1983) located a narrow, weathered and silted ditch with a considerable causeway, occupying about a fifth of its circumference, which had at its centre a pit which contained a cremation beneath an inverted Wessex biconical urn, with three horseshoe handles. Traces of scorching within the urn pointed to the cremation having been put into it when hot from the pyre. There was also a contracted inhumation burial in a secondary, rather than a satellite, situation, in that the grave might well have been dug into a berm. It had been capped with flint nodules, as had the central urn burial. Four post-holes demarcated a rectangular area around this urn burial and they were likely to have remained from a mortuary house. This, as the excavators indicated, is comparable with such as have been encountered in the Netherlands, where such structures were found in certain of the Toterfout-Halve-Mijl barrows (Glasbergen, 1954). Indeed, it is thought that there were contacts which brought about procedural similarities in funerary practices from Beaker times onwards (Glasbergen, 1954,

76-88; Smith, 1961). Careful excavation of a series of barrows in England and Wales has shown that such mortuary houses were a feature of urn burials and it should be appreciated that there are also similarities in form and fabric of the barrel- and bucket-urns of Holland and those normally included in the Deverel-Rimbury series of southern England. Indeed, it seems likely that there were reciprocal, incidental, movements of people across what may have been a then not too difficult southern North Sea. Horse-shoe handled urns have also been encountered in Belgium (de Laet, 1958, 124, fig.33). The example from Budel, in northern Brabant, is considered as closely comparable with the examples from Capel-le-Ferne (Ashbee & Dunning, 1960, 52; Parfitt & Grinsell, 1991), Stowting (Jessup, 1930, 118; Cruse & Harrison, 1985, 89) and that from this barrow at Wouldham. The usage similarities are the continuum of relationships which have been discernable from Mesolithic times onwards and will be seen later on, when Kent, via the classical writers, emerged with a positive name.

From its outset, humankind would have adhered to progressively defined tracks, the shortest distance between two points or routes which conveniently circumvented natural obstacles. Such ways were no more than worn frequented ground and would be invisible archaeologically. Exceptionally, a length of Bronze Age stone-paved and post-demarcated road survived, near Oxford, as a causeway (*British Arch.*, 36 (July 1998), 5). However, the survival in marshy areas, seemingly numerous in Bronze Age times, of lengths of wooden trackways, timbers deployed longitudinally, parallel cross-timbers or compactly bundled brushwood were effective and ensured safe passage for pedestrians and, perhaps, pack-animals (Harding, 2000, 174, fig.5, 4). Those encountered in the erstwhile wetlands of the Somerset Levels are well known (Coles & Orme, 1976; Coles & Coles, 1986) and examples, although not as yet found in Kent, have come to light beneath the flood-plain of the Thames (Crockett *et al*, 2002) The timber trackways of the Somerset Levels linked islands within a wetland regime but, elsewhere, they could form part of a route, aiding passage across incidental marshlands. Such systems could have supplemented the recognised routes of Kent, Dover to the Canterbury area, to Rochester and beyond, or from the Maidstone area to the Weald or towards Ashford, which were finally formulated into Roman roads. There is also the so-called Pilgrim's Way, along the foot of the North Downs which could have linked settlement in the vicinity of the springs that, formerly, flowed from the junction of the chalk and the gault. It is supplemented by a ridgeway which could, at times, have afforded a better passage (Margary, 1948, 259-62). In addition to the through routes, tracks and droveways, many of which still survive (Everitt, 1986, 267-70), would have developed, thus patterning the countryside.

Roads and tracks, besides being routes for the movement of men and animals, might indicate vehicles, although it is doubtful whether any of the wooden-ways across marshy grounds could have supported even light pole-sledges. Wooden wheels, single piece and composite (Piggott, 1983, 25, fig. 5), are rare or unknown in England, but during the 1960s almost a dozen came to light in wetland sites in the Netherlands (van der Waals, 1964). A composite, tripartite, disc-wheel, of lightweight durable ashwood, was found in a bog at Blair Drummond, in Scotland (Piggott, 1957), which a radiocarbon date has set into the later Bronze Age. This was found during the earlier nineteenth century and was then thought to have been a shield. Another composite, tripartite disc-wheel has been found at Flag Fen (Denison, 1994). Its sections were secured by oak dowels and it is thought to relate to an axle found at an earlier juncture. Such wheels could, at any time, come to light from the wetlands of Kent. All too often when such pieces are encountered people cannot believe that they are ancient because of their, sometimes, good state of preservation. In earlier Bronze Age times such wheels could have carried living-wagons, a widespread adjunct of a mobile society, and in later times load-carrying carts. With small, sturdy horses yoked (Piggott, 1949) to a central pole, they would have been more sophisticated than is commonly thought and extremely effective upon beaten trackways.

Intercourse with the European mainland across, if only for short distances, open waters, indicate not unsubstantial craft, rather larger than the monoxylous boats of inland waters and even the versatile coracles and curraghs, forms of which still survive (Hornell, 1938). The remains of considerable craft, plank-constructed and sewn together with withes, have been found at North Ferriby (Wright & Wright, 1947; Wright, 1990), Brigg (Roberts, 1992; McGrail, 1994) and by the Trent (Denison, 2003). They could have been used to journey across the less turbulent waters of the North Sea of Bronze Age times. The remains from beside the Trent appear to have been of a log-boat of considerable size. About a decade ago a planked craft was found deep in the mud of Dover's Roman waterfront (Parfitt & Fenwick, 1993). It is well preserved and an end part is still *in situ* beneath walling. It was, as far as can be seen, about 15m (50ft) in length and had a maximum beam of 2.2m (7ft 4in). Its planks were caulked, secured by an ingenious lath system. Angled wedges, which had been devised for this purpose, secured the bottom planks. The upper side-planking had been removed as had the timber reinforcing the bow. Dismantling may have begun as the hewn timber would have been a valuable commodity. There was no trace of a sail-mast seating so, like more modest boats, it was presumably propelled by paddles (Harding, 2000, 179). Dated by radiocarbon assay to about 1550 BC, the greater part of this craft is now housed in an especial museum and can be viewed. This boat discovered in Dover, cannot be other than representative of Bronze Age Channel traffic and is a fortunate survival. Not all sea-going craft survived, as sea-bottom scatters of Bronze Age metal artifacts, recovered by marine archaeological endeavours off Dover (Stevens, 1975; Coombs, 1976; Muckleroy, 1980, 100-3; 1981) have shown. The bronzes from .Langdon Bay show something of the magnitude of the metal trade and that usable bronzes may have been scrapped for recycling once their particular form became unfashionable.

Langdon Bay's bronzes (Coombs, 1976), found in 1974 by amateur divers, were 352 in number and all conformed to a distinctive French pattern. There were 178 swords, dirks and rapiers and 110 axes of various kinds, plus other implements. Presumably they were a consignment for melting down and recasting into local forms and fashions en route to Dover. This assemblage, undoubtedly from a wreck, illustrates metal demands, and its trade, in a manner which escaped the most perceptive of studies (Butler, 1963). This, entitled *Bronze Age Connections across the North Sea* was an appraisal of the bronzes from the Netherlands, Northern Germany and Scandinavia found in Britain, and those from Britain found in those lands. Based upon bronzes, presumably imported, and termed 'contact finds' there were no more than 14 from the British Isles of which five are from Kent, while of the remainder of the 57, 43 implements and ornaments, were in grave-groups and hoards found in the areas of the European mainland which were the subject of the study. In Kent there is the flat rivetted dagger of Unĕtice affinity from Aylesford (James, 1899; Ashbee, 1997, 154, fig.2), a dirk, or rapier, of Sögel form Chatham Dockyard (Jessup, 1930, 102, pl.5, 12), the halberd from Faversham (Jessup, 1930, 98; Ó Ríordáin, 1936, 312, fig.56, 2), the edges of which are double-outlined in the same manner as an example from Roermond, in Holland. The tanged dagger with which it is associated bears similar blade definition. A small lugged chisel from Harbledown, in Rochester Museum, is of the Dutch *Voorhout* type, a series thought to have been cast in England for use in the Netherlands. Finally there are the bracelets with incised decoration, and a ribbed bracelet, which are from the Ilmenau metal industry of Lower Saxony (Butler, 1963, 219, fig.47) found at Ramsgate (Piggott, C.M., 1949, 118-21). Reflecting upon the Langdon Bay bronzes, one must reconsider the nature of Bronze Age industry and commerce for, in the light of the few bronzes from the European mainland, and the modest number from Britain found in that territory, it could be thought that these foreign weapons and appliances were a few retained as either exemplars of their interests or as related rarities.

Collared urns (50), current from about 2100 BC to 1500 BC, are the apogee of our barrow-interred ceramics, for thereafter we are faced with urnfields. Currently no more than 10 are listed as from Kent (Longworth, 1984, 216, nos.792-801) and full details of their context and associations given. They have been further pursued by Leslie Grinsell (1992, 357, tab.1) who has shown that they are from barrows or, if listed as flat graves, probably from the sites of barrows. Apart from the sherds, these urns, which in term of Ian Longworth's (1984) classification, consist of three which are in the Southeastern Style, followed by five which are considered to be secondary

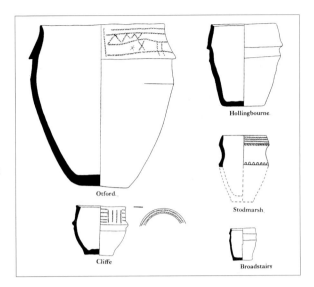

50 Kentish Collared Urns: that from Otford is of a generous average size; Hollingbourne is modest in size and plain; the examples from Cliffe, Stodmarsh and Broadstairs are of diminished dimensions but cannot be considered as miniature vessels. All ⅛. After I.H. Longworth, 1983

in style. One of the Ringwould urns, of southeastern style, is about 32.5cm (13in) in height and it is likely that the five urns from Iffin's Wood (Akerman, 1844) were of comparable size, as is that from Otford, which is in private hands. It is notable that the greater part of the small number of collared urns from Kent are of small size. That from Broadstairs is in the miniature vessel category, while those from Cliffe, Hollingbourne and Stodmarsh are also of modest, marginally larger size. Unusually the miniature urn from Broadstairs furnished a contracted inhumation burial, the small urn from Cliffe may not have been associated with an interment, while the remainder, with perhaps one exception, were inverted over cremated bones. Presumably cremations were put into urns and thereafter perishable covers were secured beneath the collar. Now and again urns display perforations which could have been used to fasten such covers. Collared urns are likely to have developed from late Neolithic Fengate forms and, indeed, two Kentish examples, which are included in the Primary Series (Longworth, 1984) from Stodmarsh and Westbere, which flank the Stour, are curiously reminiscent of earlier wares. The Hollingbourne urns were dug from sandy barrows opposite the old Whiteheath Union House, by Beale Poste in 1842. Details were found among his papers by Allen Grove (1952) in Maidstone's Museum. A quarter of a century later, the collared urns, together with a lugged miniature vessel, came to light at a sale of the residue of the Leeds Castle estate (Kelly, 1970, 232, fig.2, 1-3). By way of a postscript, a vessel unearthed from a sandpit at Potter's Corner, Ashford, in 1934, has been thought of as an enlarged food-vessel urn (Champion, 1982, 34), while W.P.D. Stebbing (Harrison, 1950, xliii) reported the discovery of 'a Bronze Age burial site with food vessels'. Sadly they have not been traced.

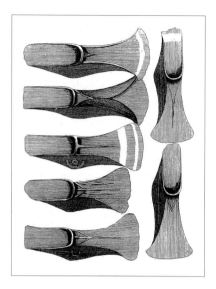

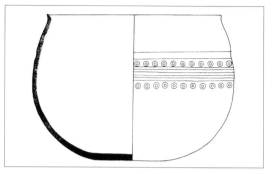

Left: 51 Seven of the hoard of 27 palstaves found close by St Mildred's Bay, Margate, in 1724. *After J. Lewis, 1736*

Above: 52 The globular urn from Birchington which was found containing 14 palstaves (1/5). *After O.G.S. Crawford, 1924*

To what extent a Middle Bronze Age can be adequately and accurately defined has for long been a matter of debate. Here in Kent are notable hoards of palstaves, accompanied by a proliferation of artifacts such as rapiers, spearheads and armlets, besides the emergence of tin-bronze. Bronzes, imported from the European mainland define what is termed the Ornament Horizon and the emergence of a range of bucket-urns and the virtual cessation of barrow burial. The first discovery of a palstave hoard to be recorded in Kent may have been at Leeds in 1708, for a letter, among the manuscripts of the Society of Antiquaries of London (Fol.162, no.202) from a Dr J.Young to Dr Thorpe dated 9 November of that year, describes the discovery near Leeds Castle of some 16 'boltheads such as the Romans used to shoot from their catapultae'. Most of these went to a brazier, but two were sent to the Royal Society which may have record of their receipt. A hoard of 27 unmistakable broad-bladed palstaves was found near Margate in 1724 and were drawn by William Stukeley (Ashbee, 2001, 78) and some were published (*51*), with comment, by John Lewis (1736, 137). More palstaves comparable with these from Margate, were found at Birchington, about two miles distant, early in the twentieth century. Fourteen were in a ceramic bowl (*52*) of Deverel-Rimbury mode, which was encountered in a brickfield almost 1m (3ft 3in) below the surface (Powell-Cotton & Crawford, 1924; Jessup, 1930, 100; Rowlands, 1976, 32, pl.10). This Birchington hoard is the basis of the Class 3 broad-bladed palstave category (Rowlands, 1976, 32). In 1986, 10 such palstaves came to light when sand was removed from the chalk in St Mildred's Bay, Westgate (Perkins, 1988). Eight such palstaves were unearthed at Goudhurst during the nineteenth century and it was observed that they had been laid out, one upon the other, in twos (Jessup, 1930, 99). Three of these found their way to the British Museum in 1855.

While Early Bronze Age times are marked by only a single hoard of bronzes, that from Buckland, Dover (Megaw & Hardy, 1938, 283, fig.10), the Middle Bronze Age has some five or six palstave hoards, and during the Late Bronze Age they proliferate, some 24 having been found. It has for long been thought that Bronze Age hoards were concealed to prevent their falling into alien hands at a time of emergency. Concealment within the surround of a house, settlement or enclosure would have been obvious and a place out and beyond, known only to the depositor, would have been more satisfactory (Hawkes & Clarke, 1963, 240). On the other hand, many hoards may have been votive, made at a particular time and place for especial reasons such as gifts to ancestors, the deceased or the deities. A further consideration is that valuable assemblages consigned to the ground, to rivers or bodies of water, was a means of obtaining social prestige, in anthropological terms potlatching. Such ideas have been current for sone time. For example, George Eogan (1964, 314) considered the Golden Bog of Cullen, a former body of water which, particularly during the eighteenth century, yielded up great numbers of bronze and golden objects, including 63 swords and various golden personalia (Wallace, 1938), a cult site. On the European mainland the many bronzes from rivers appear as votive (Torbrugge, 1972) while, more recently, it has been considered that such considerations are important as it is likely that, in prehistory, non-material factors loomed larger than is normally allowed (Bradley, 1990). Three of our Kentish Middle Bronze Age hoards are from the Thanet coast while there are two more from close by the Greater and Lesser Stour, while that from Goudhurst is at no great distance from the Teise.

Besides the palstave hoards, some 70 Middle Bronze Age singly-found bronzes are known from Kent (Rowlands, 1976, 279-430), and while about a dozen categories are represented, there are noticeable absences. In instances it may be that particular location and especial areas are significant. Thus, with one exception, that from Cliffe, the six flanged axes are all from eastern Kent, including one from Gore End, near Birchington, in Thanet. Of the 43 palstaves, there are five from the Ashford area, four from Canterbury and seven from the immediate vicinity of Sandwich. There are chisels from Canterbury and Harbledown, yet the distinctive side-looped spearheads are spread across the county; there are three from eastern Kent, Chartham, Dover and Westbere marshes, one from Sittingbourne, one from Chatham Dockyard and one more from the Darent at Horton Kirby. There is a single basal-looped spearhead from Lullingstone and a spear-ferrule, which could have been an incidental loss, appeared at Chislet (Jessup, 1930, 103). Rapiers or dirks, which developed from the Wessex II ogival daggers, are eight in number. Apart from blades from Folkestone and Thanet, there are four from the Medway at Chatham and two from the Thames at Erith and Northfleet, which are likely to have been incidental votive offerings, as were the swords, one from Chatham Dockyard (Jessup, 1933) and an Irish Ballintober blade from Strood. Early Middle Bronze Age socketed axes, knives and kite-shaped spearheads are absent from Kent, and may have been forms that were neither fashionable nor favourable for the forerunners of the *Cantiaci*.

A signal aspect of any assessment of southern English Middle Bronze Age metalwork is the Ornament Horizon (Smith, 1959) which is the appearance, largely in Somerset and the South West, of mostly bronze ornaments, which are imports, or copies thereof, of forms current in northern Germany from about 1400 to 1200 BC. The objects involved (Smith, 1959, 151-5) are torques, coiled finger-rings, ribbed bracelets, knobbed sickles and square-mouthed socketed axes. The hoards referable to this episode also normally contain wide-bladed palstaves, spearheads and quoit-headed pins. Within Kent, the hoards of low-flanged, broad-bladed palstaves from Birchington and Goudhurst, already mentioned, are a fundamental to this interlude. From Ramsgate (53) in Thanet, there are the bronze armlets, one ribbed and two with incised ornament (Piggott C.M., 1949, 118-21), said to have been found in 1891 in a chalk-cut grave, near Dumpton (Grinsell, 1992, 381), perhaps remaining from a razed barrow, which would have been almost at the end of such usages. Also from Ramsgate, found in 1929, is the urn of Deverel-Rimbury character, barrel-shaped and originally some 30cm (12in) in height, and about 20cm (8in) at the mouth. Ornamented with finger impressions upon the flat rim, and encircled with such impressions 6.5cm (2.5in) below it, this urn, clearly a votive deposit, contained horse teeth and ox bones, with a mussel shell, besides three swollen-necked bronze pins (54) of a type termed Picardy (Hawkes, 1942, 27, fig.1; 28, fig.2, 1-3). Another such pin, decorated and of the same form, had been found just inland from the South Foreland (Hawkes, 1942, 29, fig.2, 4). Their counterparts in Picardy were from close by the River Somme, and by the estuary of the River Authie (Hawkes, 1942, 29, 31, fig.4), although their origins are in a German Tumulus-Urnfield context (Childe, 1929, pl.XI, C, D series). Their associations in France point to their having come to Thanet rather later than the greater part of the Ornament Horizon material.

Although the south-western aggregate of Ornament Horizon material is apart from the Deverel-Rimbury urnfields of Wessex (Ashbee, 1978, 183, fig.54) there are, nonetheless, instances of association, as, for example, the Ramsgate urn and its pins. Clearly a local variant of a ceramic tradition which continued into the Late Bronze Age, its place and usages need determination. Although a large bucket-urn was from the Ringwould barrow (Champion, 1982, 35, fig.12.1), there are indications that the incidental discoveries of these urns may point to cremation

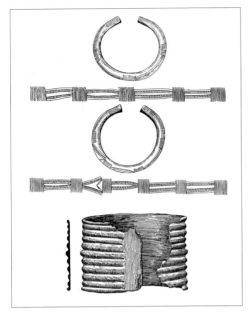

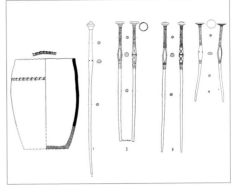

Left: 53 The bronze armlets (1/8) and ribbed bracelet from Ramsgate (1/2). *After C.M. Piggott, 1949*

Above: 54 Barrel-urn (1/5) and Picardy urns from Ramsgate (1-3) and St Margaret-at-Cliffe (4) (1/5). *After C.F.C. Hawkes, 1942 (1/12)*

cemeteries. R.F. Jessup (1930, 123) featured a massive barrel-urn from Frindsbury, found with fragments of another urn, in a deposit of black earth and wood ashes. He also records that 'barrel-shaped cinerary urns' were found at Tankerton. A bucket-urn was found on the chalk at Charing in 1935 (Cook, 1935, 239-40) and is unlikely to have been associated with a contracted inhumation burial dug out a short distance from its point of discovery. A sizeable bucket-urn has been found at Great Mongeham (Champion, 1932, 35, fig.12, 2) while the greater part of a globular urn came to light at Broadstairs (Hurd, 1914), in 1912. However, to illumine this pattern of incidental discovery, the excavation of the site of a razed barrow in the parish of Bekesbourne-with-Patrixbourne yielded 10 cremation burials, mostly adult, grouped largely in the north-western quarter and apparently secondary interments. Five of these were in pits and five in bucket- or barrel-urns. There was a mass of burnt flints in the ditch, presumably from the pyre. A note by Ian Longworth stressed that these urns, and one in particular, were akin to a series across the Thames estuary in Essex (Longworth, 1960). Perforations below the rims of three of these urns suggest that they were initially covered in a manner comparable with collared urns. Radiocarbon dates from Cremations 5 and 7 (Har-1492; Har-1493) when appropriately calibrated, should fall within the age band of the Deverel-Rimbury tradition.

The Deverel-Rimbury tradition changed abruptly by about 1000-900 BC when they were replaced by plain wares, fine and coarse, and later by pottery decorated by a wide range of techniques. These changes have been documented

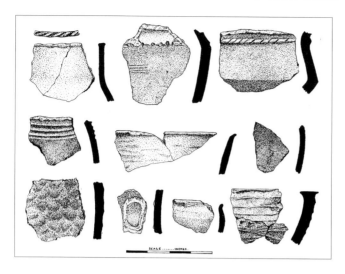

55 Sherds of Late Bronze Age pottery from Minnis Bay, Birchington. *After F.H. Worsfold, 1943*

(Barrett, 1980, 299, fig.1). Assemblages once assigned to the Early Iron Age have been reidentified as a Late Bronze Age phenomenon. In 1980 three Kentish sites, Aylesford, Mill Hill, Deal and Minnis Bay, Birchington (55) were seen as having yielded these later decorated wares. The vessels from Aylesford (Barrett, 1980, 305, fig.6, 9, 10) which bear a finger-printed cordon and a scored cordon, with short, oblique strokes below, respectively are likely to be developments from the general Deverel-Rimbury globular urn tradition (Calkin, 1962, 25, fig.10). Mill Hill, Deal (Stebbing, 1934) appears to have been a ditched circular hut site. Sherds were recovered from the floor but the mass was obtained from the ditch. Although this pottery has been thought of as Late Bronze Age (Champion, 1982, 38) there were rotary querns present which were an Iron Age innovation. Were there a clear association the dating of pottery would be in question. At Minnis Bay (Worsfold, 1943), the remains of a timber building, enclosed by pits and a gravel bank, discovered and examined on the foreshore, produced pottery which was, indirectly, associated with a Late Bronze Age hoard of 73 bronze pieces, recovered in 1938. It was possible, from the many sherds, to reconstruct the profiles of seven vessels. There were four bowls, three of which were carinated, and one ornamented, a round shouldered jar, recalling one of the Aylesford pots (Barratt, 1970, 305, fig.6, 10), and an angular *situla* urn. A remarkable series of decorated sherds (Worsfold, 1942, 38, fig.8) which were detailed, supplemented the reconstruction. The considerable range of pottery recovered from Site 5, during the construction of the Bridge by-pass (McPherson-Grant, 1980, 146-51) is to be associated with the sites which have been enumerated and their European mainland connections (Cunliffe, 1980, 174-7) need further detailed evaluation. A series from East Northdown, Margate (Smith, 1987) must also be involved.

A recent rescue excavation at Swalecliffe (Masefield *et al*, 2003) examined 17 pits and hollows, with associated woodwork, adjacent to a stream, which were dubbed 'wells'. Their prime purpose was thought to be water collection and supply. In essence a wetland site, the woodwork, mostly steps, revetments and some palisading was well preserved. Besides dramatic insights into wood workmanship, a dendrochronological sequence could be coupled to Flag Fen's (Pryor, 2003, *passim*) chronology. As with the Wilsford Shaft, at no great distance from Stonehenge (Ashbee *et al*, 1989), biological remains in some quantity, which included dung beetles, betokening cattle in the vicinity, allowed environmental investigation in various dimensions. Two discoveries of note are a cannibalised wooden ox yoke and a remnant of a basketry carrier presumably used for pottery vessels. A modest number (152) of sherds were recovered and the profiles of two fine ware bowls and a high-shouldered jar, later Bronze Age forms, were reconstructed. Radiocarbon dates are of the order of 1100 BC. Comparison was made with Minnis Bay and its various pits (Worsfold, 1943) and other comparable installations in southern England. This site at Swalecliffe is important to the pursuit of prehistory in that wetland conditions have allowed a comprehensive assessment, difficult on chalkland and gravel sites, to be made. Labelling this hollow and pit complex as 'wells' might be misleading as the possibility of rural industrial uses, rather than mere water extraction, might be considered.

It is during the later Bronze Age that positive habitation sites appear in Kent (Champion, 1980), as elsewhere (Ashbee, 1978, 181-98). Nothing more than Stebbing's details illumine the nature of the Mill Hill, Deal, house site, although the artifacts therefrom have been enumerated (Champion, 1980, figs.4, 6). The Minnis Bay, Birchington, timber house remains (Worsfold, 1943) and its pits were reduced by marine erosion. Indeed, these, thus reduced, are reminiscent of what remains of comparable sites when almost erased by deep ploughing. Traces of other such sites may remain to seaward as the erosion and innundation of Kent's northern coast has been considerable. An enclosure at Highstead, Chislet (Tatton-Brown, 1976, 236-7) produced later Bronze Age pottery, comparable with that from Minnis Bay, while similar settlement traces, labelled Hallstatt, were detected at Richborough (Bushe-Fox, 1949, 3-11, fig.2, pl.XL, 157). In Thanet, as a concomitant to his exploration of the site of the initial Monkton hoard of late bronzes, D.J. Perkins has shown not only a focus for these hoards but also something of a correlation with settlement sites. In addition to the Monkton site, he described remains at St Mildred's Bay, Westgate, in a situation reminiscent of Minnis Bay (Perkins, 1983, 243), a hilltop installation at St Nicholas-at-Wade, another at Sarre and yet another, a crop mark, on the high ground, close by the North Foreland, at Kingsgate. This pattern has been amplified by the Monkton Court Farm settlement (Perkins *et al*,1994), its range of pottery and the four late bronze hoards found within its ambit. In their discussion of this remarkable site, the authors were able to add to and clarify their exposition of the coincidence of developed Bronze Age settlement traces and hoards. It was observed (Perkins *et al*, 1994, 311) that the occupation of the Monkton site was short-lived and that there might have been a move inland, to higher ground, because of rising sea-level on the Wantsum shoreline. With the observations made regarding hoards earlier in the chapter, it could have been that the four Monkton hoards were propitiatory (Bradley, 1990) rather than the concealment of valuable metal artifacts, a frequent explanation. When a settlement is finally abandoned it is customary for all of value to be removed (Ashbee, 1996, 137).

Now that specific later Bronze Age settlement sites have been located and investigated, particularly in eastern Kent, one wonders as to the nature of the agrarian systems, notably the fields which sustained them (Bowen, 1961). In Kent, except for broken and isolated lynchets, unrelated to present-day agrarian usage patterns, the evidence for ancient fields is rare, if not entirely absent. Elsewhere in southern England complex field systems have been examined and their relationships with particular settlements established (Fowler, 1981, 144-232). At Minnis Bay (Worsfold, 1943) there is evidence that might denote a form of mixed farming, for there are domestic animal bones as well as a considerable variety of plant remains, thought to be the residue from threshing. Considerable care was exercised in their recovery and it is surprising that cereal grains were entirely absent. Elsewhere (Sheldon, 1982) palaeobotany has shown that there was woodland clearance and arable land use from earlier Bronze Age times onwards. Within Kent, field systems aligned upon Roman roads have been identified (Applebaum, 1972, 97) and, as in East Anglia (Williamson, 1987), it is not impossible that field systems of later prehistoric origin are preserved in modern dispositions. The mixture of elements of the northern coastal plain where the chalk ceases, and the sheltered, spring-lined, southern front of the North Downs, where chalk and clay mingle, makes for fertile soils and farming. Likewise the chalklands of eastern Kent and Thanet might, upon investigation, yield traces of earlier regimes preserved in present-day boundaries. Our marshlands are also awaiting investigation where, as beneath the peat of Ireland (O'Kelly, 1989, 65), field systems and their boundaries might yet survive upon ancient surfaces.

Nearly 30 later Bronze Age hoards, some considerable, have come to light in Kent. Apart from the Medway valley, south of its passage through the North Downs, and the south-eastern coast, they line the northern coastal plain. There is a remarkable concentration in Thanet (Perkins *et al*, 1994, 294, fig. 310, tab.7) To a considerable extent, the single bronzes have been found in the vicinity of the hoards, while there are some from the lower reaches of the Medway and other

Kentish rivers. These hoards, such as those from Swalecliffe, the Isle of Harty, Sittingbourne, Allhallows, Cliffe and even Higham, are from near sea-threatened land. They are matched by those hoards which line the lowlands north of the Thames, which culminate in the six hoards from the vicinity of Shoeburyness. The land losses of northern Kent, and about the Thames estuary, have been considerable (Allen, 2000), as is attested by the siting of Sheppey's causewayed enclosure. They would have been noticeable during Bronze Age times as the fully marine conditions of the Southern Bight became established and any islands which may have impeded a meeting of the waters were effaced (Coles, 1998, 76-7). Were, as perhaps at Monkton, this chain of hoards propitiatory, we may see only those which remained in situations which survived. For example, the 38 spearheads, knife and chisel, dredged from the bed of the Thames, off Broadness, Swanscombe, in 1892 (Corner, 1910), may originally have been buried in low, water-threatened land. Like the palstaves from Birchington at least three of the later Bronze Age hoards were found in urns, presumably made or selected for the quantities involved; those from Little Coombe Farm, Allhallows, Sittingbourne and Marden are recorded as in earthen pots or urns. In many instances, as the greater number of these hoards were incidental discoveries, ceramic containers, perhaps cracked or broken, because of the weight of their contents, may not have been noticed. On the other hand, some of these hoards may have been housed in leather or wooden containers, the remains of which would not have been prominent unless they had survived in a good state of preservation, as, for example, the lower part of a stave-built bucket from Stuntney, near Ely, Cambridgeshire, which had in it a hoard which comprised 431lb of metal (Clark & Godwin, 1940).

The Sittingbourne later Bronze Age hoard was 'fully described and engraved' by Charles Roach Smith in the initial issue of his *Collectanea Antiqua* (1848, 97-102), while Humphrey Wickham (1877) detailed and illustrated the hoards from Little Coombe Farm and Homewood Farm, Allhallows, in the hundred of Hoo. Sir John Evans (1881, 460-69) analysed and listed the Allhallows, Harty, Marden and Sittingbourne hoards in his *Ancient Bronze Implements of Great Britain* (1881), George Clinch enumerated six later Bronze Age hoards, those from Allhallows, Minster (Thanet), Harty, Marden, Saltwood and Sittingbourne in the first volume of Kent's *Victoria County History* (1908, 322-4) while intimating their importance and implying that others were known. Knives, a possible pommel and two socketed axes are illustrated. Ronald Jessup (1930, 107-8) listed 12 hoards and commented as to their content. He included a plate of a part of the Minster (Thanet) hoard. More recently (1982) Timothy Champion, in his discussion of the Kentish later Bronze Age, outlined the nature of the Kentish hoards in terms of present-day notation (Harding, 2000, 14-18), while latterly Thanet's hoards have been listed and their contents indicated (Perkins *et al*, 1994, 295). These sites have in some measure been investigated but, for the most part the earlier hoards, which were incidental discoveries, may have items missing.

In 1825, the clearance of a part of Clay Lane Wood, Cobham, revealed an enclosure seemingly surrounding a massive deposit of bones and bronzes, perhaps a later Bronze Age cult site (Ashbee, 2000/01). An account, by A.J. Dunkin, a founder member of the Kent Archaeological Society, appeared in the *Gentleman's Magazine* of 1846:

> In 1825 some labourers while grubbing up a piece of Clay Lane Wood came upon an entrenchment in the centre of which they discovered at the very least three wagon loads of human bones, mingled with leather, many metal belts, spearheads and armour, the latter in such preservation that a suit was actually put on by one of the labourers. The bones were collected and thrown into the fosse; the earth which formed the vallum was thrown over them and the soil levelled. Some of the belts, several portions of the armour, and pieces of the weapons are preserved in a museum at Gravesend. The armour was taken to Cobham Hall by the finders, who expected a noble reward for their pains, but the then noble owner, being no archaeologist, ordered the men some refreshment and told them to take their rubbish away. After this rebuff, and knowing no collectors of antiquities, they sorted out the metal, and after breaking it into pieces sold above a bushel of it to Mr Troughton, late a Mayor of Gravesend. So bright was the metal that one of the belts was actually tested by fire to see if it were not gold, and it still bears the mark of this ill usage.

A.J. Dunkin (1848) amplified the story and George Payne (1893, 150) cited the initial version and said that Charles Roach Smith's notebook for 1842 recorded that some of the celts were in the possession of Mr Crafter of Gravesend. However, despite the mention of celts and spearheads, neither John Evans (1881) nor Ronald Jessup (1930) record the site, the last despite having grown up in Gravesend. Bronze celts and spearheads have been recognised forms since the seventeenth century (Piggott, 1976, 56). Armour is, however, rare and known only from the European mainland (Coles & Harding, 1979, 375, fig. 135; Harding, 2000, 285-91), and broken buckets or even cauldrons (Leeds, 1930) are a possibility. Despite manifest deficiencies, the tantalising details of this earthwork enclosure, and the bronzes and bones found therein, could depict a ritual enclosure which has no direct counterpart in the English series. In this context, however, it should not be overlooked that the site is central to the later Bronze Age hoards of Thameside and the Isle of Grain (Champion, 1982, 37, fig. 14).

Besides the hoards, a considerable number, some 60 or 70 single later Bronze Age bronzes, have been found in the county. Their distribution, in the river valleys on the northern coastal plain and Thanet, differs from that of the Middle Bronze Age's bronzes in that some areas where they have been found are blank. There is, however, a marked intensification of riverine deposit; in the Darent, the lower Medway (56) and the Stour in the Canterbury area and its general vicinity numbers have been found (Champion, 1982, figs.13, 14; Perkins *et al*, 1994, fig.24) Many of these bronzes (Jessup, 1930,106; 1935c, 185), particularly those from the rivers, are clearly votive and are likely to have been cast into the waters. The remainder, single bronzes such as the socketed axe from Bearsted (Jessup, 1930, 252) or the example from Cobham (Jessup, 1930, 106) are unlikely to have been casual losses. As in earlier Bronze Age times, it should be considered that single bronzes were, in certain circumstances, votive deposits, perhaps even with something of organic material that would have decayed. Indeed, we see these bronzes devoid of their hafts and shafts, the last being attested by the wood remains often preserved in spearheads, and overlook the possibility of complete tools and weapons. Swords from the Thames and Medway are likely to have been hafted and, perhaps, in scabbards. A fine Weymouth sword (56) (Cowen, 1952) was recovered from the sea by fishermen off Folkestone which may have been a solitary deposition in what was formerly land.

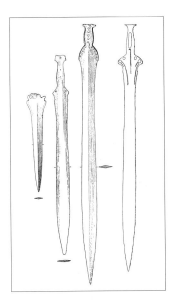
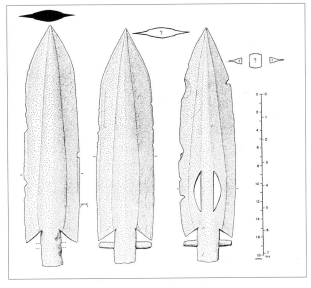

Above left: 56 Rapier and bronze swords, one of Hallstatt affinity, from the Medway at Chatham (left). Bronze sword of 'Weymouth' character from the sea off Folkstone (right). *After R. Jessup, 1933, and J.D. Cowen, 1952* (⅛)

Above right: 57 Barbed bronze spearheads from the Broadness hoard, Swanscombe, dredged from the Thames in 1892. *After C. Burgess et al, 1972* (¼)

Pieces of swords are not uncommon in the hoards, while a number of spectacular leaf-shaped swords, which are pointed at ther ends and have convex sides to their blades as in a willow leaf, have been found, mostly in the western part of the county. Two such swords, now in the British Museum, were found at Bromley. One of the number from Chatham and the Medway is spade-hilted and has an acute ricasso (Jessup, 1933c). A similar blade is said to be from Aylesford and is in the Ashmolean Museum at Oxford, while socketed axes from the same place are in the British Museum. Swords from the Thames are recorded from Erith, Greenwich and Woolwich. The last is said to have been associated with a bronze shield (Coles, 1962). Also of note are the spearheads (57), one from Broadness with barbs and lunate openings in the blade, and, from the same source, a long, lightly cast example, an angular version of the standard later Bronze Age spearhead. That with barbs and lunate openings in the blade has a counterpart in Alderney (Kendrick, 1928, 64, pl.VII), although the general form is not unknown in England (Smith, 1920, 32, fig. 26).

During the past two decades, later Bronze Age studies have refined earlier arrangements and at the present time a system of chronological order, with eponymous names, has emerged. Thus the end of the Middle Bronze Age is marked by the Penard phase, named after the Penard hoard and mindful of its impurity pattern; the later Bronze Age Wilburton phase, the bronzes of which employ metal from European mainland sources, which had a high lead content or was alloyed therewith; a Blackmoor phase during which developed sword types and socketed tools became conspicuous; and a Ewart Park style during the currency of which the numbers of hoards dramatically increase and carp's tongue swords (characterised a broad blade with a narrow tip) are present. Finally comes a Llyn Fawr climax during which iron and Hallstatt C influences from the European mainland appear (Megaw & Simpaon, 1979, *passim*; Harding, 2000, *passim*). By this time the great centres of Wessex, the henges with their supportive barrow-lined landscapes, were in the past. On the basis of the concentrations of bronze, it has been thought that power may have migrated to the Thames Valley and its environs. However, it has been seen that various hillforts emerged, presumably in embryo form, during later Bronze Age times (Ashbee, 1978, 189-90; Coles & Harding, 1979, 481; Harding, 2000, 292-306), a move which was a European phenomenon. Thus it is not impossible that in later Bronze Age Kent power resided within the earliest phases, yet to be located, of places such as Quarry Wood, Loose, Oldbury, Bigbury and Dover's heights.

Wilburton objects have been found in various hoards, for example that from Sturry, notably the indented socketed axe (Jessup, 1943; 1944). A sub-tradition termed the Broadwood is a series of hoards dominated by barbed spearheads, such as that from the Thames, off Broadness, Swanscombe (Burgess *et al*, 1972,

230, figs. 10-4). In Kent the Ewart Park style can be seen in the many hoards with their considerable numbers of swords, socketed axes and, markedly, the tools of metalworkers plus cakes of bronze and scrap metal which betokens the sophisticated intricacy of bronze cycling and recycling. Carp's tongue swords, usually in pieces, are present in at least seven major hoards, namely Allhallows, Hoo (Wickham, 1877); Minnis Bay (Powell-Cotton & Pinfold, 1939; Worsfold, 1943); Minster (Payne, 1893); Abbey Farm, Minster (Perkins *et al*, 1994, 295); Monkton Court Farm (Perkins, 1991); Swalecliffe (Worsfold, 1927, 230) and Stourmouth (Coombs & Bradshaw, 1979). The Llyn Fawr phase is present in the Hallstatt C derivative swords from Aylesford, the Bexley Heath hoard and Chatham (Cowen, 1967, 414-5, pl.LXII, 1, 9; LXIII, 1; 450, 12, 13).

Ronald Jessup, in his pioneer treatment of later Bronze Age gold ornaments from Kent (1930, 111-4), made observations that still hold good today. He pointed out that the county has no native gold and that gold ornaments, like bronzes, in terms of their gold, may safely be thought of as basically imports, perhaps from Ireland. He added that of the almost 40 gold ornaments known from Kent, there has been no instance of association with the better-known bronzes. A dearth of association is, nonetheless, common to the later series. Native gold has been found in significant quantities in Ireland and Scotland and there are sources in south-western Wales (Eogan, 1994, 9, fig.1). There are also sources on the European mainland, notably Germany and the Carpathians, the principal provenances being probably alluvial. Sheet-gold ornaments have been found in Beaker and advanced Early Bronze Age graves, and such as the Ringlemere cup were worked from suitable nuggets, but the massive bar-gold bracelets and torques of later Bronze Age times involved casting. Because England was a non-gold-producing area, there are numerous bronze ornaments, unlike Ireland where accessible gold was present. Thus gold, or the ornaments, were imported and it is significant that, of the British pennanular bracelets with expanded terminals, five major hoards are from Kent (Eogan, 1994, 93, fig.38), a concentration greater than anywhere else in England. Kent's gold hoards and objects line the northern coastal zone and have also been found in river and stream valleys and in water, notably the middle and lower Medway. They are, in terms of the later Bronze Age, clearly prestigious items. As far as can be seen their use was ultimately votive and, as has been intimated, they were destined for burial or the water. In life such things might have reinforced social distinctions and afterwards were therefore presumably potent in a votive role. There are hints of Kent, from Neolithic times onwards, having an especial role in the country's trading activities. The earliest hoards are followed by the sheer weight of metal in the later, which are augmented by quantities of bar-gold. In economic terms there could have been some commodity that would not appear in the archaeological record, one thinks of the corn and hunting dogs mentioned by Caesar. On the other hand, there is the possibility of control of a short route to the European mainland, the Thames–Medway estuary to the Rhine or even, as Dover's boat might imply, a shorter route. Indeed, although the earlier rise of Wessex was largely an internal phenomenon, the various pins and trinkets betoken a European mainland connection which could well have been channelled through Kent. By the later Bronze Age, however, Kent began to move into a European dimension, manifest during the succeeding pre-Roman Iron Age.

Kent is fortunate in that the later Bronze Age goldwork found within the county before 1980 has been classified and detailed, in common with all that has come to light in the British Isles, in Joan Taylor's (1980, 81-3) magisterial volume. Thirty-nine pieces have been listed and given reference numbers (Kt.1 etc.); there are 28 bracelets, four torques, three miscellaneous rings, a cup-ended piece, a bar-twisted ring, a piece of grooved rod and an oar-ended fragment. The golden bracelets comprise five groups: there are, first of all, those from the Medway near Aylesford (Kt.3-8; Pretty, 1863; Roach Smith, 1874), followed by the pair from Walderslade near Chatham (Kt.11, 12; Baldwin & Kelly, 1965), the group from Little Chart, near Ashford (Kt.18-20; Gordon, 1965), together with the two massive hoards from Bexley (No.1, Kt.21-28; No.2, Kt.30-38; Clinch, 1908, 338, pls.). A cup-ended piece is recorded from the Medway, below Aylesford (Kt.9; Pretty, 1863), a bar-twisted torque from Folkestone (Kt.16; Jessup, 1930, 114, 255), and, under 'Miscellaneous Types' there is a plain, tapered ring from Dover (Kt.14; Jessup, 1930, 114, 255) , a similar ring from Folkestone (Kt.17; Jessup, 1930, 114, 255) and a small ring from Gillingham (Kt.39; Roach Smith, 1874, 2) Two flanged bar-torques have been found in Kent, one from Castlemount, Dover (Kt.39; Scott Robertson, 1878), and a piece of such a torque from Gillingham (Kt.39; Roach Smith, 1874, 2). There is also a twisted torque, with no provenance other than 'Kent' attached to it (Kt.1; Roach Smith, 1874, 2) which may have been found at Aylesford.

There were two separate discoveries from the Medway at Aylesford and in its vicinity. The first group discovered in 1861 (Kt.6-9; Pretty, 1862), was 'enclosed in a box' which was alleged to have been thrown again into the river, and those 'more recently discovered in the district ... and at the same time' (Roach Smith, 1874). The records of these early discoveries, and their circumstances, are not without their ambiguities and critical investigation is undoubtedly needed. The three bracelets from Stag Paddock, Rooting Farm, Little Chart, at no great distance from the Stour, were unearthed during draining operations in 1869. Two of them, via Sir John Evans, went eventually to the Ashmolean Museum, at Oxford, while a third passed to the British Museum. They seemed unassociated but were united and once again took their place as a hoard as the result of ingenious, searching investigation (Gordon, 1965). The two Walderslade, Chatham, bracelets were dug from the ground during building operations in 1965, the site being upon the backslope of the North Downs (Baldwin & Kelly, 1965). The two seperate hoards of bracelets from Bexley were found during digging for sand and gravel in July 1906 and February 1907, at depths of about 1m (3ft), beneath 'what had been the floors of ancient hut-dwellings' (Clinch, 1908, 338). The circumstances of discovery of the various single objects are well illustrated, for example, by the torque (and perhaps the small ring) from Gillingham (Kt.39), which was found on Chatham Lines 'between the Sally Port and Brompton Barrier, by a party of soldiers throwing up a battery' (Roach Smith, 1874, 2), while the torque from Dover 'was found in a ploughed field' during the eighteenth century (Pretty, 1863, 42).

The remarkable coloured plates which illustrate the 'GOLDEN ARMILLAE found in the Medway near Aylesford (size of originals)' (Pretty, 1863) were from a drawing by Edward Pretty which was lithographed by F.G. Netherclift, also a member of the Kent Archaeological Society. The bracelets had been offered to Edward Pretty and, with thoughts for the future, he purchased them for the county. In 1861, at the October meeting of the Kent Archaeological Society, the Council secured them for its museum and they were exhibited at the Hythe Congress. Pretty described (1863, 43) the bracelets in detail and, presciently, the trumpet-shaped piece, which he compared with Irish dress-fasteners (Eogan, 1994, 88, pl.XIX). The bracelets from Little Chart (the three are considered as an average hoard (Eogan, 1994, 91), are decorated with encircling grooves at their terminals and two at a short span therefrom (Gordon, 1965) and could have been the work of a single craftsman. One of the Walderslade bracelets (Baldwin & Kelly, 1965) is plain, of round section and has trumpet terminals which are not as pronounced as those of the Irish dress-fasteners. The other, a convex–concave ribbon of some weight, with acutely everted terminals, is decorated with concentric circles, within double lines behind the terminals are line-demarcated, punch-made, circles (Jessup, 1970, 136, pl.40). This concentric patterning is reminiscent of the ornamentation of the sheet-gold cones from Germany (Eogan, 1994, pl.IX) which are thought to have Urnfield origins. The four-flanged bar-torque (58), from Castlemount, Dover (Scott Robertson, 1878) has five coils, and is in pristine condition (Jessup, 1970, 136, 136, pl.41), almost as if it were fresh from the hands of the goldsmith.

In the initial publication of the considerable hoards of bracelets from near Bexley (Clinch, 1908) there is, sadly, a capital error. The plate facing p.388 is of the first hoard (Eogan, 1994, pl.8). These bracelets, eight in all, have plain, expanded terminals, and one is in two pieces. In the second hoard (Eogan, 1994, pl.8), three of the nine bracelets have expanded, slightly everted terminals,

58 The golden twisted torque found at Dover, north-west of the castle, in February 1878. *After W.A. Scott-Robertson, 1878* (1:2)

three more have merely expanded terminals and although their compeers are of slender character, these could be considered as ribbon bracelets. The initial hoard could well be the work of a single goldsmith, as could the second, although the uniform character of the first contrasts with the mixed character of the second, which includes one bracelet which would not be amiss in the first. The piece of an oar-ended strip-ornament from Minnis Bay, Birchington, has Scandinavian affinities (Taylor, 1980, 24) and may predate the bracelets and torques.

These groups of unwarn golden bracelets, the torques and other objects, from water or close thereby, and from the ground, indicate votive deposits, a principle that must also apply to the single objects. Some of these might have been the only one of a group that was found or declared. Such artifacts cannot have been casual losses, nor does it seem that they were concealed with an intent to recover them. It is perhaps significant that gold was consigned to the Medway in the vicinity of Aylesford, for the area was clearly of some importance. On both sides of the Medway there were the considerable megalithic long barrows, the earlier Bronze Age burials and, later, the spectacular Iron Age burials, a temple and finally the substantial Roman villa at Eccles. The consignment of gold and valuable bronzes to water invariably invites allusions to Arthur (Bradley, 1996, 1-4) while deposition in the ground may well have had its origins in the pits with pottery and the buried polished flint and stone axes of Neolithic times. That such deposition continued into Iron Age times is shown by such as the Snettisham and Ipswich torques (Clarke, 1955; Cunliffe, 1991, 482-5).

The Bronze Age, in time lasting about two millennia – the first copper daggers, with Beaker incomers, and their distinctive drinking cups, appeared in about 2500 BC and the initial Iron Age Hallstatt swords from 750 BC onwards – was a time in which the fundamental nature of society changed. The Mesolithic people's pattern of life was one of measured mobility, punctuated by periodic recourse to particular places. This order of things continued into Neolithic times when, notwithstanding developed agricultural undertakings, there was the visitation of long barrows and causewayed enclosures. In the later Neolithic the henges, particularly in Wessex where huge round-houses and Stonehenge came into being, and the round barrow cemeteries dominated certain landscapes, there was a continuum of long-lasting modes of life which came to an end in about 1450 BC. From this time onwards we see small settled units, ditched and embanked enclosures around round-houses, on a more modest scale than earlier (Ashbee, 1978, 181-98) with continuing occupation centred upon developed agricultural endeavour which provided an assured level of sustenance. In many places, and especially in Kent, the settled peoples had a territorial identity and are likely to have looked to the first strongholds.

SEVEN

THE PRE-ROMAN
IRON AGE *CANTIACI*

A notion of a pre-Roman Iron Age had been a part of Thomsen's 'Three Age' system and, in the guise of 'Late Keltic' antiquities, it was afoot in Kent by the middle of the nineteenth century. The concept had been given depth and perspective by the spectacular furnishings from almost a thousand graves dug up at Hallstatt in the Austrian Salzkammergut, before 1864. The Emperor Franz-Josef was interested and visited the excavations in person (Daniel, 1975, 109-11). At about the same time a mass of ancient material, mainly iron swords, had been recovered by Colonel Schwab from the Neuchatel Lake at La Tène in Switzerland. Ferdinand Keller gave us details of this great assemblage when his work on Pfahlbauten was translated into English as *The Lake Dwellings of Switzerland and other parts of Europe* (1866). In Kent there was knowledge of these things and Iron Age antiquities were recognised as such when they were found in quantity when gravel digging was undertaken on Bigbury Hill. John Brent (1861, 33) recorded them, labelling them Roman, and after they were shown to the British Archaeological Association meeting the pieces were seen as 'Celtic'. R.C. Hussey (1874), of Harbledown, thought of Bigbury as a 'British settlement of high antiquity, in all probability of prehistoric origin' and published the first plan of the earthworks. He indicated where the iron- and bronze-work had been disinterred, saying that much had been dispersed without examination. Notice of Bigberry was given at the meeting of the Kent Archaeological Society at Cranbrook in 1873 and the intention to plan commended. In 1866 John Brent had written a letter to Charles Roach Smith detailing yet another discovery there of iron and bronzes, about 1m (3ft) below the surface and upon a burnt layer (Gomme (ed.),1887, 141). In 1878, General Pitt Rivers excavated the ramparts of Caesar's Camp, at Folkestone, as he considered it similar to Mount Caburn in Sussex (Pitt Rivers, 1883). He thought the earthwork medieval (Bowden, 1991, 86). Now known as Castle Hill, a motte-and-bailey site, later Neolithic pottery was, nonetheless, found beneath the rampart (Rady & Ouditt, 1989). Excavation was small-scale amd the possibility of the later use of a small hillfort remains. In 1886, Sir John Evans, and his son Arthur, visited the gravel pit by the church at Aylesford (Evans, 1890) where they obtained from the workmen the many vessels and bronze objects which had accompanied cremation burials. It should not be forgotten that the well-known picture (Evans, 1890, 318, fig.1) is labelled 'Diagrammatic sketch, from account given' and that the associations and arrangements (Evans, 1890, 322, fig.4) are from the memories of the workmen. Notwithstanding this, the Aylesford assemblages allowed Evans to associate them, ultimately, with northern France and the Illyro-Italic cultures of the fifth century BC. They became the basis for the identification of Belgic culture (Hawkes & Dunning, 1931), and having been supplemented by the Swarling urnfield discovered in 1921 (Bushe-Fox, 1925), allowed comparison with rich graves of similar form encountered north-east of the Thames. The problems pertaining to Aylesford and the alleged Belgic ethnic influx have generated a considerable literature (Birchall, 1963; 1965; Stead, 1971; 1976).

The pre-Roman Iron Age began in about 700 BC, when iron Hallstatt swords had their currency, and continued, with the increasing use of wrought iron for tools, appliances and weapons, until the Roman incursion of AD 43, by which time an integrated, named people, the *Cantiaci*, had emerged. *Cantium*, rendered in Greek, was applied to either the South or North Foreland by Pytheas, sailing from Massilia in about 300 BC. Later, various early writers use the term for what is now Kent, a peninsula at the south-eastern corner of Britain. C.A. Raleigh Radford (1954, 6) considered the place name *Durovernum Cantiacorum*, Canterbury, as likely to have incorporated the official tribal name, which was prefaced by a notice of the *oppidum* which, after Caesar's campaigns, grew up upon the site of what became the riverine Roman city. *Durobrivae*, riverside Rochester, had, it seems likely, similar roots as an *oppidum*, the beginnings of urbanisation (Collis, 1984). As a name *Cantium* is ancient and, even with the endeavours of the ancient geographers in mind, there is no reason why it should not have had ethnic application. Alec Detsicas (1987, 6-8) evaluated the perplexing, if not intractable, sources, and despite the divisions observed by Caesar, considered that there would have been a comprehensive name for those of such a distinctive terrain.

The divisions of Kent – four 'kings' are recorded by Caesar – had their origins in earlier prehistory and were apparent by Bronze Age times. They are difficult to define with exactitude but are likely to have been bounded by local topography. Thus in eastern Kent there could have been an area incorporating the Stour and Thanet, a central enclave around the Medway, and, to the west, the lands flanking the Darent and its valley. Further to the west, an area bounded by the Thames to the north, and the Mole or Wey to the west, would have had the Ravensbourne as its waters. Alternatively, eastern Kent, mid-Kent and western Kent, together with a Wealden area, incorporating the headwaters of the Medway and Rother are a possibility. Such territories would have looked to a hillfort and, later, a near-urban *oppidum* and, although defendable, they are the apex of complex social systems. Such major installations are not necessarily the central point of a territory; indeed, they may have grown up at a boundary where they could have been a source of social prestige. Away in the countryside there were defended enclosures and demarcated farmsteads, served by extensive field systems and woodlands. All were linked by ways and tracks, routes that were formalised in a later age. Principal places, and the territory at large, were supported, here and there, by temples, sacred places, perhaps enclosures that may have demarcated particular groups of trees, and recourse to the greater monuments of an earlier age. Cemeteries were in the vicinity of principal places and other, lesser, installations.

Certain Kentish earthworks of Iron Age times are best considered as *oppida*. First and probably foremost there is Quarry Wood, Loose (Kelly, 1971) just to the east of the Medway. Like *Camulodunum* (Hawkes & Hull, 1947; Cunliffe, 1991, *passim*) there is a citadel, with scattered supplementary enclosures, the whole complex being confined by dykes. Almost 25 miles to the east, on a hilltop above the Stour, there is Bigbury (or Bigberry), patently an enclosed *oppidum*, the earthworks of which contain some 7.3ha (30 acres) (Jessup, 1933b; 1938; Jessup & Cook, 1936; Jenkins, 1962, 10; Thompson, 1983). It was attacked by Caesar in 54 BC and thereafter this focus moved to the site of Canterbury and spanned the Stour. Just over 18km (12 miles) to the west of Quarry Wood is Oldbury (Ward-Perkins, 1939; 1944), on a site not unreminiscent of Bigbury, which encloses a remarkable 50ha (123 acres). Other and lesser works, considered hillforts, have been investigated near Tonbridge and Tunbridge Wells (Money, 1968; 1975), Keston (Piercy Fox, 1969) and Squerryes, near Westerham (Piercy Fox, 1970). Thus Bigbury and, later, Canterbury were the foci for eastern Kent. The considerable Loose *oppidum*, from which a move to the site of Rochester may have been made, dominated mid-Kent and the Medway valley, while Oldbury, supplemented by Keston and Squerryes held sway over the western region. The lengthy, indistinct, Wealden division looked to the Tonbridge or Tunbridge Wells installations by the headwaters of the Medway.

Kent's wealth in the pre-Roman Iron Age, as shown by, for example, cemeteries and the considerable incidence of gold coins, was from its trade in commodities such as iron and control of sea-links with the European mainland.

Dover, with what would have been a spectacular multivallate hillfort (Colvin, 1959; Bayley, 1962), now surmounted by the medieval castle and multiples of lesser, later, works, would have dominated the estuarine harbour, which served the shortest sea route. Lesser works on the western heights, destroyed by early nineteenth-century fortifications, could have housed beacons and navigational aids later supplanted by Roman phari (Wheeler, 1929). At Richborough traces of Iron Age occupation, albeit early, were found (Bushe-Fox, 1949, 8-11) as were a number of 'Celtic' coins, British, Gaulish and from distant Massilia (Allen, 1968). Although it has been considered that this Iron Age occupation was at an end by about 100 BC (Cunliffe, 1968, 232) it seems unlikely that there was no use of the harbour facilities proffered by the eastern end of the erstwhile Wantsum Channel. As has been observed, the Roman harbour has yet to be found (Hawkes, 1968, 226). Iron Age pottery, notably 'Belgic' combed wares have been found at Reculver (Thompson, 1955, 54, pl.1, b). They are comparable with pieces from Richborough and Bigbury. An installation to guide coastal craft at the entrance or exit of the Wantsum Channel seems likely. However, the Great Stour, although flowing to a mean sea-level some 7-8m (25-30ft) lower than today, would have allowed appropriate craft to serve Cantebury, and even Bigbury, by unloading, as in later times, in the vicinity of Fordwich. It is also likely that there were port facilities, with communications to the hinterland, somewhere in the Medway estuary, even at Rochester, the site of the later *oppidum*. Indeed, the Medway, in a deeper channel attuned to the lower sea-levels, could have been navigable to the vicinity of the Quarry Wood, Loose, *oppidum*. Western Kent, however, may have relied upon the Thames and transhipment therefrom. Down the English Channel from Kent, entrepots have been identified at Poole (Markey *et al*, 2002), Hengistbury Head (Cunliffe, 1987) and probably Mount Batten, a promontory protruding into Plymouth's sheltered sound (Cunliffe, 1988). There is evidence that these down-channel havens handled wine and minerals; the Kentish entrepots, serving short sea routes, could have transmitted commodities such as the corn, hunting dogs and slaves, as mentioned by Caesar.

Although H.A. Colvin's (1959) notion of a hillfort, preceding the castle on Dover's eastern heights, has been considered as unproven, it should not be overlooked that Iron Age pottery, as yet unpublished in detail, has been found in its interior (Bayley, 1962). The earthworks follow no known later plan and are not inconsistent with a number of hillforts (Wheeler, 1943) which occupy important sites (59). Furthermore, the white cliffs of Dover are in a continual process of recession, sometimes more than 1m (4-5ft) in a decade, and it is manifest that the earthworks, which are likely to have clung to the contours of the heights upon which they had been constructed, have been truncated and that as much as a third of the enclosed area has been lost to the sea. A hillfort

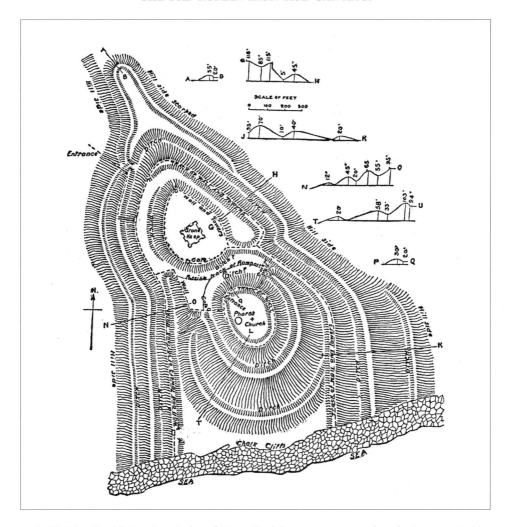

59 I. Chalkley-Gould's (1908, 414) plan of Dover Castle's encompassing earthworks. It is conceivable that the outer contour-clinging banks and ditches remain from an Iron Age hillfort, of Maiden Castle magnitude, which has been halved by the erosion of the chalk cliffs. Iron Age pottery has been found within the remaining interior. *After I. Chalkley-Gould, 1908*

on such a commanding height would have been an appropriate accompaniment for what may have been later prehistoric Britain's most important port. Indeed, like many hillforts its origins may well have been in the later Bronze Age, as is, perhaps, shown by the many bronzes and gold ornaments from the immediate area. Moreover, the boat remains, considered in the previous chapter, and the bronzes from the sea-bed, combined with the generalities of 'Celtic' seafaring (McGrail, 1995) are further, albeit indirect, indications of Dover's prehistoric maritime role.

Besides their control of routes such as the Medway estuary to the Scheldt and the Rhine, it should not be overlooked that even today the chalk cliffs of Dover look across to Cape Griz Nez. There has been considerable coastal erosion during the past three millennia and in later Bronze Age times the Channel could have been no more than about 17km (11-12 miles) in breadth. Thus the Straits of Dover would have been a narrow through which all sea-borne trade from the west, and to the west, had to pass. Ingress to the Rhine and Elbe, corridors into Germany's heartland, besides the Baltic, could have been controlled. Conversely, access by those from that quarter, to the Atlantic areas, could have been regulated. A symbol of the authority of the *Cantiaci* would have been the considerable ramparts of the *oppidum*, upon which Dover Castle now stands, looming above Dover's estuarine haven. Indeed, this may well have been a replacement, built in Iron Age times, for a work that succumbed to the sea. At this time tidal flow could have had its difficulties and dangers, and thus a system of pilotage may have operated.

Bigbury (*60*), some 3km (2 miles) to the west of Canterbury, besides being a major factor in the early development of Iron Age archaeology, has entered history as the fastness stormed by Caesar's Seventh Legion on the second day of his 54 BC incursion (BG, V, 9). Its investigation and excavation was a major part of the life's work of Ronald Jessup (1933b; 1938; Jessup & Cook, 1936). More recently Frank Jenkins (1962), Hugh Thompson (1983) and the brothers Blockley (1989), building upon the earlier work, have also adressed themselves to its problems. In addition to his carefully sited excavations, which followed his investigation of Anstiebury, Holmbury and Hascombe (Thompson, 1979), Hugh Thompson (1983) undertook the compilation of a critical catalogue of the iron and bronze material recovered from Bigbury during the nineteenth century, which included horse-gear vehicle fittings, firedogs, cauldron chains, slave chains (*61*) and fetters. A single bank and ditch encloses 10.7ha (26 acres) and surrounds a gravel-capped plateau which has a maximum height of 71m (233ft) OD. There are entrances to the east and west, while, attached to the northern side, there is a largely bivallate annexe, adding 3.3ha (8 acres) to the enclosed area. The main defences are only about 9m (30ft) in breadth and the present crest of the bank rises no more than just over 3m (11ft) above the original ditch bottom, which would have been heightened by a timber revetment. Hugh Thompson (1983) located a probable hut, a water-hole and gullies in the interior. Occupation of the hilltop may have begun during the later Bronze Age, perhaps even earlier than the fifth century BC. A west-facing cross-ridge dyke preceded the enclosure and its annexe which emerged during the second century BC. At some time after 54 BC the site was abandoned and a move was made to Canterbury and the Stour. Normally when an occupation site is abandoned everything of use is taken and only the inutile abandoned. However, considerable deposits of serviceable metalwork were buried, presumably in pits, as votive deposits.

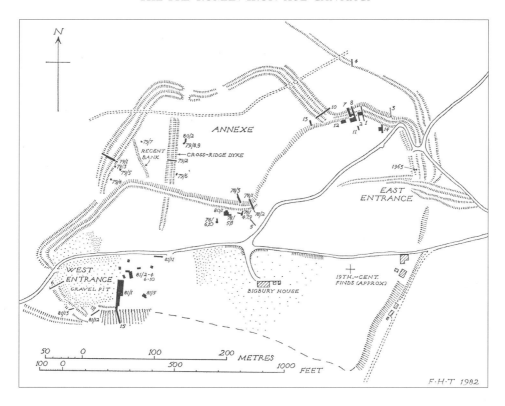

Above: 60 Hugh Thompson's general plan of the Bigberry Hillfort, showing the positions of excavations of 1933-4 (Jessup and Cook, 1-14); 1965 (Jenkins); 1978-80 (Thompson, 1978 1-10, 1979 1-9, 1980 1-2) and 1981 (K. and P. Blockley, 1-13). *After F.H. Thompson, 1983*

Right: 61 Bigberry: iron cauldron-hangers and slave chain neck-rings. *After F.H. Thompson, 1983* (1:7)

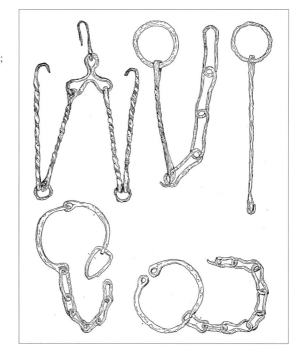

Down the years various traces of Iron Age occupation have been encountered in Thanet, at that time separated from the Kentish mainland by the Wantsum Channel, perhaps a discrete territory in its own right and not subservient to the generalities of eastern Kent. Crop marks, denoting ditches, have for long been known upon the chalky eminence of North Foreland Hill (Jessup, 1957, 13; Perkins, 1993, 411). In 1995 sections were cut across these ditches and, despite deep-ploughing-reduction, they proved to have been not inconsiderable (Hogwood, 1995). Pottery indicated their digging in about 300 BC. Scouring is not mentioned although later pottery has been found, presumably in the upper silts. They have emerged as the double ditches of a hillfort, if not a minor *oppidum*, with an area of some 24ha (60 acres). With the ports, local sea-passage routes and the trade of pre-Roman Iron Age Kent in mind, an aspect of this not inconsiderable enclosure may have been a beacon, precursor of the renowned lighthouse.

Recently, a part of a palisade and ditch-defended Iron Age installation has been traced on Fort Hill at Margate and it may have been some 6ha (15 acres) in extent. Traces of round houses and other structures were found and settlement traces were visible between its ditches and further down the hill. Gaulish and other pottery in quantity has been found together with loom-weights and the burial of a young woman. This settlement is thought to have lasted from about 250 BC until Roman times. Fort Hill, indicated by such early nineteenth-century houses as Fort Crescent and the Fort Paragon Hotel, is some 20m (about 75ft) above the low lying land which backs Margate's harbour, the King Street area, which might conceal traces of an earlier haven. It is likely that much of this defended enclosure, which was not inconsiderable, was destroyed without record when the Winter Gardens were constructed during the 1920s, although, as at Dover, chalk sea-cliff erosion may have destroyed a part (Denison, 2003).

As has been observed, the dyke-protected Quarry Wood Camp at Loose (Kelly, 1971) is the focal point of a considerable dispersed *oppidum*, and was, for the *Cantiaci*, probably their principal installation (*62*). In close association with the principal stronghold were various enclosures which would have fulfilled specific functions. To the north, by Mangravet Wood, less than a mile distant, was a considerable kite-shaped earthwork (Chalkley-Gould, 1908, 438-9; Allcroft, 1908, 153), upon which a route, considered Roman, was aligned (Margary, 1948, 214). Little is known of the function of the kite-shaped enclosures which have been encountered in Hampshire and Wiltshire (Crawford & Keiller, 1928, 252-6) but, nonetheless, within such a system as Quarry Wood they could have bounded a grove, some shafts or even an assemblage of effigies (Ross, 1967, 40-3; Webster, 1995, 453-60). Also distant from the fortified focus of the *oppidum* is, at Coxheath (Jessup, 1930, 160), a denuded rectilinear enclosure, divided by a cross-bank. In the north-eastern corner there is a low flat-topped mound, perhaps a barrow.

This enclosure is at no great distance from a possible terminal of the southern boundary dyke of the complex. The Quarry Wood Camp, although cut away at its northern end by quarrying, displays ramparts of simple, single-period dump construction, which are still about 5m (15-16ft) in height, with a flat-bottomed ditch, and enclosure about 15-16ha (30 acres). Pottery was found in 1911, which included a stamped amphora handle, while sherds emerged when the considerable bank and ditch sections were excavated (Kelly, 1971, figs.10, 11). The second quarter of the first century BC, a date indicated by the pottery, is considered to be that of the raising of this earthwork. Unless there are earlier features as yet undetected, the establishment of this *oppidum* may mark a move from elsewhere. Millbay's Camp at Nettlestead, on the other side of the Medway, of which little is known, has the look of an unfinished, abandoned site (Chalkley-Gould, 1908, 399-400). A rectangular enclosure at Barming, sited on the high ground above the Medway (Jessup, 1930, 159) looks at the site of the cemetery wherein local principals, probably from Quarry Wood, were interred.

Like Bigbury, Oldbury (*63*), beloved by Benjamin Harrison (Harrison, 1928, *passim*; 1933) is for the most part a work with but a single bank and ditch. They encircle the edge of a steep-sided, stoney plateau, near the northern edge of the Weald, and enclose some 49ha (123 acres). Excavation during 1938 showed that there had been two periods of bank and ditch construction. First of all there

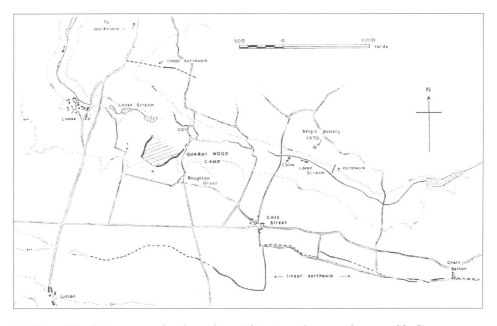

62 Quarry Wood, Loose, an enclosed oppidum with its immediate area demarcated by linear earthworks. *After D. Kelly, 1971*

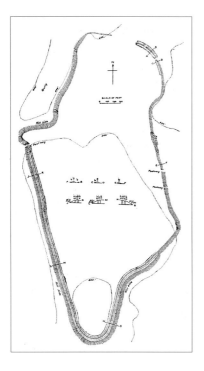

63 I. Chalkley-Gould's (1908, 396) plan of Oldbury Camp, near Ightham. The eastern ramparts were destroyed by nineteenth-century quarrying and only a modest escarpment remains. *After I. Chalkley-Gould, 1908*

was a simple bank of dump construction from a ditch, which was followed by a programme of modification and amplification and, in places, an additional bank and ditch, while the ditch was enlarged and given a wide, flat-bottomed, character. There is also reason to believe that the ramparts were augmented, revetted, and topped with wooden breastwork and a parapet walk. The distinguished excavator, J.B. Ward-Perkins, published details of his excavation, which was, in view of the size of Oldbury, on a necessarily modest scale, first of all in *Archaeologia Cantiana* (1939), on the eve of World War II, and, later, in the *Archaeologia* (1944), where he discussed the wider issues raised by his diagnostic work. Various beads (1939, 162, fig.9) came to light, as did pottery termed Patch Grove (1944, 149, fig.9) plus storage jars and bead-rimmed bowls. He was also able to define what he termed Wealden pottery, plain vessels with footrings (1939, 159-60; 1944, 145-6, fig.6). This material suggested occupation during the first centuries BC and AD. If the flat-bottomed ditch of the second phase of the ramparts is comparable with the northern French Fécamp style (1944, 137-41, fig.4) it would have been dug during the first century BC. This form of ditch, nonetheless, may have had a longer history than is commonly supposed. Surprisingly, six gold coins were found when a road was driven into Oldbury in 1923. Two of these came into the possession of Mr Hooker of Ightham and proved to be from the Gaulish *Bellovaci*; both were worn and one had been clipped. Another such coin was located in the British Museum, while three others are known from the vicinity. A piece of a rotary quern of Niedermendig lava, bearing signs of considerable use, was found near the crest of the reconstructed rampart (1939, 181) and points to their early import from the Rhineland, perhaps even as ballast for boats crossing the North Sea.

During 1983 and 1984 Hugh Thompson (1984) sectioned Oldbury's defences near the north-eastern entrance for comparison with the 1938 work, and also investigated anomalies revealed by a magnetic survey. As a result of this work he was adamant that there was no clear evidence of refortification and was of the view that it had been rapidly constructed and abandoned by about 50 BC. Traces of iron-working were detected as was a hearth, the charcoal from which yielded a radiocarbon date BM-2292 BC 40± 80. A later, local Romanised native population used the site as a quarry.

Excavation has taken place in two of the western hillforts, Caesar's Camp, at Keston (Piercy Fox, 1970) and Squerryes, Westerham (Piercy Fox, 1970). Hulbury, a razed hillfort by the Darent has, besides pottery of of the Oldbury Wealden series, produced wares appropriate to the later Bronze Age (Ward-Perkins, 1939, 166, fig.11), which points to an early beginning for that site. Caesar's Camp at Keston, sited upon the Blackheath Pebble Beds, which rise to a height of some 150m (430-500ft) above sea-level, has attracted attention since the eighteenth century. Hasted (1775) produced a plan, it was surveyed for the Society of Antiquaries of London by Thomas Milne, when the ramparts were almost complete, and engraved by James Basire in 1790. It was Pitt the Younger, who lived at Holwood House, who caused so much to be levelled (*64*). The early plan shows that 16.8ha (4-3 acres) were enclosed by a double bank and ditch, showing perhaps strengthening of the defences, with, in places, a counterscarp bank. The excavation of 1956-9 consisted of an examination of the north-western entrance and sections of the banks and ditches. The posts of a presumably gated entrance were found while the inner rampart, which was of dump construction, still stood in places almost 2.5m (8ft) above the ancient soil surface, and almost 3m (9ft 6in) close by the gate. Some of the pottery, found beneath and in the primary rampart, was patterned with curvilinear motifs. The ancient soils were studied by Dr I.W. Cornwall and the soil pollen by Professor G.W. Dimbleby. There had been forest in the vicinity when the work was initially raised. Indeed, some of the original rampart material may have been augmented by supplies carted from a distance and not dug from the ditch. A considerable linear ditch, still some 8m (25ft) in depth, flanks the Downe road from Keston church to Holwood Farm. It may show movement control exercised from this hillfort. The work undertaken at Squerryes, Westerham, consisted of two sections cut across its defences, one close by the south-western entrance and another upon

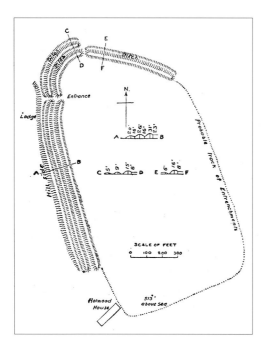

64 I. Chalkley-Gould's (1908, 398) plan of Holwood Camp, Keston. A considerable run of the ramparts was erased by an eighteenth-century landscape enhancement scheme. *After I. Chalkley-Gould, 1908*

the western side. Squerryes is sited upon a headland of the Hythe Beds of the Lower Greensand, the ragstone, and its ramparts enclose about 7ha (18 acres). By the south-western entrance the ditch proved to be of V-form, almost 3m (10ft) in depth and 9m (30ft) in breadth. The height of the inner bank, which was of dump construction, sealed a podsolised ancient soil. Traces of tumbled stone revetting were in the ditch. The section on the western side unearthed what were possibly sherds from the first century BC, beneath the modest bank, which was high above a slighter ditch, which yielded five sherds of handmade pottery from its primary infill. There were traces of tumbled revetment from the facing of both banks, and Squerryes, seen when first built, would have been formidable and spectacular. It was thought to have been of a later construction than Caesar's Camp at Keston.

The hillforts on High Rocks, near Tunbridge Wells (Money, 1968), and on Castle Hill, near Tonbridge (Money, 1975; 1978), are conceivably foci for the Wealden territory and may have been designed to protect, or even dominate, the entreprenurial iron industry of that area (Cleere & Crossley, 1985, 52-56). High Rocks, discovered only in 1939, was sited upon the Lower Tunbridge Wells Sandstone, of which use was made, and 9.7ha (some 20 acres) were involved. An initial bank and ditch was, during the first century BC, replaced by formidable double stone-faced ramparts and ditches, together with an elaborate inturned south-eastern entrance, with complex outworks, which involved a flat-bottomed ditch as at Oldbury. G.W. Dimbleby's soil pollen analysis pointed to arable farming in the vicinity, while iron-working may also have been undertaken. Despite scepticism (Thompson, 1978), two hillforts were located and excavated on Castle Hill, Capel, near Tonbridge (Money, 1975; 1978). The first, bivallate and enclosing 1.8ha (2.9 acres), raised in about 300 BC, was thought to have exercised control over a crossing of the Medway and appears to have had little use before abandonment. It was replaced by another, not dissimilar work, on the same elevation (Money, 1975, 63, fig.1), adjacent to the first and to its south-west. It enclosed 1.01ha (2.5 acres) and, again, it had but a brief period of use before abandonment. The knoll upon which these modest, but not unformidable, works were successively raised rises to a height of about 100m (about 325ft) and normally one would have expected its entire encirclement by ramparts, as had been suspected. However, it is clear that there were successive works. Importantly radiocarbon dates were obtained from charcoal found in the ancient soil surfaces beneath the ramparts. They are, for the first fortification BM-810 315± 50 bc, and for the second, BM-809 225± 61 bc, and are, sadly, scarcely statistically separable. A function for the forts is difficult to determine, with the nature of the area in mind, and an adverse association, pertaining to the site, is not an impossibility. In 1978 the earthworks were razed in the interests of totalitarian agriculture (Money, 1978, pl.3) and no action was taken by the Inspectorate of Ancient Monuments, of the Ministry of Works, regarding this wanton destruction.

An explanation for the hillforts, as distinct from the manifest *oppida*, is far from easy. Demographic changes have been invoked (Cunliffe, 1982, 43) as have economic factors, the control of internal trade (Drewett *et al*, 1988, 159). Their excavation has been for the most part no more than modest sampling of considerable sites and thus traces of the early use and development of many may remain. By and large, however, there was, if not initial construction, a spate of development of the hillforts of Kent during the third and second centuries BC. Here and there, is an indication that particular works may be intrusions into hitherto underdeveloped areas.

Incidental discoveries and recent rescue archaeology show that Kent was settled and farmed as in other areas of southern England. Such open settlement may well have been of two kinds, first of all farms, sometimes substantial and ditch-demarcated, together with often indeterminate traces of occupation which may have resulted from trade and industry. An inhibiting factor is likely to have been areas of podsolised heathland, the clays and woodlands of the Weald and of the backslopes of the North Downs. Conversely, the chalklands of eastern Kent, as in earlier times, supported settlements, as did the broad lowlands of our river valleys and the loamy, fertile soils of the north-western areas. A later Iron Age farmstead was located on the chalk of Farningham Hill (Philp, 2002, 125-7) and is an enterprise against which further such work in the county must be measured. Indeterminate traces of Iron Age activity at Richborough and Reculver have already been thought of as indicative of maritime enterprise and they illustrate the fragmentary nature of much of the evidence for the many and various undertakings which would have sustained the lives of the *Cantiaci* at large.

Farningham Hill's farm was about 0.2ha (less than an acre) in extent and was within an angular ditched enclosure which had, initially, four entrances and later only three. There were three groups of pits, infilled with domestic debris as they passed out of storage use, and the traces of a modest, circular house. There were also pairs of post-holes, thought to denote drying racks. Besides pieces of more than 40 vessels in one of the pits, 2,500 potsherds from the site were from some 165 ceramic containers. The enditchment had in it the bones of oxen, ovicaprids, pigs, horse and deer. The last are likely to have been hunted. The farm's fields would have been at no great distance and cattle could have been watered in the nearby Darent. The site was detected from the air and the degree to which it had been denuded by deep ploughing bodes ill for other installations, still unknown elsewhere in the county. Its use-life, unlike some of its kind, was no more than a century, from about 50 BC to AD 50. There are in the Darent Valley (Pyke, 1978) traces of land division which could have restrained this farming enterprise. By way of contrast, a considerable palimpsest of enclosures encountered on the Isle of Grain (Philp, 2002, 139-41), some of which surrounded posted structures, was largely industrial. Sadly limited resources precluded a more detached examination than periodic sampling ahead of destruction. Nonetheless, details were recovered and it emerged that the site, at the confluence of the Thames and Medway, although concerned with farming and fishing, was geared to salt production, a commodity which would have been traded inland. Iron Age activity, as shown by the pottery, took place during the second and first centuries BC, with indications of continuity into Roman times. Besides these informative undertakings, Brian Philp has been able to investigate traces of Iron Age occupation at Charing, North View and Snodland. Another Iron Age site of note was at Greenhithe (Detsicas, 1966) where a number of circular enclosures had, it would appear, contained circular houses of which but a few traces remained. Quantities of pottery were recovered and it was possible for comparison to be made with the Wealden wares from Oldbury (Ward-Perkins, 1944). At Fawkham an example of the distinctive banjo-enclosures has been detected (Fowler, 1981, 113; Drewett *et al*, 1988, 143), one of the first to be found in Kent.

Whereas the various countryside installations of the pre-Roman Iron Age west of the Medway have been revealed by rescue archaeology, similar sites to the east of that river have been encountered and investigated since the early days of the twentieth century. Near Dumpton Gap, Broadstairs, in Thanet, Howard Hurd

(1909; 1914), between 1907 and 1909, investigated, in advance of a building scheme, a considerable system of pits, enclosures, and, at no great distance, the surround of a circular house and some burials. He recovered combed and cordoned pottery, loom-weights, a bone weaving comb and a bracelet of Kimmeridge shale; the burials were inurned cremations. The pits had in them bones, broken pottery, oyster, mussel and limpet shells, having become receptacles for rubbish when they went out of use. The results of this comprehensive excavation programme were published, with exemplary promptitude, first of all in the *Archaeologia* (1909) and also in *Archaeologia Cantiana* (1914). In 1925, Dr Arthur Rowe of Margate (Perkins, 1938, 234-6) investigated the site of the new tennis courts at Tivoli Park Gardens, finding abundant traces of Iron Age occupation, which included some scroll-ornamented Glastonbury wares. J.P.T. Burchell's work at Lower Halstow (1928) located an early Iron Age surface, in a marshland area, which yielded a considerable quantity of mostly cordoned and combed wares, which were illustrated photographically. Briquetage was also found, as were pieces of elegant pedestal urns, and this pottery is housed in Ipswich Museum. The site would repay location and further investigation with a programme of environmental evaluation in mind. While the Worth temple has yet to be discussed, it should not be overlooked that settlement traces, yielding a considerable quantity of pottery, examined and reported upon by R.A. Smith, were close by (Klein, 1928). In 1940, C.F.C. Hawkes published a note describing a La Tène I bronze brooch, together with what was termed Marnian pottery, from Worth-next-Sandwich (Hawkes, 1940). As early as 1930 Iron Age pottery from Mill Hill, Walmer (now Deal) had interested Hawkes (1930) in that he propounded the likely techniques for the production of combed wares. From 1939 onwards F.H. Worsfold (1948) monitored brickearth extraction at Borden where he was able to record a system of pits and ditches. Gold coins had been found in the adjoining parish of Tunstall and it was thought that there should have been an occupation site in the vicinity. Quantities of pottery were recovered, a good measure of which was coarse, early and handmade. There were also pieces of vessels which were compared with those from the considerable site encountered at Crayford in 1936 (Ward-Perkins, 1938), which are thought to have been made some 70 years before AD 43. The site at Crayford was a discovery that did not permit excavation but the quantities of pottery (65) therefrom allowed classification into Iron Age A and B, the notions of that time (Hawkes, 1931). Thus Ward-Perkins was able to draw together, as appendices to his examination of the Crayford pottery, decorated wares from Essex, Kent and Sussex, terming it South-Eastern B, to separate it from the Glastonbury series. Indeed, such cultural groups were seen as the way forward (Hawkes, 1939).

One of the accomplishments of rescue archaeology has been the revelation of the nature of Iron Age occupation in eastern Kent. Timothy Tatton-Brown (1976,

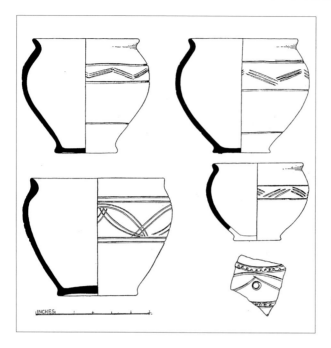

65 Decorated Iron Age pottery from Crayford. *After J.B. Ward-Perkins, 1938*

236-8) planned the remarkable palimpsest of occupation, detected from the air as crop marks by J.K. St Joseph flying from Cambridge, at Highstead, Chislet. Investigation showed that that a four-entranced enclosure was a component, and excavation, which yielded pottery of the fifth to third centuries BC, was presciently described as of importance to the development of Iron Age studies in north-eastern Kent. The crop marks are also of significance in that there has been occupation from Mesolithic and Neolithic times onwards, a factor which shows the part played by particular places in prehistory, a concept that has as yet to be examined in detail. Although enclosed farms and enclosures are likely to be involved, the exigencies of rescue excavation mean that all too often only a part of a considerable site can be examined. This applies to such as was detected and examined (MacPherson-Grant, 1980) on the line of the Bridge by-pass on Barham Downs. There was an enclosure with pits, likely to have been storage silos, used as usual for rubbish when they fouled. The considerable quantity of pottery was examined by B.W. Cunliffe (1980, 174-9) who saw the assemblage as early and embodying quirks and styles which were close to European mainland forms. Canterbury's by-pass construction also disclosed pits with pottery and evidence of iron-working in their vicinity (Hearne *et al*, 1995). The ditches, gullies, pits and post-holes detected, plus abundant pottery found at Whitfield (Parfitt, 2002) may well mark another not unsubstantial farmstead which was worked during the later Iron Age and after AD 43. Many of the post-holes may have marked drying-frames. The features of this considerable site, as revealed by excavation, were carefully tabulated, size, form and pottery content being indicated.

The possibility of field-systems serving settlements was looked at in the last chapter and there are allusions to such systems which may be related to Iron Age installations in their vicinity. One of the earliest was to lynchets in the Lullingstone area which were traced as far north as Farningham and south to Shoreham (Greenfield *et al*, 1948, 183). In eastern Kent ancient fields were first recognised by R.F. Jessup (1937, 122) and have recently been referred to by T. Tatton-Brown (1988, 85). 'Belgic' field boundaries are possibly a part of the Highstead, Chislet, complex (Tatton-Brown, 1976, 238). There are possible fields at Chestfield (Blockley, 1987), while a field system has been identified on Abbots Land Farm between Folkestone and Dover (Rady, 1991, 285) that might well be prehistoric. At Dolland Moor, near Folkestone (Bennett, 1988, 10, 14), traces of square Iron Age fields have been found, while, just to the east of this area, fields succeeded an enclosure.

Shortly after Caesar's incursions various hillforts, and even dispersed major settlements, were abandoned and we see the emergence of *oppida*, the first towns (Collis, 1984). Thus, Bigbury was abandoned and a move made to a site which spanned the Stour. Excavations, mostly in pursuit of the Roman city, have shown something of its nature (Frere, 1954, 103-14, figs.1-6, pl.1, 2; Jenkins, 1962, 4) and the present-day city walls, which follow the Roman walls, are substantially the boundaries of the *oppidum*. As a Roman city it became *Durovernum Cantiacorum* (Rivet & Smith, 1979, 353), the *Duro-* element being a reference to what must have been a substantial conurbation. It seems likely that the Loose enclosures were abandoned and that a move was made to an *oppidum* that was eventually Romanised and became Rochester. Up to the present little more than coin-flan moulds have come to light and it is not impossible that the Roman walls follow an earlier boundary. The name *Durobrivae* (Rivet & Smith, 1979, 346), with *Duro-* as the initial element could refer to an enclosed entity on low ground as it contrasts with *duno*, a hillfort. It is said that there was no bridge before Roman times but this is unproven, for Iron Age times were far more sophisticated and formidable than is commonly allowed. The recovery of foundation timbers and their radiocarbon assay would be a step forward.

Within Kent and south-eastern England many who pursue the problems of the pre-Roman Iron Age use, for its later manifestation, the term Belgic or refer to the arrival of the Belgae. Caesar noted an incursion of the Belgae into Britain at some time before his own landings and it has for some time been argued that they settled in Kent and the Thames valley (Hawkes & Dunning, 1931; Cunliffe, 1991, 110). This notion is strengthened by the incidence of Gallo-Belgic coins in these areas (Cunliffe, 1991, 111, fig.6.2). However, it could be thought that the coinage came about from mutual gift-giving and the exotic grave furniture of the Aylesford-Swarling culture, with which the Belgae are identified, originated from the sophisticated trade which was backed by, in certain areas, specialised production, which developed in concert with neighbouring areas of the European mainland. Were there an incoming it could have been on a modest scale and in Hampshire (Jones & Mattingly, 1990, 154, map 5.11) where by Roman times Winchester was styled *Venta Belgarum*. Although this name may incorporate a copyist's error (Rivet & Smith, 1979, 492) the sense is likely to have been 'market of the Belgae', an appelation which points to such people in that region.

In contrast with the large cemeteries of the European mainland, Iron Age burials were for the most part, until recently, a rarity. Indeed, apart from the cist burials of the South West (Whimster, 1978) and the vehicle burials of Yorkshire (Stead, 1965; Ramm, 1978; Dent, 1985) careful burials in the South East of the country are not common and there is a considerable incidence of the disposal of bodies in such as ditches and disused storage pits. In general, inhumation burials are infrequent and there but few barrow burials (Whimster, 1977; 1981). In the South East, and particularly in Kent, cremations became the standard mode of disposal from the outset of the first century BC, the burned bones being contained in ceramic urns, and other vessels, and buried in cemeteries. Considerable quantities of wood would have been required, in various locations, for the cremation pyres, a factor which would have accelerated deforestation.

Iron Age inhumation burials, however, are not unknown in Kent. The cist graves found at Aylesford (Evans, 1890, 325-7) because of the contracted burials they contained, have for long (Jessup, 1930, 116; Ashbee, 1997) been thought of as of Beaker origin, but may have been later. There are examples of this usage in places other than the South West (Fox, 1955, *passim*). Accelerated radiocarbon dating of a small sample from the bones, some of which may survive in Maidstone's Museum, should resolve our doubts. In later Iron Age times, however, inhumation burial was restricted, as will be seen from the burials at Deal, to the upper levels of society. At Walmer an extended female inhumation burial was furnished with a pair of cast-bronze spoons (*66*), one having been placed at each side of the head (Woodruff, 1904, 11; Parfitt, 1995, 105-7, figs.46, 47). Other inhumation burials, some with brooches, are known from the area. Of particular note, and also from Deal, is the extended inhumation burial, in a grave which was furnished with a crown, La Tène II sword, shield, suspension ring, brooch and girdle fitting (Parfitt, 1995, 18-20, pls.II, III, VIII-X). As the writer, Keith Parfitt, remarked (1995, 157), there were poorly recorded burials from Highsted, near Sittingbourne (Vale, 1987, 368) and one furnished with an iron brooch from Dumpton, near Broadstairs. The Mill Hill inhumation cemeteries are unique in England although the rite obtains upon the European mainland, where such burials in flat graves are not infrequently encountered. However, as was said, the Mill Hill grave furnishings do not reflect cross-channel fashions and usages. Caesar, when he came to Kent in 55 and 54 BC was nonplussed by the use of chariots against him; Cassivelaunus commanded, it was said, 4000. It is curious therefore that chariot and cart burials have not been found in Kent, although fitments such as the Bapchild terret (*67*) are not unknown (Jessup, 1930, 142, fig.25). With such burials confined to a particular area of Yorkshire one has for long thought that it could have been a supra-tribal cemetery for charioteers and prestigious vehicle drivers.

A recent rescue excavation at Brisley Farm, Ashford (Stevenson & Johnson, 2004) disclosed two encoffined warrior burials enclosed by the ditches of two reduced square barrows of eastern Yorkshire style, or even northern French enclosure form. After their establishment a large rectangular enclosure had been attached to their western sides. In pride of place was the barrow of a poorly preserved male of about 1.80m (more than 6ft) in height, supine, furnished with sword and shield, while in the grave-pit was a spear, a bronze ring, and a large ceramic butt-beaker from Amiens, in northern France. Several sherds were present and the burial could have been made as late as AD 50, after the Claudian invasion. A supplementary barrow, at the south-eastern corner of the enclosure, was of an adult, perhaps young, only 1.57m (about 5ft) in height. His coffin was in an irregular grave-pit hardly long enough to accommodate him; his corpse had been twisted and the head was in the opposite direction to that of the other interment. His furnishings were, however, more elaborate: an inverted sword, with remains of

Left: 66 The pair of cast-bronze spoons from an inhumation grave at Walmer, Deal (1:2). *After C.H. Woodruff, 1904*

Above: 67 The crimson and cobalt blue enamelled bronze terret from Bapchild. (1:2). *After R.F. Jessup, 1930*

scabbard, with three suspension rings, and hilt, a spear (bent to fit the grave), and a shield, with a conical iron boss lay over the body. There was also a brooch, and some iron nail-like pieces were across the ankles. A butt-beaker, a platter, with a maker's mark CANICOS, from the Marne region of northern France, and a small cup were also present. Near the platter was half of a *Sus scrofa* (pig's) head. Indeed, boar's heads and joints of pork make an early appearance in such burials, the boar being the premier cult animal of the period. It may have been a hero's portion! Platters such as that in the grave were current in France between about AD 20 and AD 45, but sherds in the barrow's ditch point to activities in the vicinity into the later part of the first century AD. The archaic character of these burials make for a reassessment of the warrior in later Iron Age society.

Later in the pre-Roman Iron Age there evolved within Kent a number of cemeteries for the burial of cremated remains contained within ceramic urns and other receptacles in an appropriate pit. The best known are Aylesford (Evans, 1890) and Swarling (Bushe-Fox, 1925), which are important for prehistory immediately prior to the AD 43 Roman annexation of Britain. Besides the cemeteries, there are apparently isolated burials, such as have been found in the Maidstone area (Kelly, 1963), which were incidental discoveries and may indicate as yet unidentified cemeteries. Indeed, small numbers of cremations in urns, such as were found on Hothfield Common in 1942 (Brinson, 1943), are similarly likely to have been a part of a larger entity. As well as Aylesford and Swarling, urn cemeteries and indications thereof are known from Allington (Thompson, 1978), Cheriton and Folkestone (Bushe-Fox, 1925, 20), Deal (Ogilvie & Dunning 1967; Parfitt, 1995, 145), Hothfield, already mentioned, Sittingbourne (Kelly, 1978, 267) and Stone (Cotton & Richardson, 1941). Burials encountered incidentally are known from Ashford (Kelly, 1963, 188-9), Charing (Cook, 1935, 239-40), Deal (Ogilvie & Dunning, 1967), Folkestone (Bushe-Fox, 1925, 20), Maidstone (Kelly, 1963) and Plaxtol (Ward-Perkins, 1939, 168) and they are likely to have been indicative of larger groups.

Aylesford's cemetery is well known as it was the basis of a pioneer study of the nature of the pre-Roman Iron Age (Evans, 1890). It was dated to after 150 BC and, following Caesar, was attributed to the Belgae. Arthur Evans' illustrations, fundamental to any consideration of the assemblages (1890, figs.1 & 4) have been regularly reproduced for a century. The principal burial (fig. 1), a cremation contained within an ornate bucket, with accessory vessels, interred within a chalk-lined pit, is clearly captioned 'Diagrammatic sketch from account given'. Similarly, the various urn burials (fig.4), the 'family circle', are from memories of discoveries made during the removal of surface soil over a number of years (68). In the light of the procurement of antiquities from Aylesford alluded to in earlier chapters, the accounts of the Iron Age cemetery should be accorded critical

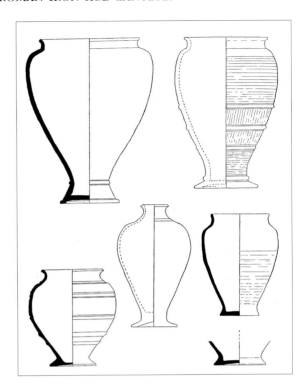

68 Ungrouped pedestal urns from
Aylesford (1:8). *After A. Birchall, 1965*

caution. Nonetheless, there have been reconstructional endeavours, employing the
basic account together with information in the registers of the Ashmolean and
British Museums, which have not been unsuccessful (Birchall, 1965). The principal,
oft-illustrated burial appears to have been a cremation with a brooch, contained
within a wooden stave-built bucket, bronze-banded, the top band bearing an
embossed, scrolled frieze with confronting grotesque horses. Its handle was secured
by human-head masks, perhaps of warriors, with large crescentic headdresses. It
was said to have been in the chalk- (block?) lined cylindrical grave with a bronze
jug and pan (*oenochoe* and *patella*) of Italian origin and various ceramic urns. Other,
possibly similar, graves may have had between them a large iron-bound stave-built
bucket, ceramic urns and a bronze-mounted tankard. These richly furnished graves
are likely to have been the principals of the Loose *oppidum* and the other burials
those of immediate supporters. The revaluation (Birchall, 1965, 283-91) suggests,
however, that burials may have been made at Aylesford after the presumed move
to the riverside location which became Rochester.

Swarling (Bushe-Fox, 1925) bracketed with Aylesford (Birchall, 1965), a
site adjacent to Chartham Downs and about 4km (3 miles) from Canterbury,
consisted of two groups of inurned cremations, an eastern and a western, clearly
separate. Class distinction may well have been indicated by accompanying vessels,

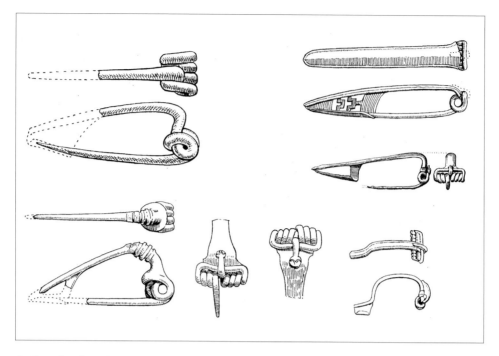

69 Brooches from the Swarling Urnfield (2:3). *After J.P. Bushe-Fox, 1925*

fibulae (brooches) (69) and even the care with which graves were dug. The departure from a near-egalitarian pattern of deposition was Grave 13 which was, as at Aylesford, a roughly circular pit, more than 1m (3ft 3in) in diameter and of almost the same depth. Its principal feature was the remains of a wooden iron-bound bucket, some 70cm (2ft 6in) in diameter, which contained charcoal and calcined bone in quantity, together with two bronze brooches. It was surrounded by six ceramic vessels which had presumably contained sustenance (Bushe-Fox, 1925, pl.II, fig.2). There is the sad possibility that these groups remained from a much larger cemetery which had been destroyed by gravel extraction. An unusual feature was the proximity of an iron-working installation which may have preceded the interments.

Bucket burials were observed and examined at Alkham no great distance from Dover, when three pedestal-urn burials were examined in 1989 (Philp, 2002, 160). One of these buckets had decorated bronze bands and an iron handle, and the other multi-bands, traces of feet, with the bronze handle attached by horned human face-masks. The only comparison is the Aylesford bucket. It is, indeed, fortunate for Kentish prehistory that these three burials were the subject of a present-day excavation, evaluation and recording. Besides its bucket, which contained the cremated bones of a male, about 25 years of age, one burial was furnished with a spectacular pedestal urn and two cordoned pots, all wheel-made, and three brooches. Another burial of note, one furnished with a mirror (*70*) and two bronze brooches, was found at Chilham in 1993 (Parfitt, 1998; Stead, 1998, 141): the cremated remains were thought to have been those of a female. The mirror's closest loop-handled counterpart is that from Trelan Bahow, St Keverne, in Cornwall (Hencken, 1932, 120-1, fig.33, B) which, like this from Chilham, was rather smaller than many (Rook *et al*, 1988, fig.9). By virtue of its accompanying brooches it appears as early in the series and a copy, albeit a skilled one, of a more sophisticated example. The circumstances of this discovery illustrate the dangers of untrammeled metal detection and the necessary diplomacy deployed to enable publication and illustration.

As in earlier times, the pre-Roman Iron Age communities of Kent had various cult sites, where expression could be given to their patterns of belief. Some such sites may have been similar to that described by Lucan, travelling in the first century BC. Of a Gaulish sanctuary he wrote 'And there were many dark springs running there, and grim-faced figures of gods uncouthly hewn by the axe from the untrimmed tree trunk rotted to whiteness'. Such a frightening scene would, however, leave no more than confusing tree-holes, and, perhaps, some post-holes for an archaeologist. A sanctuary such as Lucan described could have been one of the *nemeton* category, a location sometimes indicated by a present-day place name derived from or incorporating that term (Piggott 1975, 63-4; 1978, 37).

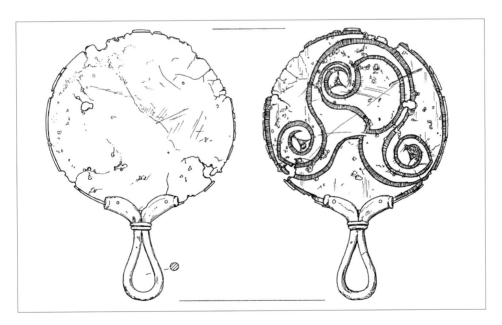

70 The mirror from the Chilham Castle burial (1:3 approx). *After K. Parfitt, 1998*

With the Greek word *temenos*, in Latin *templum*, one need not be dealing with a structure but an enclosed area with appropriate qualities. It might, however, have within it a *fanum*, which could have been a shrine, sanctuary or temple. Another aspect of pre-Roman Iron Age ideological activity is the *bothros*, *mundum* in Latin, which is an imprecise term pertaining to, among other things, the earth at large, a pit or shaft, which could be an access to the deities deep in the earth and the departed souls confined therein. Into this libations could be poured and offerings made. Like other things, a pit or shaft could have been within an enclosure (Piggott, 1978).

Such places and their attributes would have demanded ministrants and, via Caesar and Tacitus, a prehistoric priesthood, the Druids, is known (Kendrick, 1927; Piggott, 1975). They are thought of as figures of later prehistory yet, from early times onward, particular people would have been concerned with such as the specifications for barrows and other monuments where traces of cult usages have been observed and claimed. Druidical practices as detailed by Greek and Roman writers are often more appropriate to earlier prehistory than to Iron Age times. For example, Strabo (Geog. IV, 4) relates how victims were shot to death with arrows which can only relate to a time when archery was current (Clark, 1963; Piggott, 1971). Such a victim has been incorporated into Christian hagiology as St Sebastian, a handsome Roman youth martyred by being pierced with a multiple of arrows. Curiously he is the patron saint of athletes.

Of the 10 or more ostensible Roman temple sites in Kent, two have yielded positive evidence of having been initially established in pre-Roman Iron Age times. At Worth, near Sandwich (Klein, 1928; Jessup, 1930, 213; Harding, 1974, 10), beneath the square Roman masonry construction, there were post-holes and flooring from which earlier Iron Age pottery was recovered. A bone weaving-comb and a brooch pointed to activity as early as the fourth century BC. Three miniature bronze votive shields (71), two no more than fragments, point to a warrior cult. This continued into later times, for the broken pieces of a war-god statue were found. Twenty-four such miniature votive shields were a feature of the notorious Salisbury hoard (Stead, 1998, 114-5). As shown by the later pottery, this site continued in use throughout Roman times. Clearly, if not entirely eliminated by modern agriculture, it would repay re-excavation, as further features of the earlier installation might still survive. Another temple, high on Blue Bell Hill and close by the descent of the Roman road from Rochester, was subjected to an investigation during the nineteenth century; subsequently numerous small objects and coins were incidentally collected (Lewis, 1966, 124; Detsicas, 1987, 145). It looked down upon the megalithic long barrows, but was at a distance from Aylesfords dynastic cemetery. Recourse was made to it before and throughout Roman times, as is shown by the number and variety of Iron Age and Roman

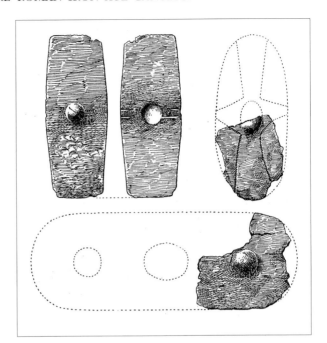

71 Worth-next-Sandwich: a votive model shield, and the fragments of two others (⅔). *After W.G. Klein, 1928*

coins (Charles, 1844, 536; Evans, 1864, 122, 197, 354). Various other temples are likely to have been established during pre-Roman Iron Age times in Kent. A possible square structure has been detected from the air at Barham, while a similar building may have been associated with the Boxted Roman villa (Detsicas, 1987, 130). The temple in Greenwich Park (Lewis, 1966, 126) may have initially been an early shrine in a mode similar to the circular shrine at Lullingstone which was dismantled in about AD 180 (Detsicas, 1987, 108)

Various modest Kentish earthworks are comparable with the *viereckschanzen*, numerous in southern Germany (Piggott, 1965, 232; Webster, 1995, 453-4), although for the most part little is known of them. As long ago as 1722, William Stukeley (1776, 53, 2d) drew such an enclosure on Barham Downs. Ronald Jessup (1930, 159) noted the characteristics of such enclosures and recorded an example in a wood near Shingleton Farm, at no great distance from the Worth temple and the Hammill shaft, to be discussed below. Some enclosures are patently components of the dispersed Quarry Wood, Loose *oppidum* (Kelly, 1971). That in a wood at Coxheath, the Mangravet kite-shaped enclosure and the near-square enclosure in Well Woods, Barming, have already been noticed. A rectangular enclosure in West Kent, near St Paul's Cray, now destroyed, was some 43m x 21m (140ft x 70ft), had entrances through its longer sides and post- and stake-holes in opposite corners (Parsons, 1961). A flint industry was a feature of the hilltop which may well have been only indirectly associated with the earthwork.

Shafts (bothroi), some of which contained occupation debris, are a feature of southern England (Ross, 1968, 280, fig.67; Piggott, 1975, 72-6). The Wilsford Shaft (Ashbee *et al*, 1989) in Wiltshire, and its contemporary at Swanwick, in Hampshire (Fox, 1928, 1930; Piggott, 1963) appear as the earliest of the formalised examples and belong to the later Bronze Age. Possibly one of the first of such shafts, apart from the enigmatic series on Blue Bell Hill described by Thomas Wright (1854, 177), to be recorded in Kent was that associated with the later Iron Age cemetery at Aylesford (Evans, 1890, 317) which was 'some 8 feet in diameter and from 12 to 15 feet deep, entirely filled with animals' bones mostly much decayed'. Some modest flint-lined pits were close by. However, in terms of archaeological endeavour one of the first of the deeper shafts to have been thought of as ritual, rather than utilitarian, was at Hammill (*72*), near Sandwich (Ogilvie, 1982). It came to light in 1946, and was examined and excavated by J.P.T. Burchell during the next two years. He found a large broken Belgic pot at the bottom and established its depth as 22m (70ft). He gave an account of his work with this shaft, together with the notions that he had developed therefrom, to the Society of Antiquaries of London which apparently gave them a mixed reception. Indeed, there is a reluctance to examine the evidence, coupled with claims that they must have been wells (Pitts, 2003, 173), which persists to this day.

Thomas Wright (1854, 177) described the sarsen-stone covered flint-filled shafts on Blue Bell Hill, which were at no great distance from the temple site, as follows: 'An immense stone was laid over the mouth of a large circular pit which had been filled to the top with flints'. Cottagers told him that 'these pits were frequently found on that hill, and that generally they had one or two of the large stones at the mouth'. E.H.W. Dunkin (1871, 75) associated them with the pattern of prehistoric activity that he saw in the area, but, although they may have been of considerable depth, nothing of their origins emerged. There are other shafts in Kent which, as far as can be seen, were dug and dedicated during the pre-Roman Iron Age and continued in use until well into Romano-British times. Seven shafts are in eastern Kent, there are three in the vicinity of the Medway and six in western Kent (Ross, 1963, list). Only one shaft, that encountered at Ramsgate, conforms, more or less, to the European mainland norm, about 35m (115ft) in depth, while another, at Birchington, descends to the more modest depth of about 9-10m (almost 33ft). The Hammill shaft (Ogilvie, 1982, 148, fig.2) was about 22m (77ft) in depth and its upper half had been dug through the Thanet Sands, the lower into the chalk. The letter 'L' on the section might denote a fall-in of the friable clay when it was initially dug. At this point, it is recorded that the infill was 'extremely sticky black earth'. The top might result from weathering and it could eventually have been sealed with timber and chalk blocks. Although dug, perhaps, in early Roman times, as is shown by the pottery at the bottom,

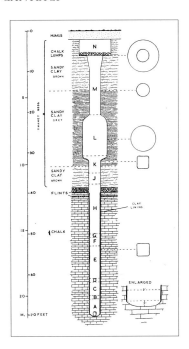

72 The Hammill ritual shaft and its geology. *After J.D. Ogilvie, 1982*

it was an element of the ritual monuments of the area. It is at no great distance from the Ringlemere barrow, at that time of some substance, and the three shafts close by Richborough's temples (Roach Smith, 1850, 55), as well as the Worth temple (Klein, 1928). Such juxtapositions show that the past development of the monumental landscape was understood and appreciated. One of two shafts at Bekesbourne (Brent, 1859), about 3.5m (12-13ft) in depth, had been lined with massive oak timbering, horizontal planks and principals pegged together; its contents were urns and horses teeth. A model of this timbering was at one time to be seen in Canterbury's Beaney Institute Museum. The second shaft, unlined and flint-filled, was close by. A shaft at Frittenden some 4m (14ft) deep, with urns at its bottom, was, it would seem, timber-lined and comparable with that examined at Bekesbourne (Kelly, 1968, 263). A group of pits at Strood (Ross, 1968, 273), all about 3m (10ft) in depth had in them Samian ware and Upchurch beakers. In western Kent, a shaft at Crayford had a depth of some 12m (40ft). That at Keston (Piercy Fox, 1967), adjacent to the circular temple, examined in 1828, was about 5m (17ft) in depth and more than 3m (10ft) in diameter. An adjacent shaft at Warbank (Philp, 2002, 64, 13.5) had horse skeletons at its bottom. The diameters of these pits and shafts vary; while some are modest, others are considerable. The pit, 3m (10ft) deep, at no great distance from Thunor's Pit (Crawford, 1933), on the Isle of Thanet, was some 12m (40ft) across. At Greenhithe the 11m (35ft) deep pit had a 7m (23ft) diameter, while that at Northfleet, of about the same depth, was more than 6m (20ft) in width. This last, examined by J.P.T. Burchell, had at its bottom what was described as an oval chamber, perhaps cleared collapse. In this, besides early Romano-British pottery, was a considerable inventory of bird and animal bones. A recent discovery of a 2.5m (8ft) deep shaft at Deal revealed that its bottom was an oval chamber in which was a chalk-carved figurine (Green, 1986, 135, fig.64). Footholds gave access.

Besides the various installations which may be demonstrative of cult practices, there are assemblages of serviceable artifacts which have been buried in the ground (Stead, 1998, 109-24). At Bigbury Camp, Harbledown (Jessup, 1933B; Thompson, 1983), the mass of objects, found during gravel digging between 1861 and 1895, could well represent a series of votive deposits made in pits, rather than a single assemblage buried, as has been suggested, when the move was made to the Canterbury *oppidum*. It is unlikely that the gravel diggers would have seen such pits as they pursued thair onerous labours. Furthermore, as has already been emphasised, when a particular site is abandoned all that is functional is removed and only the inutile remains. With the exception of the gang chains and fetters, probably indicative of a lucrative slave trade, the objects represented routine rural life and activities. Iron axes, adzes, hammers, chisels, plough coulters, sickles and billhooks were there in numbers. There were also iron pot-hooks, hangers for cauldrons with their tripods, as well as firedogs. With these there was a piece of an iron vehicle tyre, linchpins with bronze mounts, three-link snaffle bits and harness fittings. All appear to have been in a usable condition when consigned to the ground.

As has been observed, cremated bones contained in spectacular buckets is the norm for a number of Kentish later pre-Roman Iron Age burials. As furnished burials they are substantial but perhaps not princely, that is *fürstengräber* in the German sense, and the possibility that they are of a powerful, priestly caste is a possibility. Anne Ross (1967, 70) has pointed to their possible use as containers for 'alcoholic liquid for feasts of a ritual nature'. The pair of heads or masks on the better preserved Aylesford bucket (Megaw, 1970, pl.187; Brailsford, 1975, 83-89) have been considered as examples of the *tête coupée* cult (Lambrechts, 1954; Ross, 1957-8, 31). It is thought that the severed human head character of the handle-mount heads of the comparable Baldock buckets (Stead, 1971, 251) could support this contention. The spectacular, though mutilated, human mask bucket-mount (*73*) from Boughton Aluph (Megaw, 1970, 133, pl.210) could also be considered in this context, although its European mainland stylistic affinities suggest a *Cernunnus* attribution (Megaw, 1970, 157; Green, 1986, 195-9). A stone janiform head, perhaps from a figure, recorded by Horsley (1732, p.192, N76; Ross, 1957-8, 17) as from Kent, with youthful and aged faces, is apart from the essentials of the head cult, as is the Richborough sherd bearing a horned

73 Boughton Aluph, the mutilated face-masked bronze ?bucket mount. Traces of red enamel still survive in the ridged hair-line (⅓ approx). *After E.J.E. Pirie, 1958*

female head (Bushe-Fox, 1949, pl.LXII, 347; Ross, 1957-8, 31). Depictions of local deities may have been intended. Two of the Deal furnished inhumation burials may have been those of cult functionaries (Cunliffe, 1995, 106). One was accompanied by the pair of spoons and the other, although armed, was wearing a diadem. This last is comparable with those found at Cavenham, in Suffolk, and Hockwold-cum-Wilton in Norfolk (Layard, 1925; Clarke, 1960, 128, pls. 41, 42; Toynbee, 1962, 178, pl.139).

Coins first appeared in Britain, the last European region to adopt them, from about 150 BC onwards and soon thereafter distinctive tribal examples were struck. Initially they may have been for gift exchange and votive deposition. It was only after Caesar's incursions that diversity and denomination appeared, factors which may reflect the emergence of a monetary system. An aspect is the considerable number of Gallo-Belgic coins that have been found in Kent (Cunliffe, 1991, 110-16; 1995, 62-4) and the various developments therefrom. Cast bronze were the first, to be followed by gold in about 70 BC (Haselgrove, 1993). Apart from the pioneer works of J.V. Akerman (1846) and the Rev. Beale Poste (1853), the effective beginning of pre-Roman Iron Age numismatics was the publication of *The Coins of the Ancient Britons* (1864) by Sir John Evans, in which those coins considered were engraved by F.W. Fairholt. He remarked (1864, 187) upon the comparitive abundance of copper alloy coins and that there were none attributable to the four kings of Kent mentioned by Caesar. Of named coins he said that the greater numbers are EPPILLUS, followed by DUBNOVELLAUNUS and VOSENOS, while observing that the coins of AMMINUS are probably Kentish. Ronald Jessup (1930, 149) described the Kentish golden coins as dish-shaped, from Gaul, and derived from the golden stater of Phillip II of Macedon (c.382-336 BC), which had, obverse, a wreathed head and, reverse, a warrior in a chariot. Continued copying, it was observed, debased the design to the extent that the wreathed head had become a cruciform pattern and the reverse dots and pellets. He called especial attention to the Higham and Westerham hoards of gold coins, which in each instance had been concealed within hollow spherical flints (1930, 150). The Higham hoard consisted of 11 coins and that from Westerham 14.

In our own age there has been D.F. Allen's magisterial appraisal of *The Belgic Dynasties of Britain and their Coins* (1944) his reappraisal of *The Origins of Coinage in Britain* (1961), followed by his *Coins of the Ancient Celts* (1980). *The Origins* is accompanied by a gazetteer of coins and, where possible, the circumstances of their discovery. This, as far as Kent is concerned, is particularly detailed and, as the county is a tribal area, the further study of its coins could be both rewarding and illuminating. Writing in 1982, B.W. Cunliffe saw the Kentish Gallo-Belgic golden staters as having been used for high-level transactions, a prestigious monetary system. He mapped (1982, 46, fig.20) almost 90 such coins as from Kent, the dispersed spread in the eastern region, the Medway and northern concentrations being notable, as is the western scatter to the Thames. He was moved to remark on the density of the distribution of gold coinage in use during the first century BC. Like the golden torques and other such objects from early times, golden coins were precious objects, the hoards being of even greater prestige. Thus particular attention should be given to the circumstances of discovery, for it seems extremely unlikely that they were simply lost! Thus like the Snettisham torques (Stead, 1998, pls.22, 23) the coins, their flint containers and single coins in bag or pouch, are likely to have been votive deposits in places which were, to those who performed the act of deposition, of especial significance. Within erstwhile enclosures or at the bases of particular trees are but some of the possibilities that must be considered. Another aspect of the golden coinage distribution is that it loosely defines the territories of Iron Age, and probably earlier, Kent, whose principals were dignified by the title of 'king' by Caesar.

While these words concerning Kent's Iron Age coinage were being written, a considerable hoard, more than 200 coins and pieces were being dug from a high place on the North Downs, at Thurnham (Richardson, 2003/4). They are of potin, a tin-bronze alloy, and may, perhaps, predate many of the golden series. They bear, obverse, a stylised human head and on the reverse a Gaulish butting bull. Hoarded potin coins are rare in England and it is likely that the assemblage was votive. High places, for example Chanctonbury, on the South Downs, sometimes had upon them an enclosure, followed by a temple (Curwen, 1954, 288), and it is not impossible that such installations were upon certain heights of the North Downs, as might be indicated by Coldharbour place names. Thus a votive deposit in this vicinity should not be surprising. However, potin coins came early to Kent, and they may have been used in a monetary economy. Their circulation was surprisingly long-lasting, even into early Roman times when villas were being constructed.

A dimension of pre-Roman Iron Age studies has been the many books and papers in learned journals which, in various ways, pursue particular aspects of what has for long been termed 'Celtic Art'. Its arcane, ambiguous attractions, which would have been redolent with meaning for all who saw such things, are mostly confined to ceramics and metal pieces, which were the prerogative of the upper social stratum. Nonetheless, in various places careful excavation has revealed remains which hint at the adornment of buildings and perhaps even palisades, evidence which, when accumulated, may alleviate the gloom of the incessant log-cabin reconstructions. The notion of Celtic Art was manifest in the Arthur Evans' (1890) consideration of the Aylesford material but was introduced by J. Romilly Allen's *Celtic Art in Pagan and Christian Times* (1904), followed by the *Celtic Ornament* of E.T. Leeds (1930). He reminded us that, following upon his reconstruction of the Aylesford cemetery, Arthur Evans, in 1898, had given as a Rhind Lecture an unpublished survey of Celtic Art. Allen and Leeds included pieces from Aylesford, Canterbury and Folkestone Warren in their surveys. It was, however, the publication by the Oxford University Press, in 1944 (2nd ed., 1969) of Paul Jacobstahl's *Early Celtic Art* in two prodigious volumes, text and illustrations, that made English prehistorians fully conscious of this remarkable heritage. Jacobstahl had left Hitler's Germany, when dismissed from the University of Marburg, and was given haven in Oxford. The work, begun in 1933, is essentially an examination of the European mainland's material. However, domicile in Oxford allowed the inclusion of English pieces, for Kent the Aylesford bucket and a brooch from Deal. There are gaps in the narrative because of the war and mention is made of a work on *Celtic Art in the British Isles* then in preparation. Shortly thereafter, inspired by the metalwork found at Llyn Cerrig, in Anglesey (Fox, 1946), Sir Cyril Fox detailed British Celtic Art in a work entitled *Pattern and Purpose* (1958), published by the National Museum of Wales. Aylesford's artifacts loomed large and various pieces from the county are noted and put into perspective (ox, 1958, *passim*, pl.26). After Jacobstahl's demise in 1957, his work was continued by Martyn Jope, at that time Professor of Archaeology in Belfast. Although much of *Early Celtic Art in the British Isles* (2000) was written during the 1960s, it was concluded in 1996, a short while before his death. Although the textual volume is analytical and geared to the remarkable illustrations, which comprise a second considerable volume, a wealth of Kentish material, some 25 pieces, is described and depicted. As in Jacobstahl's volumes, the exotic oblects salvaged by Arthur Evans and his father, Sir John, in 1886 at Aylesford (Evans, 1890), take pride of place, with eight revealing illustrations. Thereafter, there is the famous Bapchild terret, followed by pieces from Canterbury, Deal, Faversham, Minster and Richborough. Each is accorded description, provenance and primary source, and it is abundantly clear that many pieces, particularly those from Kent, displayed a considerable originality and that their artificers were at the forefront of their craft. Indeed, it may emerge that their skills were, from time to time, a valuable export to the European mainland. At the same time this dazzling array expresses the ethos and timbre of the *Cantiaci* at, broadly, their zenith, the time at which they were specified by the classical writers but before their incorporation into the Roman imperial system.

A further aspect of 'Celtic' art is that it is definitive of society at large (Jope, 1995). Thus in eastern Kent earthworks such as Bigbury, or the hillfort which dominated the port of Dover, indicate strong, centralised authorities, as do the Loose *oppidum* and Oldbury. Such personages as we see via their grave furniture, and infer from their earthworks, are likely to have had substantial houses which have yet to be found. Within the county we should be looking for the remains of princely houses such as have, for example, been encountered in Germany (Bittell *et al*, 1981, 124, abb.53) or upon a hilltop near Thetford, in Norfolk (Gregory, 1991). Upon the introduction of sophisticated wheel-thrown ceramics, potters would have had an especial place within society, as would the smiths, forging iron weapons, tools and appliances. There were also the wheelwrights and carriage builders constructing chariots and carts, while horses demand skilled maintenance. Barrels are known, having developed from the staved buckets of the Bronze Age, pieces of which were found in the Wilsford Shaft (Ashbee *et al*, 1989) and the coopers would have had their place among the craftsmen. Cult ministrants, who can now be termed Druids (Piggott, 1975), are likely to have had social prominence, as may those whose farms were considerable and who produced corn for export to the expanding Roman Empire, together with the slaves and hunting dogs. Building and the layout of particular installations are also likely to have been specialised undertakings. Within the tribal bounds of the *Cantiaci* there are likely to have been modes of communication, while port management would have been necessary at Dover, Richborough and Rochester.

All in all, pre-Roman Iron Age society in Kent was intricate and sophisticated, and was, because of its involvement with commerce and communications a unique insular development. Direct evidence of liason with the European mainland is infrequent, which may point to the considerable sense of identity in insular society. While certain features of Iron Age society can be seen during the later

Bronze Age, change began in about the third century BC and there came about a rapid intensification of all kinds of production. From about the beginning of the first century BC, production begat population and the increased population brought about even more production, while the status of the various elites would have become even more polarised. Trade with Romanised Gaul is likely to have led, particularly in Kent, to the emergence of a powerful commercial class whose demands upon production, even of prestigious objects of the 'art' category, would have increased with time. It is not unlikely that entreprenurial power fuelled the opposition to Caesar's incursions. It should be remembered that when he landed with his forces in Kent he was surprised by the contrasts, numerous settlements and the considerable population that he encountered. Indeed, his clashes with the *Cantiaci* are likely to have further impressed upon him the desirability of bringing parts of Britain, particularly prosperous Kent and the south-eastern parts of the country, into the Roman order of things.

Caesar's attempts in 55 and 54 BC to carry Roman dominion across the English Channel, which he documented, are considered as the point at which Britain strode upon the stage of history. Yet about a century was to elapse before Claudius would emulate him and end the vaccillation regarding the need to bring Britain into the imperial system. Despite the emergence in the south east of philo- and anti-Roman factions, this century saw the further dynamic development of the various communities of Kent, which was marked by the emergence of the first towns, the *oppida* of Canterbury and Rochester. What is becoming ever more evident, however, is the extent to which many have so sadly misjudged the complexity and sophistication, likely, as in early Ireland (Jackson, 1964), to have been bonded by oral tradition and ordinances, of our later prehistoric past.

EPILOGUE

Caesar's invasions in 55 and 54 BC impressed upon those who encountered his forces the nature of their power. The minutiae of these operations, and of those in the name of Claudius a century later, have often been detailed, so they should not unduly detain us (Ashbee, 1978, 236-67). That Caesar's forces stormed Bigbury has for long been accepted but, notwithstanding, neither nineteenth-century gravel extraction nor twentieth century archaeological excavation has found any trace of this operation. His landing place, oft-debated, has succumbed to the eustatic rise of mean sea-level. It would have been some 6m (20ft) lower when he sailed from Gaul than it is today. The lowlands of Deal would have reached out to the Goodwin Sands and all that is now the marshes of northern Kent would have been extensive low-lying loamy lands. Furthermore the remains of an archipelago of low islands may have broken the clash of the waters of the North Sea and Channel, as does the Danish series of the Baltic outflow. Thus he would have experienced broad, shallow, sandy shores, with low, open lands beyond. Using prevailing Channel winds, they would have been ideal for his transports.

Claudius' forces landed at Richborough, the harbour at the eastern end of the Wantsum Channel. A ditch, located beneath and beyond the Saxon Shore fort, marks his base camp (Cunliffe, 1968, 232-4). He moved on to the Medway where, for two days, he battled a formidable native force. Archaeologically, the only association with this great engagement is a hoard of gold coins, some in mint condition, found at Bredgar in 1959 (Dudley & Webster, 1965, 69; Jessup, 1970, 165; Detsicas, 1987, 14). Four of the 34 coins were of Claudius, struck during AD 41 and 42. Bredgar, on the backslope of the North Downs, is about 10 miles from the likely site of the battle and it has been thought that the coins were savings, buried and never recovered. There may have been a war cemetery, yet to be found, in the vicinity of Cuxton. It is likely that a salvage corps ranged over the ground and that serviceable weaponry and vehicles were collected and sequestered. It appears that the *Cantiaci*, as shown by the Thurnham Roman villa (Oxford Arch. Unit, 2000), accepted Roman mores and exploited its advantages. The conflicts that continued for a generation in Britain passed them by, although human remains, with sword-cuts and swords, found in the ditch of an erstwhile fort at Canterbury (Tatton-Brown, 1977, 213-5) point to a violent incident at about the time that Boudicca's forces assembled for her campaign of liberation from Roman rule. Kent may have been one of the first tribal areas to have been constituted as a *civitas* for it was *Durovernum Cantiacorum* that the *oppidum* astride the Stour became (Rivet & Smith, 1979, 353), an inevitability because of its place of convergence of roads, trackways and river transport.

Land and people were moulded by imitation and decree into the imperial matrix, a process that has made for characteristics which have endured to this day. Yet within five or six generations the pattern of Roman sway began to unravel and the earlier indigenous social and economic systems were returned to. What has been thought of as a Roman decline was the re-emergence of earlier usages. A casualty was the insular, inevitably Latin-laced language, extinguished by the Germanic *foderati*. Yet there was a Roman reassertion; its Christianity came to Kent and Canterbury with Augustine, who landed at or near Richborough in AD 597.

It has emerged during the past half-century that there are many more ancient sites in Britain than earlier generations ever thought. Our landscapes, and Kent is no exception, are a palimpsest of traces of occupation and it is almost impossible to undertake earth-moving or agriculture without encountering ancient remains. Sir David Walsh (1969, 60), when investigating the arrangements for the protection of field monuments, which he found wanting, said that they were just as important to the study of our past as the papers and parchments in our public record offices.

In one of the lists (1961) of ancient monuments issued by the now disbanded Inspectorate of Ancient Monuments, Kent had, in the prehistoric sector, 19 'Burial Mounds and Megalithic Monuments', nine 'Camps' and a single 'linear earthwork'. Officialdom has from the first used neutral terms for such remains to be seen and found in our landscapes. As for long in Ireland (Ashbee, 1960, 199), the term 'National Monument' should be used.

Of the megalithic long barrows, and the remains thereof, on Blue Bell Hill, only three sites have been accorded protection, namely Kit's Coty House, the Lower Kit's Coty House and the White Horse Stone. Yet, besides these monuments, there are the spreads of sarsen stones, many of great size, now sorely depleted, used for the long barrows, the descent of the early, termed Roman, way to the Weald, an associated pre-Roman and later temple site, the perhaps surviving Warren Farm remains, and, at a lower level, the Coffin Stone and its long barrow, besides the ingathering of sarsen stones by Tottington's springheads. Even at the end of World War II in 1946, the long barrow of which Kit's Coty House is a chamber remnant, was about 1m (3ft) in height, although spread. By 1976, however, the barrow remnant, which was about 60-70cm (almost 2ft) of barrow and 30cm (about 1ft) of ancient soil, had been completely destroyed and the naked chalk exposed, flanked by the reduced ditches (Ashbee, 2000, 329, pl.II). The considerable long barrow, of which a stone from the chamber, the Coffin Stone, survives, was apparent in much reduced form until the 1950s but can today hardly be traced. Whereas the Inspectorate of Ancient Monuments considered that ploughing did little damage to the Kit's Coty House long barrow, a recent correspondence with English Heritage regarding damage to the Coffin Stone, and the setting of another substantial sarsen stone upon it, elicited the reply that it was natural, and thus could not be protected, and that the early reports of human remains from its proximity were to be associated with the erstwhile medieval chapel close by. Tottington's sarsen stones, some of which are likely to have been removed from the Coffin Stone's long barrow are, as far as can be ascertained, an ingathering for an early sarsen stone splitting industry, as in Wiltshire (King, 1968). Yet again, an overture to English Heritage was met with the tired reply that natural phenomena were not their concern. This, despite the fact that the stones could be considered as an early industrial monument! It has, however, for long been manifest that English Heritage is more concerned with commercialisation than affording appropriate protection to our national monuments.

Across the Medway at Addington, the road-transected long barrow survives, although smaller stones have been removed. When last seen, there were patent traces of metal-detector activity. Although the Chestnuts, because of careful, skilled excavation, can now be seen as a restored chamber (Alexander, 1961), the construction of the adjacent house was a lamentable mistake, as access is often impossible. Coldrum, difficult to visit because of barred private tracks, is hedged by massive trees which damage the subsoil and obscure the monument while preventing appreciation of its siting.

It is clear that as soon as possible Blue Bell Hill, its long barrow remnants and all pertaining to them, should be accorded Heritage status, with appropriate protection, like the supportive landscapes of Stonehenge and Avebury. Indeed, public bodies are empowered to designate such areas (Pugh-Smith & Samuels, 1996, 40). The Blue Bell Hill and other long barrow remains are the only major monuments employing sarsen stones beyond Wiltshire. It has been seen that Goddard's Keep, on the North Downs above Thurnham, has been cleared and conserved as a county undertaking. In the absence of responsible concern by English Heritage, it is surely time for Kent to seize the initiative and safeguard Blue Bell Hill and its unique monuments. Many books (Manley, 1989, 60, 154) consider the Kentish megalithic long barrows as sites of considerable importance.

Almost all the later Bronze Age and pre-Roman Iron Age camps, as they have for long been termed, are listed. In eastern Kent, the earthwork enclosures on Barham Downs are notionally protected, as is Bigbury Camp at Harbledown. This is in great measure wooded and is traversed by a road. The gravel pits are still prominent and until recently in use, while all is open to the activities of treasure seekers (Philp, 2002, 243). Dover is included in the list of castles but no mention is made of the complex system of earthworks of earlier origin, which, when last seen, needed protection against burrowing rabbits and denudation from visitor pressure. The Loose *oppidum* is listed but its outworks, which include a considerable linear earthwork, are entirely unprotected. The Mangravet Wood kite-shaped enclosure has long since been built over, although the disposition of the houses has preserved its lineaments (Margary, 1948, 216, H-I). A modest excavation might recover the dimensions and nature of its ditch. The earthwork in Milbay's Wood, Nettlestead, is difficult of access and this may afford it protection but, sadly, the huge expanse of Oldbury, at Ightham, is a regular venue for treasure seekers and unauthorised diggers. The listed camp in Cobham Park is possibly no more than a series of hollow ways: a different kind of monument. The hillforts of western Kent, Holwood, Keston, and Squerryes Park, Westerham, are listed and, although on private land, they are accessible to marauders. In many instances the scheduling notices for camps appear to refer to no more than the ramparts; the interiors are unprotected (Fowler, 1972, 105). On the Wessex chalklands the interiors of a number of hillforts have been deeply ploughed and all traces of occupation destroyed. In many places where the destructive character of deep ploughing has not been appreciated, a generation is purveying the notion that prehistoric ditches were shallow, having seen no more than surviving ditch bottoms and fragments of erstwhile systems.

Legislation for the preservation and protection of our national monuments has been in place for more than a century and it was, in great measure, formulated within Kent. The 1882 'Act for the Better Protection of Ancient Monuments' was for the most part brought about by the political acumen of Sir John Lubbock, later Lord Avebury, of High Elms, Farnborough, and was the outcome of the mounting concern of a lifetime (Saunders, 1983; Pugh-Smith & Samuels, 1996, 5). The first and prestigious Inspector of Ancient Monuments, General Augustus Henry Lane Fox Pitt Rivers (Bowden, 1991, 95-102), visited Kit's Coty House in April 1883. It caused him considerable concern, for pieces had been smashed from the stones, while ploughing was up to their feet. He recommended iron railings and said that should they become unstable an iron frame would support them. In the event the stones of Kit's Coty House became a protected monument in 1885. The erection of the iron railings, now rusted and distorted, occasioned some two years of bureaucratic obstruction and delay, while a quarter of the entire ancient monuments budget for the year, £25, was spent upon them (Saunders, 1983). Pitt Rivers also visited the Lower Kit's Coty House for which the owner readily accepted protection, which took effect from 1887 after an Order in Council.

It has been said (Thompson, 1981) that since the main Ancient Monuments Act of 1913, some 20,000 monuments have been listed, that is scheduled, in England, Scotland and Wales, a total which includes the 124 considered worthy in Kent. Difficulties of enforcement were mentioned and it was claimed that the system had at least slowed interference. Nonetheless, it is manifest that our national monuments in their totality make for a situation impossible to police. A cogent illustration of what has come to pass is the wholesale destruction of the barrows and earthworks of Stonehenge's supportive landscape, in the stewardship of the National Trust since 1925. Initially incidental, the devastation intensified in 1954 when parts of the Normanton barrow cemetery were razed. By 1960 only one relatively undamaged barrow group remained (Ashbee, 1960, 196). In 1954, a prosecution was embarked upon but the then acting Chief Inspector of Ancient Monuments, P.K. Baillie-Reynolds, unversed in prehistory, said that barrows were numerous and that little damage had been done.

There was, during the 1970s, the setting up of what were termed Archaeological Units in cities and counties. This followed overtures, from 1971 onwards, by RESCUE, the Trust for British Archaeology (Barker, 1974), and could be thought of as the establishment of a national archaeological service, beyond the civil service. All this had been anticipated in Kent by Brian Philp (2002) who, with his dedicated supporters, as early as 1952 began to examine threatened sites. His remarkable achievements are well known, and have been referred to in this volume. Indeed he was a key figure whose experiences were drawn upon in the 1970s. Elsewhere, and later, in Kent there has been the emergence of the Canterbury and Thanet Archaeological Trusts. Such bodies, as a part of their work, set up effective Sites and Monuments records for their areas of activity. At the outset they were financially vulnerable but since the publication of PPG 16 (Planning Policy Guidance: Archaeology and Planning) in 1990, appropriate investigation has become a prelude to all forms of development, and is paid for by those concerned.

Following the precept of Sir Mortimer Wheeler (1954, 182) citing Pitt Rivers, there has been an exemplary pattern of publication within our county. Brian Philp (2002, 248-50) besides his contributions to established journals, such as our *Archaeologia Cantiana* has devised serial and especial publication, a policy followed in eastern Kent (Parfitt, 1995). As a result of the great accumulations of archaeological material, published and in the records of the many units, it has emerged that works of synthesis, such as Gordon Childe's *Prehistoric Communities of the British Isles* (1940, 2nd.ed. 1947) or, more recently, Timothy Darvill's *Prehistoric Britain* (1987) may no longer be possible. A related difficulty is that museums currently exhibit no more than illustrative material and that quantities are stored and difficult of access, or have been discarded. Narrow, thematic studies are now becoming the rule and broader assessments avoided. Another development has been the treatment of regions by coordinated teamwork as in Germany (Köln, 1990) which includes environmental issues. This formula has, indeed, been not unsuccessful when applied to the broader European scene (Cunliffe, 1994) of which Britain is an essential element.

From this examination of Kent's prehistory it is evident that its sites and artifacts had intrinsic qualities which were exceptional within England at large. This individuality is manifest in Neolithic times when we had become an island people and access to the European mainland involved travel by water. Indeed, the North Sea and English Channel are likely to have been a stimulus for much that came to pass. The megalithic long barrows sited in the Medway Valley are unique in terms of their erstwhile scale and size. The round barrows of the Bronze Age are numerous and some were richly furnished, while the later weight of metal consigned to water and the ground was phenomenal. With the advent of iron and the first record of the *Cantiaci*, there are the exceptional hillfort centres, succeeded by *oppida* at Canterbury and Rochester. Control of the short sea routes to the European mainland, likely from Bronze Age times onwards, is clear at Dover and probable elsewhere around our coast. Some six millennia of prehistory preceded the mere two millennia of history that separate us from our ancient British ancestors, the people who determined the nature of our identity.

BIBLIOGRAPHY

Abercromby, J., 1904. A Proposed Chronological arrangement of the Drinking Cup or Beaker Class of Fictilia in Britain, *Proc. Society of Antiquaries of Scotland*, 38, 323-410

Abercromby, J., 1912. *The Bronze Age Pottery of Great Britain and Ireland* (2 vols), Oxford

Ackeroyd, A.V., 1972. Archaeological and historical evidence for subsidence in Southern Britain, *Phil. Trans. Royal Society*, London A272, 151-69

Akerman, J.Y., 1844. Account of the opening by Matthew Bell of an Ancient British Barrow in Iffin's Wood, near Canterbury, in January 1842, *Archaeologia*, 30, 57-61

Akerman, J.Y., 1846. *Ancient Coins of Cities and Princes Geographically Arranged and Described: Hispania, Gallia, Britannia*, London

Alexander, J., 1961. The Excavation of the Chestnuts Megalithic Tomb at Addington, Kent, *Archaeologia Cantiana*, 76, 1-57

Alexander, J., 1978. Frontier Studies and the earliest farmers of Europe, *Social Organisation and Settlement*, BAR International Series (supp.), 47 (i), 13-29

Allcroft, A. Hadrian, 1908. *Earthwork of England*, London

Allen, A.F., 1970. Investigation and excavations during the year: Gravesend Area, *Archaeologia Cantiana*, 85, 182-7

Allen, D.F., 1970. The Belgic dynasties of Britain and their coins, *Archaeologia*, 90, 1-46

Allen, D.F., 1961. The Origins of Coinage in Britain: a reappraisal, *Problems of the Iron Age in Southern Britain*, ed. S.S. Frere, Institute of Archaeology Occ. Paper II, 97-303

Allen, D.F., 1968. The Pre-Roman Coins, *Fifth Report on the Excavations of the Roman Port at Richborough, Kent*, ed. B.W. Cunliffe, Reports of the Research Committee, Society of Antiquaries of London, 23, Oxford, 184-8

Allen, D.F., 1980. *The Coins of the Ancient Celts*, Edinburgh

Allen, J. Romilly, 1904. *Celtic Art in Pagan and Christian Times* London

Allen, T., 2000. The Origin of the Swale; an archaeological interpretation, *Archaeologia Cantiana*, 120, 169-86

Annable, F.K. & Simpson, D.D.A., 1964. *Guide Catalogue of the Neolithic and Bronze Age Collections in Devizes Museum*, Devizes

Anon., 1934. Flint Dagger from Upchurch, *Antiquaries Journ.*, 14, 298-9

Anon., 1939. A remarkable flint core, *Antiquaries Journ.*, 19, 317-8

Applebaum, S., 1972. Roman Britain, *The Agrarian History of England and Wales*, I.ii, ed. H.P.R. Finberg, Cambridge, 3-287

ApSimon, A., 1954. Dagger Graves in the Wessex Bronze Age, *Ann. Rpt. Univ. London Institute of Archaeology*, 10, 37-62

Ashbee, P., 1950. Addington, Kent, *Archaeological Newsletter*, 3.5, 86-7

Ashbee, P., 1952. Two Early Bronze Age Axes, *Archaeologia Cantiana*, 65, 180-3

Ashbee, P., 1960. *The Bronze Age Round Barrow in Britain*, London

Ashbee, P., 1966. The Fussell's Lodge long barrow excavations, 1957, *Archaeologia*, 100, 1-80

Ashbee, P., 1967. The Wessex Grave (Portsdown, Portsmouth), *Proc. Hampshire Field Club*, 24, 7-14

Ashbee, P., 1976. Bant's Carn, St Mary's, Isles of Scilly, An entrance grave restored and reconsidered, *Cornish Archaeology*, 15, 11-26

Ashbee, P., 1978. Amesbury barrow 51: Excavations 1960, *Wiltshire Archaeological & Nat. Hist. Mag.*, 70/71, 1-60

Ashbee, P., 1978. *The Ancient British*, Norwich

Ashbee, P., 1982. A Reconsideration of the British Neolithic, *Antiquity*, 56, 134-8

Ashbee, P., 1983. Halangy Porth, St Mary's, Isles of Scilly, Excavations 1975-76, *Cornish Archaeology*, 22, 3-46

Ashbee, P., 1984. *The Earthen Long Barrow in Britain* (2nd ed.), Norwich

Ashbee, P., 1993a. The Medway megaliths in perspective, *Archaeologia Cantiana*, 111, 57-111

Ashbee, P., 1993b. William Stukeley, The Kit's Coty Houses and his Coves: a Note, *Archaeologia Cantiana*, 112, 17-24

Ashbee, P., 1996. Julliberrie's Grave. Chilham: Retrospection and Perception, *Archaeologia Cantiana*, 116, 1-33

Ashbee, P., 1996. Halangy Down, St Mary's, Isles of Scilly, Excavations 1964-1977, *Cornish Archaeology*, 35, 1-201

Ashbee, P., 1997. Aylesford's Bronze Age Cists and Burials, *Archaeologia Cantiana*, 117, 147-59

Ashbee, P., 1998. Coldrum Revisited and Reviewed, *Archaeologia Cantiana*, 118, 1-43

Ashbee, P., 1999. The Medway Megaliths in a European Context, *Archaeologia Cantiana*, 119, 269-84

Ashbee, P., 2000. The Medway's Megalithic Long Barrows, *Archaeologia Cantiana*, 120, 319-45

Ashbee, P., 2000/01. Clay Lane Wood, Cobham: A Bronze Age Cult Site? *Kent Archaeological Society Newsletter*, 48, 8-9

Ashbee, P., 2001. William Stukeley's Kentish Studies of Roman and other Remains, *Archaeologia Cantiana*, 121, 61-102

Ashbee, P., 2002. The Ringlernere Gold Cup and its Affinities, *Kent Archaeological Society Newsletter*, 53, 4-5

Ashbee, P. & Dunning, G.C., 1960. The Round Barrows of East Kent, *Archaeologia Cantiana*, 74, 48-57

Ashbee, P., Bell, M. & Proudfoot, E., 1989. *Wilsford Shafts: Excavations 1960-1962*, English Heritage Archaeological Report No.11, London

Ashbee, P. & Jewell, P.A., 1998. The Experimental Earthworks Revisited, *Antiquity*, 72, 485-504

Baldwin, R.A. & Kelly, D.B., 1965. Walderslade (gold bracelets), *Archaeologia Cantiana*, 80, 283-4

Barber, M., 1997. Landscape, the Neolithic and Kent, *Neolithic Landscapes, Neolithic Studies Group Seminar Papers 2* (ed. Topping, P.), Oxbow Monograph 86, 77-85

Barber, M., Field, D. & Topping, P., 1999. *The Neolithic Flint Mines of England*, Swindon, RCHME

Barker, C.T., 1984. The Long Mounds of the Avebury region, *Wiltshire Archaeological & Nat. Hist. Mag.*, 79, 7-38

Barker, H & Mackey, J., 1961. British Museum Natural Radiocarbon Measurements III, *Radiocarbon*, 3 39-45

Barker, P., 1974. The Scale of the Problem, *Rescue Archaeology* (ed. Rahtz, P.A.) 28-34, Harmondsworth

Barrett, J. & Collis, J., 1996. *Barrows of the Peak District, Recent Research*, Sheffield

Barrett, J.C., 1980. The Pottery of the later Bronze Age in Lowland England, *Proc. Prehistoric Society*, 46, 297-319

Bayley, E.H., 1962. Activities round Dover, 1962, *Archaeologia Cantiana*, 77, xlviii

Beck, H.O. & Stone, J.F.S., 1936. Faience Beads of the British Bronze Age, *Archaeologia*, 85, 203-52

BIBLIOGRAPHY

Bell, M., Fowler, P.J., & Hillson, S.W., 1996. *The Experimental Earthwork Project, 1960–1992*, London, Council for British Archaeology Research Report, 100

Bennett, F.J., 1907. *Ightham, the story of a Kentish village and its surroundings*, London

Bennett, F.J., 1913. Coldrum Monument and Exploration, *Journ. Royal Anthropological Inst.*, 43, 76-85

Bennett, P., 1988. Archaeology and the Channel Tunnel, *Archaeologia Cantiana*, 106, 1-24

Bennett, P., 1991. *From Ice Age to Tunnel*, Folkestone

Bennett, P., MacPherson-Grant, N. & Blockley, P., 1980. Four minor sites excavated by the Canterbury Archaeological Trust, 1978-1979, *Archaeologia Cantiana*, 96, 267-302

Bersu, G., 1940. Excavations at Little Woodbury, Wiltshire, Part I, The settlement as revealed by excavation, *Proc. Prehistoric Society*, 6, 30-111

Birchall, A., 1963. The Belgae problem: Aylesford revisited, *British Museum Quarterly*, 27, 21-9

Birchall, A., 1965. The Aylesford-Swarling culture: the problem of the Belgae reconsidered, *Proc. Prehistoric Society*, 31, 241-367

Bittell, K., Kimmig, W. & Schiek, S., 1981. *Die Kelten in Baden-Württemberg*, Stuttgart

Black, S.B., 2001. *A Scholar and a Gentleman, Edward Hasted the Historian of Kent*, Otford, Kent

Blockley, P., 1987. Chestfield, *Archaeologia Cantiana*, 104, 321

Blockley, K. & P., 1989. Excavations at Bigberry, near Canterbury, *Archaeologia Cantiana*, 107, 239-51

Boast, E. & Gibson, A., 2000. Neolithic, Beaker and Anglo-Saxon Remains, Laundry Road, Minster-in-Thanet, *Archaeologia Cantiana*, 120, 359-72

Bowen, H.C., 1961. *Ancient Fields*, London, British Assn. for the Advancement of Science

Bowen, H.C. & Smith, I.F., 1977. Sarsen stone in Wessex: the Society's first investigation in the evolution of Landscape project, *Antiquaries Journal*, 57, 185-96

Bowden, M., 1991. *Pitt Rivers, the life and archaeological work of Lieutenant-General Augustus Henry Lane Fox Pitt Rivers, D.C.L., F.R.S., F.S.A.*, Cambridge

Bradley, R., 1976. Maumbury Rings, Dorchester: the Excavations of 1908-1913, *Archaeologia*, 105, 1-97

Bradley, R., 1989. Herbert Toms – A Pioneer of Analytical Field Survey, *From Cornwall to Caithness, Some Aspects of Field Archaeology, Papers presented to Norman V. Quinnell* (eds. Bowden, M., Mackay, D. & Topping, P.), BAR British Series 209, 29-47

Bradley, R., 1990. *The Passage of Arms*, Cambridge

Bradley, R., 1993. *Altering the Earth*, Soc. Antiquaries Scotland, Monograph Series 8, Edinburgh

Bradley, R. & Lewis, E., 1974. A Mesolithic site at Wakeford's Copse, Havant, *Rescue Archaeology*, Hampshire, 2, 5-18

Bradshaw, J. 1968. Report of the Ashford Archaeological Society Excavation Group, *Cantiana*, 83, 251-4

Bradshaw , J., 1970 Investigations and excavations during the year, Reports from Local Secretaries and groups, *Archaeologia Cantiana*, 85, 175-94

Brailsford, J.W., 1953. *Later Prehistoric Antiquities of the British Isles*, London (British Museum)

Brailsford, J.W., 1975. *Early Celtic Masterpieces from Britain in the British Museum*, London (British Museum)

Brent, J., 1859. Ancient Sepulchral Shaft at Bekesbourne, *Archaeologia Cantiana*, 2, 43-8

Brent, J., 1861. Roman Cemeteries in Canterbury, with some conjectures regarding its earliest, *Archaeologia Cantiana*, 4, 27-42

Brinson, J.G.S., 1943. Two Burial Groups of Belgic Age, Hothfield Common, near Ashford, *Archaeologia Cantiana*, 56, 41-7

Britten, D., 1963. Traditions of Metal-working in the Later Neolithic and Early Bronze Age of Britain, Part 1, *Proc. Prehistoric Society*, 29, 258-325

Britten, D., 1961. A Study of the Composition of Wessex Culture Bronzes, *Archaeometry*, 4, 39-52

Broadfoot, D.N., 1975. The Flint Material, Philp. 1973, 14-19

Brothwell, D. & P., 1969. *Food in Antiquity*, London

Burchell, J.P.T., 1925. The shell mound industry of Denmark as represented at Lower Halstow, Kent. *Proc. Prehistoric Society of East Anglia*, 5, i, 73-8

Burchell, J.P.T., 1927. Further report on the Epi-Palaeolithic factory site at Lower Halstow, Kent, *Proc. Prehistoric Society of East Anglia*, 5, ii, 217-23

Burchell, J.P.T., 1928. A Final Account of the Investigations carried out at Lower Halstow, Kent, *Proc. Prehistoric Society of East Anglia*, 5, iii, 289-96

Burchell, J.P.T., 1931. Early Neanthropic Man and his relation to the Ice Age, *Proc. Prehistoric Society of East Anglia*, 6, 253-303

Burchell, J.P.T., 1938. The Mesolithic 'floors' in the Ebbsfleet Valley of the Lower Thames, *Antiquaries Journal*, 18, 399-401

Burchell, J.P.T., & Erdtman, 1950. Indegenous Tilia platyphyllos in Britain, *Nature* (London), 165, 411

Burchell, J.P.T. & Piggott, S., 1939. Decorated Prehistoric Pottery from the bed of the Ebbsfleet, North Fleet, Kent, *Antiquaries Journal,* 19, 405-20

Burgess, C., 1980. *The Age of Stonehenge*, London

Burgess, C., Coombs, D. & Davies, D.G., 1972. The Broadland Complex and Barbed spearheads, *Prehistoric Man in Wales and The West, Essays in Honour of Lily F. Chitty,* (eds. Lynch, F., Burgess, C.) Bath, 211-83

Bushe-Fox, J.P., 1915. *Excavations at Hengistbury Head, Hampshire, in 1911-12,* Reports of the Research Committee of the Society of Antiquaries of London, 3, London

Bushe-Fox, J.P., 1925. *Excavation of a Late-Celtic Urn-Field at Swarling, Kent.* Reports of the Research Committee of the Society of Antiquaries of London, 16, Oxford

Bushe-Fox, J.P., 1949. *Fourth Report on the Excavations of the Roman Fort at Richborough,* Reports of the Research Committee of the Society of Antiquaries of London, 16, Oxford

Butler, J.J., 1963. Bronze Age connections across the North Sea, *Palaeohistoria,* 9, 1-286

Calkin, J.B., 1962. The Bournemouth Area in the Middle and Late Bronze Age, with the Deverel-Rimbury problem reconsidered, *Archaeological Journal,* 119, 1-65

Canterbury Archaeological Trust Ltd., 1991. *From Ice Age to Tunnel* (ed. Bennett, P., Folkestone)

Case, H.J., 1977. The Beaker Culture in Britain and Ireland, *Beakers in Britain and Europe,* (ed. Mercer, R.), BAR (Int. Series), 26, 71-101, Oxford

Case, H.J., 2003. Beaker Presence at Wilsford 7, *Wiltshire Studies,* 96, 161-94

Casson, S., 1940, *The Discovery of Man,* London

Chalkley-Gould, I., 1908. Ancient Earthworks, *The Victoria History of the Counties of England, Kent,* Folkestone & London, 339-455

Champion, T.C., 1980. Settlement and Environment in Later Bronze Age, Kent, *Settlement and Society in the British Later Bronze Age* (eds. Barratt, J.C. & Bradley, R. J.), British Archaeological Reports, 83, 223-46

Champion, T.C., 1982. The Bronze Age in Kent (ed. Leach, P.E.), *Archaeology in Kent to AD 1500,* 31-9, CBA Research Report No. 48, London

Champion, T.C. Gamble, C., Shennan, S. & Whittle, A., 1984. *Prehistoric Europe,* London

Charles, T., 1844. Roman Antiquities found at and near Maidstone in Kent, *Archaeologia,* 30, 535-37

Childe, V.G., 1929. *The Danube in Prehistory,* Oxford

Childe, V.G., 1930. *The Bronze Age,* Cambridge

Childe, V.G., 1931. The Continental Affinities of British Neolithic Pottery, *Archaeological Journal,* 88, 37-66

Childe, V.G., 1932. The Danish Neolithic Pottery from the Coast of Durham, *Archaeological Aeliana* (4th Ser.) 9, 84-88

Childe, V.G., 1940. *Prehistoric Communities of the British Isles,* London & Edinburgh (2nd ed., 1947)

Christensen, C., 1999. Mesolithic Boats from around the Great Belt, Denmark, *Bog Bodies, Sacred Sites and Wetland Archaeology* (eds. Coles, B., Coles, J. & Jørgensen, M.S.), Exeter

Clark, J.G.D., 1932. The curved flint sickle blades of Britain. *Proc. Prehistoric Society of East Anglia* 7, 67-81

Clark, J.G.D., 1932. *The Mesolithic Age in Britain,* Cambridge

Clark, J.G.D., 1934. A Late Mesolithic settlement at Selmeston, Sussex, *Antiquaries Journal,* 14, 134-58

BIBLIOGRAPHY

Clark, J.G.D., 1936. *The Mesolithic Settlement of Northern Europe,* Cambridge

Clark, Grahame, 1938. The Reindeer Hunting Tribes of Northern Europe, *Antiquity,* 12, 154-71

Clark, Grahame, 1938. Reindeer Hunters' Summer Camps in Britain, *Proc Prehistoric Society,* 4, 1, 229

Clark, J.G.D., 1952. *Prehistoric Europe, The Economic Basis,* London

Clark, J.G.D., 1954. *Excavations at Star Carr,* Cambridge

Clark, J.G.D., 1963. Neolithic Bows from Somerset, England, and the prehistory of archery in North-Western Europe, *Proc. Prehistoric Society,* 29, 50-98

Clark, J.G.D., 1975. *The Earlier Stone Age Settlement of Scandinavia,* Cambridge

Clark, J.G.D. (Grahame), 1980. *Mesolithic Preluse,* Edinburgh

Clark, J.G.D., 1989. *Economic Prehistory,* Cambridge

Clark, Grahame, 1989. *Prehistory at Cambridge and Beyond,* Cambridge

Clark, J.G.D. & Rankine, W.F., 1939. Excavations at Farnham, surrey (1937-8): the Horsham culture and the question of Mesolithic sites in the Farnham District, *Proc. Prehistoric Society,* 5, 61-118

Clark, J.G.D. & Godwin, H., 1940. A late Bronze Age find near Stuntney, Isle of Ely, *Antiquaries Journal,* 20, 52-71

Clark, J.G.D., Higgs, E.S. & Longworth, I.H., 1960. Excavations at the Neolithic site at Hurst Fen, Mildenhall, Suffolk, *Proc. Prehistoric Society,* 27, 202-45

Clarke, A.F., 1982. The Neolithic in Kent, *The Archaeology of Kent to AD 1500* (eds. Leach, P.E. & Clarke, A.F.), CBA Research Report, 48, 25-30

Clarke, D.L., 1970. *Beaker Pottery of Great Britain and Ireland,* I & II, Cambridge

Clarke, D., 1976. Mesolithic Europe: the economic basis, *Problems in Economic and Social Archaeology* (eds. Sieveking, G. de G. Longworth, I.H. & Wilson, K.E.), London, 449-81

Clarke, R.R., 1955. The Early Iron Age treasure from Snettisham, Norfolk, *Proc. Prehistoric Society,* 20, 27-86

Clarke, R.R., 1960. *East Anglia,* London

Cleal, R., 1992. Significant forms: ceramic styles in the earlier Neolithic of Southern England, *Vessels for the ancestors, Essays on the Neolithic of Britain and Ireland in honour of Audrey Henshall* (eds. Sharples, N. & Sheridan, A.) Edinburgh, 286-304

Cleal, R.M.J., Walker, K.E. & Montague, R., 1995. *Stonehenge in its Landscape, twentieth century excavations,* London, English Heritage Arch. Rpt., 10

Cleere, H. & Crossley, D., 1985. *The Iron Industry of the Weald,* Leicester

Clinch, G., 1908. Early Man, *Victoria County History,* Kent, I, London, 307-338

Clough, T.H. McK. & Cummins, W.A. (eds.) 1988. *Stone Axe Studies,* 2, CBA Research Report, 67, London

Clough, T.H. Mck. & Wooley, A.K., 1985. Petrography and Stone Implements, *World Archaeology,* 17.1, 90-110

Clutton-Brock, J., 1981. *Domesticated Animals from Early Times,* London, British Museum Natural History

Coffey, G., 1913. *The Bronze Age in Ireland,* Dublin

Coleman, A.M. & Lukehurst, C.T., 1967. *East Kent,* The Geographical Association, Sheffield

Coles, B.J., 1998. Doggerland: a Speculative Survey, *Proc. Prehistoric Society,* 64, 45-81

Coles, B. & Coles, J., 1986. *Sweet Track to Glastonbury, The Somerset Levels in Prehistory,* London

Coles, J., 1962. European Bronze Shields, *Proc. Prehistoric Society,* 28, 156-90

Coles, J.M. & Orme, B.J., 1976. The Meare Trackway: excavation of a Bronze Age Structure in the Somerset Levels, *Proc. Prehistoric Society* 42, 298-318

Coles, J.M. & Harding, A.F., 1979. *The Bronze Age in Europe,* London

Coles, J.M. & Lawson, A.J., 1987. *European Wetlands in Prehistory,* Oxford

Coles, J.M. & Orme, B.J., 1983. Homo sapiens or Castor fiber?, *Antiquity,* 57, no. 220, 95-102

Coles, J. & Taylor, J., 1971. The Wessex Culture: a minimal view, *Antiquity,* 45, 6-14

Coles Finch, W., 1927. *In Kentish Pilgrimland, its Ancient Roads and Shrines,* London

Collins, D.M. & A., 1968-9. Excavations at Oldbury in Kent: cultural evidence for Last Glacial occupation in Britain, *Bulletin Institute of Archaeology, University of London,* 8-9, 151-76

Collins, D., 1986. *Palaeolithic Europe,* Tiverton, Devon

Collingwood, R.G., 1939. *An Autobiography*, Oxford

Collingwood, R.G., 1946. *The Idea of History*, Oxford

Collis, J., 1984. *Oppida, earliest towns north of the Alps*, Sheffield

Colt Hoare, R., 1810. *The History of Ancient Wiltshire,* London

Colvin, H.M., 1959. An Iron Age Hill-fort at Dover, *Antiquity*, 33, 125-7

Cook, N.C., 1934. Archaeology in Kent, 1933, *Archaeologia Cantiana*, 46, 195-7

Cook, N.C., 1935. Archaeology in Kent, 1935, *Archaeologia Cantiana*, 47, 239-41

Cook, N.C., 1936. Archaeology in Kent, 1936, *Archaeologia Cantiana*, 48, 234-5

Cook, N.C., 1937. Report of Society's Curator, Maidstone, *Archaeologia Cantiana*, 49, 284-6

Cook, N.C., 1950. Arthur Charles Golding, FSA, *Archaeologia Cantiana*, 63, 166

Cook, N. & Jessup, R.F. 1933. Excavations in Rose Wood, Ightham, *Archaeologia Cantiana*, 45, 162-7

Coombs, D., 1976. The Dover harbour bronze find – a Bronze Age wreck?, *Archaeologia Atlantica*, 1, 193-5

Coombs, D. & Bradshaw, J., 1979. A Carp's Tongue hoard from Stourmouth, Kent *Bronze Age Hoards*, eds. Burgess, C.B. & Coombs D., *British Archaeological Reports*, 67, Oxford, 181-96

Corner, F., 1910. Bronze Age Hoard from the Thames, off Broadness, *Proc. Society of Antiquaries of London*, 23, 160-71

Cornwall, I.W., 1958. *Soils for the Archaeologist*, London

Cornwall, I.W., 1964. *The World of Ancient Man,* London

Cotton, M.A. & Richardson, K.M., 1941. A Belgic Cremation Site at Stone, Kent, *Proc. Prehistoric Society*, 7, 134-41

Couchman, J.E., 1919. Neolithic Spoons and bronze loops and palstaves found in Sussex, *Proc. Society of Antiquaries of London*, 31, 108-18

CBA (Council for British Archaeology), 1948. *A Survey and Policy of Field Research in the Archaeology of Great Britain,* London

Cowen, J.D., 1952. A Bronze Sword from Folkestone, *Archaeologia Cantiana*, 65, 90-2

Cowen, J.D., 1967. The Hallstatt Sword of Bronze: on the Continent and in Britain, *Proc. Prehistoric Society*, 33, 377-454

Craddock, P.T., Cowell, M.R., Leese, M.N. & Hughes, M.J., 1983. The trace element composition of polished flint axes as an indicator of source, *Archaeometry*, 25, 135-63

Crawford, O.G.S., 1924. The Birchington Hoard, *Antiquaries Journal*, 4, 220-4

Crawford, O.G.S., 1933. Some recent Air Discoveries, *Antiquity*, 7, 290-6

Crawford, O.G.S., 1934. Field Notes in the Canterbury District, *Archaeologia Cantiana*, 46, 57-62

Crawford, O.G.S., 1955. *Said and Done*, London

Crawford, O.G.S. & Keiller, A., 1928. *Wessex from the Air,* Oxford

Crockett, A.D., Allen, M.J. & Scaife, R.G., 2002. A Neolithic Trackway within a Peat Deposits at Silvertown, London, *Proc. Prehistoric Society*, 68, 185-213

Combe, P. Perdaen, Y., Sergant, J. van Roeyen, J-P. & van Strydonck, M., 2002. The Mesolithic Neolithic transition in the sandy lowlands of Belgium: new evidence, *Antiquity*, 76, 699-706

Cruse, R.J. & Harrison, A.C., 1983. Excavation at Hill Road, Wouldham, *Archaeologia Cantiana*, 99, 81-108

Cunliffe, B.W. (ed.), 1968. *Fifth Report on the Excavation of the Roman Fort at Richborough* Kent, Reports of the Research Committee of the Society of Antiquaries of London, 23, Oxford

Cunliffe, B.W., 1980. The Evolution of Romney Marsh: a Preliminary Statement, *Archaeology and Coastal Change* (ed. Thompson, F.H.), Society of Antiquaries of London, London, 37-55

Cunliffe, B.W., 1980. Overall Discussion of the Iron Age Pottery, Macpherson-Grant, 1980, 174-79

Cunliffe, B.W., 1982. Social and Economic development in Kent in the pre-Roman Iron Age, *Archaeology in Kent to AD 1500* (ed. P. Leach), CBA Research Report, 48, 40-50, London

Cunliffe, B.W., 1987. *Hengistbury Head, Dorset, I, Prehistoric and Roman Settlement*, Oxford University Committee for archaeology, Monograph, 13, Oxford

Cunliffe, B.W., 1988. *Mount Batten, Plymouth, A Prehistoric and Roman Port,* Oxford University Committee for Archaeology, Monograph 26, Oxford

Cunliffe, B.W., 1991. *Iron Age Communities in Britain,* London

Cunliffe, B.W. (ed.), 1994. *The Oxford Illustrated Prehistory of Europe,* Oxford

Cunliffe, B.W., 1995. *Book of Iron Age Britain,* London, English Heritage

Curwen, E.C., 1954. *The Archaeology of Sussex,* London

Daniel, G.E., 1950. *The Prehistoric Chamber Tombs of England and Wales,* Cambridge

Daniel, G.E., 1975. *A Hundred and Fifty Years of Archaeology,* London

Daniel, G.E., 1986. *Some Small Harvest,* London

Daniel, G.E. & Chippindale, C., 1989. *The Pastmasters,* London

Daniel, G.E. & Renfrew, C., 1988. *The Idea of Prehistory,* Edinburgh

Darvill, T.G., 1982. *The Megalithic Chambered Tombs of the Cotswold-Severn Region,* Highworth

Darvill, T., 1987. *Prehistoric Britain,* London

Darvill, T., 1996. Neolithic Buildings in England, Wales and the Isle of Man, *Neolithic Houses in Northwest Europe and Beyond* (eds. Darvill, T. & Thomas, J.), Neolithic Studies Group Seminal Papers, I, Oxbow Monograph 57, Oxford

Davis, S.J.M., 1987. *The Archaeology of Animals,* London

Degerbøl, M., 1961. On a find of a Preboreal domestic dog (Canis familiaris L) from Star Carr, Yorkshire, with remarks on the other Mesolithic dogs, *Proc. Prehistoric Society,* 27, 35-55

Denison, S., 1994. Flag Fen Wheel, *British Archaeology News,* Oct. 94, 8

Denison, S., 1999. Neolithic House and Roman Temple on rail link route, *British Archaeology,* 44, May, 4

Denison, S., 2003. Tale of the Bronze Age barge sunk in the Trent, *British Archaeology,* 69, 4

Denison, S., 2003. Iron age hilltop 'town' found at Margate, *British Archaeology,* 71, 5

Dent, J.S., 1985. Three cart-burials from Wetwang, Antiquity, 59, 85-92

Desmond, A. & Moore, J., 1991. *Darwin,* London

Detsicas, A.P., 1966. An Iron Age and Romano-British site at Stone Castle Quarry, Greenhithe, *Archaeologia Cantiana,* 81, 139-90

Detsicas, A.L., 1987. *The Cantiaci,* Gloucester

Devoy, R.J.N., 1979. Flandrian Sea level changes and vegetational history of the lower Thames Estuary, *Phil. Trans. Royal Society,* London B285, 355-407

Devoy, R.J.N., 1980. Post-glacial Environmental Change and Man in the Thames Estuary: A Synopsis, *Archaeology and Coastal change* (ed. F.H. Thompson), Society of Antiquaries of London, London, 134-48

Dewey, H., 1932. The Palaeolithic deposits of the Lower Thames Valley, *Quart. Journal, Geological Society, London,* 88, 35-54

Dewey, H. & Smith, R.A., 1924. Flints from the Sturry Gravels, *Archaeologia,* 79, 117-36

Dimbleby, G.W., 1963. Pollen analysis of a Mesolithic site at Addington, Kent, *Grana Palynalogia,* 4 (I), 140-8

Dimbleby, G.W., 1967. *Plants and Archaeology,* London

Dimbleby, G.W., 1968. Pollen Analysis, J.H. Money, Excavations in the Iron Age Hillfort at High Rocks, near Tunbridge Wells, 1957-1961, *Sussex Archaeological Collections,* 106, 193-7

Dimbleby, G.W., 1969. Report on Pollen analysis, N.Piercy-Fox, Caesar's Camp, Keston, *Archaeologia Cantiana,* 84, 196

Dimbleby, G.W., 1970. Pollen Analysis, N. Piercy-Fox, The Iron Ace Camp at Squerryes, Westerham, *Archaeologia Cantiana,* 85, 32-3

Dines, H.G., 1928. The Palaeolithic Site at Bapchild, near Sittingbourne, *The South-Eastern Naturalist and Antiquary, 1928* (trans. South-Eastern Union of Scientific Societies), 100-7

Dines, H.G., 1929. The flint industries of Bapchild, *Proc. Prehistoric Society of East Anglia,* 6.1,12-26

Dixon, P., 1988. The Neolithic Settlements on Crickley Hill, *Enclosures and Defences in the Neolithic of Western Europe,* (eds. Burgess, C., Topping, P., Mordant, C. & Maddison, M.), B.A.R. (Int. Series), 403, Oxford, 75-88

Donaldson, P., 1977. The Excavation of a Multiple Round Barrow at Barnack, Cambridgeshire, *Antiquaries Journal*, 57, 197-231

Douglas, J., 1793. *Nenia Britannica : or a Sepulchral History of Great Britain*, London

Drew, C.D. & Piggott, S., 1937. Two Bronze Age Barrows excavated by Mr. Edward Cunnington *Proc. Dorset Nat. Hist. & Archaeological Society*, 58, 18-25

Drewett, P.L., 1977. The Excavation of a Neolithic Causewayed Enclosure on Offham Hill, East Sussex, 1976. *Proc. Prehistoric Society*, 43, 201-41

Drewett, P., Rudling, D. & Gardiner, M., 1988. *The South East to AD 1000*, London

Dudley, D.R. & Webster, G., 1965. *The Roman Conquest of Britain, AD 43-57*, London

Duff, A.G., 1934. *The Life-Work of Lord Avebury (Sir John Lubbock), 1834-1913*, London

Dunkin, A.J., 1848. *Memoranda of Springhead and its Neighbourhood during the Primaeval Period*, London

Dunkin, E.H.W., 1871. On the Megalithic Remains in Mid-Kent, *The Reliquary*, 12, 67-80

Dunning, G.C., 1966. Neolithic Occupation sites in East Kent, *Antiquaries Journal*, 46, 1-25

Dyson, E., Shand, G. & Stevens, S., 2000. Causewayed enclosures (Kent), *Current Archaeology*, Vol. 14, No. 12, 470-2

Eddison, J., 2000. *Romney Marsh, Survival on a Frontier*, Stroud

Eddison, J., Gardiner, M. & Long, A., 1998. *Romney Marsh, Environmental Change and Human Occupation in a Coastal Lowland*, Oxford University Committee for Archaeology, Mon. No. 46, Oxford

Elworthy, S.D. & Perkins, D.R.J., 1987. Newly Discovered Archaeological sites in the Isle of Thanet, *Archaeologia Cantiana*, 104, 333-39

Eogan, G., 1964. The Later Bronze Age in Ireland, *Proc. Prehistoric Society*, 30, 268-351

Eogan, G., 1994. *The Accomplished Art, Gold and Gold working in Britain and Ireland during the Bronze Age (c.2300-650 BC)*, Oxbow Monograph, 42, Oxford

Evans, A.J., 1890. On a Late-Celtic urnfield at Aylesford, Kent, *Archaeologia*, 52, 315-88

Evans, J., 1864. *The Coins of the Ancient Britons*, London

Evans, J., 1881. *The Ancient Bronze Implements, Weapons and Ornaments of Great Britain and Ireland*, London

Evans, Sir John, 1897. *The Ancient Stone Implements, Weapons and Ornaments of Great Britain*, London

Evans, J.G., 1972. *Land Snails in Archaeology*, London

Evans, J.G., 1975. *The Environment of Man in the British Isles*, London

Evans J.G. & Limbrey, S., 1974. The experimental earthwork in Morden Bog, Wareham, Dorset, *Proc. Prehistoric Society*, 40, 170-202

Evans, J.H., 1948. Smythe's Megalith, *Archaeologia Cantiana*, 61, 135-40

Evans, J.H. 1950. Kentish Megalith Types, *Archaeologia Cantiana*, 63, 63-81

Evans, J.H., 1953. Archaeological Horizons in the North Kent Marshes, *Archaeologia Cantiana*, 66, 103-46

Everitt, A., 1986. *Continuity and Civilisation, the Evolution of Kentish Settlement*, Leicester

Evison, V., 1956. An Anglo-Saxon Cemetery at Holborough, Kent, *Archaeologia Cantiana*, 70, 84-141

Evison, V., 1987. *Dover: the Buckland Anglo-Saxon Cemetery*, London, H.B.M.C. Archaeological Report, No. 3

Fagan, B., 2001. *Grahame Clark*, Cambridge, Perseus

Field, N.H., Matthews, C.L. & Smith, I.F., 1964. New Neolithic Sites in Dorset and Bedfordshire, with a note on the Distribution of Neolithic Storage-Pits in Britain, *Proc. Prehistoric Society*, 30, 352-81

Filkins, E.W., 1924. Coldrum Exploration, 1923, *Antiquaries Journal*, 4, 265

Filkins, E.W., 1928. Excavations at Coldrum, *Antiquaries Journal*, 8, 356-7

Fisher, C.E., 1938. Archaeology in Kent, 1938, *Archaeologia Cantiana*, 50, 147-8

Fitzpatrick, A., 2003. The Amesbury Archer, *Current Archaeology*, No.184, Vol.16, No. 4, 146-52

Fowles, J. (ed) 1980. John Aubrey, *Monumenta Britannica*, I, II (1982), Dorchester

Fowler, P.J., 1972. Field Archaeology in Future, the Crisis and the Challenge, *Archaeology and the Landscape : Essays for L.V. Grinsell* (ed. Fowler, P.J.), London, 96-126

Fowler, P.J. (ed), 1972. *Archaeology and the Landscape : Essays for L.V. Grinsell*, London

Fowler, P.J., 1981. *Later Prehistory, The Agrarian History of England & Wales*, 1.1, *Prehistory*, Cambridge, 63-288

Fox, Charles, F., 1928. A Bronze Age Refuse Pit at Swanwick, Hants., *Antiquaries Journal*, 8, 331-6

Fox, Charles, F., 1928. The Bronze Age pit at Swanwick, Hants., further finds, *Antiquaries Journal*, 10, 30-33

Fox, Cyril F., 1933. *The Personality of Britain*, Cardiff

Fox, C.F., 1946. *A Find of the Early Iron Age from Llyn Cerrig Bach, Anglesey*, Cardiff

Fox, Sir Cyril, 1958. *Pattern and Purpose: a survey of Early Celtic Art in Britain*, Cardiff

Fox, Sir Cyril, 1959. *Life and Death in the Bronze Age*, London

Fox, C.F. & Grimes, W.F., 1928. Corston Beacon: an Early Bronze Age Cairn in South Pembrokeshire, *Archaeologia Cambrensis*, 83, Pt.L, 137-74

Frere, J., 1800. Account of Flint Weapons discovered at Hoxne in Suffolk, *Archaeologia*, 13, 204-5

Frere, Sheppard, 1954. Canterbury Excavations, Summer 1946, The Rose Lane Site, *Archaeologia Cantiana*, 68, 101-43

Gallois, R.W., 1965. *The Wealden District* (British Regional Geology), London, HMSO

Garraway Rice, R., 1911. Contribution to discussion of R.A. Smith's paper on Baker's Hole, *Proc. Society Antiquaries London*, NS, 23, 450

Garrod, D.A.E., 1926. *The Upper Palaeolithic Age in Britain*, Oxford

Gerloff, S., 1975. *The Early Bronze Age Daggers in Great Britian and a Reconsideration of the Wessex Culture*, Munich, Prehistorische Bronzefunde, Ab VI, Bd. 2

Glass, H., 1999. Archaeology of the Channel Tunnel Rail Link, *Archaeologia Cantiana*, 119, 189-220

Glass, H., 2000. White Horse Stone, A Neolithic Longhouse, *Current Archaeology*, No. 168, Vol. 14, No. 12, 450-453

Glass, H., 2000. The Channel Tunnel Rail Link, *Current Archaeology*, No 168, Vol. 14, No 12, 448-466

Glasbergen W., 1954. Barrow Excavations in the Eight Beatitudes, *Palaeohistoria*, II, III

Godwin, H., 1962. Vegetational history of the Kentish chalk downs as seen at Wingham and Frogholt, *Veroff, Geobot, Inst., Zurich*, 37, 83-99

Gomme, G.L. (ed.), 1887. *The Gentleman's Magazine Library, Romano-British Remains*: Part 1, 141, London

Gordon, M.S., 1965. Gold Bracelets from Little Chart, *Archaeologia Cantiana*, 80, 200-204

Green, M., 1986. *The Gods of the Celts*, Gloucester

Green, M.J. (ed.), 1995. *The Celtic World*, London & New York

Green, S., 1981. *Prehistorian, a Biography of Gordon Childe*, Bradford-On-Avon

Greenfield, E., 1960. A Neolithic Pit and other finds from Wingham East Kent, *Archaeologia Cantiana*, 74, 58-72

Greenfield, E., Meates, G.W. & Birchenough, E., 1948. Schedule of new Discoveries in the Darent Valley, *Archaeologia Cantiana*, 61, 180-3

Gregory, T., 1991. Excavations in Thetford 1980-82, Fison's Way, *East Anglian Archaeology*, No 53

Grimes, W.F., 1948. Pentre-Ifan Burial Chamber, *Archaeologia Cambrensis*, 100, pt.1, 3-23

Grimes, W.F. (ed.), 1951. *Aspects of Archaeology in Britain and Beyond, Essays presented to O.G.S. Crawford*, London

Grinsell, L.V., 1936. *The Ancient Burial Mounds of England*, London (2nd ed., 1953)

Grinsell, L.V., 1941. The Bronze Age Round Barrows of Wessex, *Proc. Prehistoric Society*, 7, 73-113

Grinsell, L.V., 1948. Bronze implements in the Avalon Museum, *Archaeologia Cantiana*, 61, 185

Grinsell, L.V., 1989. *An Archaeological Biography*, Gloucester

Grinsell, L.V., 1992. The Bronze Age Round Barrows of Kent, *Proc. Prehistoric Society*, 58, 355-84

Grove, L.R.A. 1952. The Whiteheath Excavations, *Archaeologia Cantiana*, 65, 160-66

Hallam, J.S., Edwards, B.J.N., Barnes, B. & Stuart, A.J., 1973. The remains of a Late Glacial Elk associated with barbed points from High Furlong, near Blackpool, Lancashire, *Proc. Prehistoric Society*, 39, 100-128

Harbison, P., 1969a. *The Daggers and Halberds of the Early Bronze Age in Ireland*. Praehistorische Bronzefunde, Abt.VI, Bd. 1, Munchen

Harbison, P., 1969b. *The Axes of the Early Bronze Age in Ireland,* Praehistorishches Bronzefunde, Abt. IX, Bd. 1, Munchen

Harding, A.F., 2000. *European Societies in the Bronze Age,* Cambridge

Harrison, Sir Edward R., 1928. *Harrison of Ightham,* Oxford

Harrison, Sir Edward R., 1933. Oldbury Hill, Ightham, *Archaeologia Cantiana,* 45, 142-61

Harrison, Sir Edward, 1943. Report for the Year ended 31st December, 1942, *Archaeologia Cantiana,* 56, xxxii

Harrison, Sir Edward, 1950. Report for the Year ended 31st December, 1949, *Archaeologia Cantiana,* 63, xli-xlvi

Harrison, R.J., *The Beaker Folk,* London

Harden, D.B., 1948. *Guide to an Exhibition of Air-Photographs of Archaeological Sites* (G.W.R. Allen), Oxford

Harding, A.F. & Lee, G.E., 1987. *Henge Monuments and Related Sites of Great Britain,* British Archaeological Reports (British Ser.,), 175, Oxford

Harding, D.W., 1974. *The Iron Age in Lowland Britain,* London & Boston

Haselgrove, C., 1993. The development of British Iron Age Coinage, *Numismatic Chronicle,* 153, 31-64

Hasted, E., 1782. *The History and Topographical Survey of the County of Kent,* ii, Canterbury

Haverfield, F. (MacDonald, G.), 1924. *The Roman Occupation of Britain,* Oxford

Hawkes, C.F.C., 1930. Patterns on Early Pottery, *Antiquaries Journal,* 10, 166-7

Hawkes, C.F.C., 1931. Hillforts, *Antiquity,* 5, 60-97

Hawkes, C.F.C., 1939. The Caburn Pottery and its Implications, *Sussex Archaeological Collections,* 80, 219-62

Hawkes, C.F.C., 1940. The Marnian Pottery and La Tène I brooch from Worth, Kent, *Antiquaries Journal,* 20, 115-21

Hawkes, C.F.C., 1942. The Deverel Urn and the Picardy Pin: a phase of Bronze Age Settlement in Kent, *Proc. Prehistoric Society, 8,* 26-47

Hawkes, C.F.C. & Clarke, R.R., 1963. Gahlstorf and Caistor-On-Sea, *Culture and Environment, Essays in Honour of Sir Cyril Fox* (ed. Foster, I. Ll & Alcock, L.), London, 193-250

Hawkes, C.F.C. & Dunning, G.C., 1931. The Belgae of Gaul and Britain, *Archaeological Journal,* 87, 150-335

Hawkes, C.F.C. & Hull, M.R., 1947. *Camulodunum,* Society of Antiquaries of London Research Report, 14, Oxford

Hawkes, J., 1982. *Mortimer Wheeler, Adventurer in Archaeology,* London

Hawkes, S.C., 1968. Richborough-The Physical Geography (ed. Cunliffe, B.) 224-31

Hawkes, S.C., 1990. Bryan Faussett and the Faussett Collections, An Assessment, *Anglo-Saxon Cemeteries, A Reappraisal* (ed. E. Southworth), Stroud Gloucestershire, 1-24

Hearne, C.M., Perkins, D.R.J. & Andrews, P., 1995. The Sandwich Bay wastewater treatment scheme archaeological project, 1992-94, *Archaeologia Cantiana,* 2115, 239-354

Hedges, J. & Buckley, D.G., 1978. Excavations at a Neolithic Causewayed Enclosure, Orsett, Essex, 1975. *Proc. Prehistoric Society,* 44, 219-308

Hencken, H.O'Neill, 1932. *The Archaeology of Cornwall and Scilly,* London

Henshall, A.S., 1963. *The Chambered Tombs of Scotland,* I, Edinburgh

Henshall, A.S., 1972. *The Chambered Tombs of Scotland,* II, Edinburgh

Hicks, R., 1878. Roman Remains found at Ramsgate, *Archaeologia Cantiana,* 12, 14-18

Higginbotham, E., 1978. Excavations at Whiting's Yard, Ospringe, Kent, 1978, *Archaeologia Cantiana,* 94, 259-60

Higgs, E.S., 1959. The Excavation of a Late Mesolithic site at Downton, Near Salisbury, Wiltshire, *Proc. Prehistoric Society,* 25, 209-32

Hodder, I., 1990. *The Domestication of Europe,* Oxford

Hodder, I. & Shand, P., 1988. The Haddenham long barrow, an interim statement, *Antiquity,* 62, 349-53

BIBLIOGRAPHY

Hogg, A.H.A, 1941. Earthworks in Joyden's Wood, Bexley, Kent, *Archaeologia Cantiana*, 54, 10-27

Hogg, A.H.A., 1981. The Causewayed Earthwork and the Elizabethan Redoubt on West Wickham Common, *Archaeologia Cantiana*, 97, 71-8

Hogg, A.H.A. & O'Neil, B.H. St. J, 1937. A causewayed earthwork in West Kent, *Antiquity*, 11, 223-5

Hogg, A.H.A., O'Neil, B.H. St. J. & Stevens, C.E. 1941. Earthworks on Hayes and West Wickham Commons, *Archaeologia Cantiana*, 54, 28-34

Hogwood, P., 1995. Investigations at North Foreland Hill, *Archaeologia Cantiana*, 115, 475-8

Holgate, R., 1981. The Medway Megaliths and Neolithic Kent, *Archaeologia Cantiana*, 97, 221-34

Hornell, J., 1938. *British Coracles and Irish Curraghs*, London

Horsley, J., 1732. *Britannia Romana or the Roman Antiquities of Britain*, London

Houlder, C.H., 1963. A Neolithic Settlement on Hazard Hill, Totnes, *Proc. Devon Archaeological Exploration Soc.*, 21, 2

Hubbard, R.N.L.B., 1982. The environmental evidence from Swanscombe and its implications for Palaeolithic archaeology, *Archaeology in Kent to AD 1500* (ed. Leach, P.E.), CBA, London, 307

Hurd, H., 1909. On a Late-Celtic Village near Dumpton Gap, Broadstairs, *Archaeologia*, 61, 427-38

Hurd, H., 1914. Late-Celtic Discoveries at Broadstairs, *Archaeologia Cantiana*, 30, 309-12

Hussey, R.C., 1874. The British Settlement in Bigbury Wood, *Archaeologia Cantiana*, 9, 13-15

Ilett, M., 1984. The early Neolithic in North-Eastern France, *Ancient France, 6000-2000 BC* (ed. Scarre, C.) Edinburgh, 6-33

Jacobi, R.M., 1982. Late Hunters in Kent: Tasmania and the earliest Neolithic, *Archaeology in Kent to AD 1500* (ed. Leach, P.E.), CBA Research Report, 48, London, 12-24

Jacobi, R. & Tebbutt, C.F., 1981. The excavation of a Mesolithic rock shelter at Hermitage Rocks, *Sussex Archaeologica Collect.*, 119, 1-36

Jacobstahl, Paul, 1944. *Early Celtic Art*, Oxford (2 vols)

Jackson, K.H., 1964. *The oldest Irish tradition: a window on the Iron Age*, Cambridge

James, F., 1899. Bronze Age Burials at Aylesford, *Proc. Society of Antiquaries of London*, 17, 373-37

Jay, L., 1990. Researches and discoveries in Kent, *Archaeologia Cantiana*, 108, 275

Jay, L., 1993. Barrow reconstruction, *Archaeologia Cantiana*, 112, 420-21

Jenkins, F., 1962. *Men of Kent before the Romans, Cantium in the Early Iron Age*, Canterbury

Jessup, F.W., 1955. Annual Report for the Year ended 31st December, 1955, *Archaeologia Cantiana* 69, xl-xlvii

Jessup, F.W., 1956. The Origin and First Hundred Years of the Society, *Archaeologia Cantiana* 70, 1-43

Jessup, R.F., 1930. *The Archaeology of Kent*, London

Jessup, R.F., 1933a. Early Bronze Age Beakers, *Archaeologia Cantiana*, 45, 174-78

Jessup, R.F., 1933b. Bigbury Camp, Harbledown, Kent, *Archaeological Journal*, 89, 87-115

Jessup, R.F., 1933c. Bronze Age Antiquities from the Lower Medway, *Archaeologia Cantiana*, 45, 179-87

Jessup, R.F., 1936. "Incense Cup" from Canterbury, *Archaeologia Cantiana*, 48, 243-44

Jessup, R.F., 1937. Excavations at Julliberrie's Grave, Chilham, Kent, *Antiquaries Journal*, 17, 122-37

Jessup, R.F., 1938. Objects from Bigberry Camp, Harbledown, Kent, *Antiquaries Journal*, 18, 174-76

Jessup, R.F., 1939. Further Excavations at Julliberrie's Grave Chilham, *Antiquaries Journal*, 19, 260-81

Jessup, R.F., 1943. A Bronze Hoard from Sturry, Kent, *Antiquaries Journal*, 23, 55-56

Jessup, R.F., 1944. Additions to the Bronze Hoard from Broadoak, Sturry, Kent, *Antiquaries Journal*, 24, 148-49

Jessup, R.F., 1954. Excavation of a Roman Barrow at Holborough, Snodland, *Archaeologia Cantiana*, 68, 1-61

Jessup, R.F., 1957. The Follies of Kingsgate, *Archaeologia Cantiana*, 71, 1-13

Jessup, R.F., 1964. *The Story of Archaeology in Britain*, London

Jessup, Ronald (R.F.), 1970. *South East England*, London

Jessup, R.F., 1975. *Man of Many Talents, An Informal Biography of James Douglas, 1753-1819*, London & Chichester

Jessup, R.F. & Cook, N.C., 1936. Excavations at Bigbury Camp, Harbledown, *Archaeologia Cantiana*, 48, 151-68

Jewell, P.A. (ed.), 1963. *The Experimental Earthwork on Overton Down, Wiltshire*, London, British Association for the Advancement of Science

Jewell, P.A., 1993. Natural history and experiment in archaeology revisited, *Skeletons in her Cupboard, Festschrift for Juliet Clutton-Brock* (eds. Clason, A., Payne, S. & Uerpmann, H-P.), Oxbow Monograph, 34, Oxford

Jones, B., 1984. *Past Imperfect, the Story of Rescue Archaeology*, London

Jones, B. & Mattingly, D.J., 1990. *An Atlas of Roman Britain*, Oxford

Jones, E.C.H., 1952. Orpington Mesolithic Site, *Archaeologia Cantiana*, 65, 174-78

Jones, M. 1983. Palaeobotanical Report on filling of Water-hole, Thompson, 1983, 276

Jope, E.M., 1995. The social implications of Celtic art: 600 BC to AD 600, *The Celtic World* (ed., Green, M.J.), London & New York

Jope, E.M., 2000. *Early Celtic Art in The British Isles* (2 Vols,) Oxford

Keef, P.A.M., Wymer, J.J. & Dimbleby, G.W., 1965. A Mesolithic site on Iping Common, Sussex, England, *Proc. Prehistoric Society*, 31, 85-92

Keith, Sir Arthur, 1913. Report on the Human Remains found by F.J. Bennett Esq., F.G.S., in the Central Chamber of a Megalithic Monument at Coldrum, Kent, *Journal Royal Anthropological Institute*, 43, 86-100

Keith, Sir Arthur, 1925. *The Antiquity of Man* (2nd ed), London

Keller, Ferdinand, 1866. *The Lake Dwellings of Switzerland and other parts of Europe*, London

Kelly, D.B., 1961. Researches and Discoveries in Kent, Archaeological Notes from Maidstone Museum, *Archaeological Cantiana*, 76, 191-202

Kelly, D.B., 1963. Belgic Cremation at Maidstone, *Archaeologia Cantiana*, 78, 194-6

Kelly, D.B., 1968. Archaeological Notes from Maidstone Museum, *Archaeologia Cantiana*, 83, 262-65

Kelly, D.B., 1971. Quarry Wood, Loose: a Belgic oppidum, *Archaeologia Cantiana*, 86, 55-84

Kelly, D.B., 1976. Researches and Discoveries in Kent, *Archaeologia Cantiana*, 92, 225-33

Kelly, D.B., 1976. Archaeological Notes from Maidstone Museum, *Archaeologia Cantiana*, 94, 264-68

Kelly, D.B., 1989. Archaeological Notes from Maidstone Museum, *Archaeologia Cantiana*, 107, 395-409

Kelly, D.B., 1992. Archaeological Notes from Maidstone Museum, *Archaeologia Cantiana*, 110, 404-15

Kendrick, T.D., 1927. *The Druids,* London

Kendrick, T.D., 1928. *The Archaeology of the Channel Islands*, I, *The Baliwick of Guernsey*, London

Kendrick, T.D. & Hawkes, C.F.C., 1932. *Archaeology in England and Wales 1914-1931*, London

Kennard, A.S., 1944. The Crayford Brickearths, *Proc. Geological Society London*, 55, 121-69

Kerney, M.P., 1965. Weichselian deposits in the Isle of Thanet, East Kent, *Proceedings Geological Association*, 76, 269-74

Kerney, M.P., Braun, E.H. & Chandler, T.J., 1964. The Late-Glacial and Post-Glacial history of the Chalk Escarpment, near Brook, Kent, *Phil. Transactions Royal Society, London*, B248, King, N.E., 1968. The Kennet Valley Sarsen Industry, *Wiltshire Arch. & Nat. History. Magazine*, 63, 83-93, 135-204

Kinnes, I, 1992. *Non-Megalithic Long Barrows and Allied Structures in the British Neolithic,* British Museum Occ. Papers, 52, London

Kinnes, I., 1994. The Neolithic in Britain, *Building on the Past, Papers celebrating 150 years of the Royal Archaeological Institute* (ed. Vyner, B.) 90-102, London

Kinnes, I. & Longworth, I.H., 1985. *Catalogue of the excavated Prehistoric and Romano-British M-aterial in the Greenwell Collection,* London (British Museum),

Klein, W.G., 1928. Roman Temple at Worth, Kent, *Antiquaries Journal* 8, 76-86

Köln, Romisch-Germanisches Museum, 1990. *Archaeologie in Nordrhein-Westfalen,* Mainz

Laet, S.J. de,1958. *The Low Countries*, London

Lambarde, W., 1596. *A Perambulation of Kent, containing the description, hystorie, and customs of that shire, collected and written (for the most part) in the yeare 1570* (2nd ed.), London

Lambrechts, P., 1954. *L'Exaltation de la Tête dans la Pensee et dans l'art des Celtes,* Bruges

Lanting, J.N. & van der Waals, J.D., 1972. British Beakers as seen from the Continent, *Helinium*, 12, 20-46

Layard, N.F., 1925. Bronze crowns and a bronze head-dress, from a Roman site at Cavenham Heath, Suffolk, *Antiquaries Journal*, 5, 258-65

Layard, N.F., 1932. Solutrean blades from South-eastern England, *Proc. Prehistoric Society East Anglia*, 6, 54

Leach, P.E., 1977. Reports from Local Secretaries and Groups, Sevenoaks Branch, *Archaeologia Cantiana*, 93, 225

Leakey, L.S.B., 1951. *Preliminary excavation of a Mesolithic site at Abinger Common, Surrey*, research Paper Surrey Archaeological Society, 3, 1-44

Leeds, E.T., 1913. *The Archaeology of the Anglo-Saxon Settlements*, Oxford

Leeds, E.T., 1927. Neolithic Spoons from Nether Swell, Gloucester, *Antiquaries Journal*, 7, 61-2

Leeds, E.T., 1930. A Bronze Cauldron from the River Cherwell, Oxfordshire, with notes on cauldrons and other bronze vessels of allied types, *Archaeologia*, 80, 1-36

Leeds, E.T., 1930. *Celtic Ornament*, Oxford

Legge, A., 1995. *A Horse Burial and other grave offerings*, Parfitt, K., 1995, 146-52

Lewis, J., 1736. *History and Antiquities… of the Isle of Tenet in Kent*, London

Lewis, M.J.T., 1966. *Temples in Roman Britain*, Cambridge

Lewis, W.V., 1932. The Formation of Dungeness Foreland, *Geographical Journal*, 30, 309-24

Longworth, I.H., 1960. A Bronze Age Urnfield on Vinces Farm, Ardleigh, Essex, *Proc. Prehistoric Society*, 46, 178-92

Longworth, I.H., 1983. The Whinny Liggate Perforated Wall Cup and its affinities, *From the Stone Age to the Forty-Five, Studies Presented to R.B.K. Stevenson* (eds. O'Connor, A & Clark, D.V.), Edinburgh, 65-86

Longworth, I.H., 1984. *Collared Urns of the Bronze Age in Great Britain and Ireland*, Cambridge

Lubbock, J. (Lord Avebury), 1865. *Prehistoric Times* (1st ed), Cambridge

Lyell, Sir Charles, 1863. *The Geological Evidence of the Antiquity of Man*, London

Lynch, Frances, 1997. *Megalithic Tombs and Long Barrows in Britain*, Princes Risborough

Lynch, F., Aldhouse-Green, S. & Davies, J.L., 2000. *Prehistoric Wales*, Stroud

Macalister, R.A.S., 1921. *A Text-Book of European Archaeology*, Cambridge

McCrerie, A., 1956. Kit's Coty House, *Archaeologia Cantiana*, 70, 250-1

McGrail, S., 1994. The Brigg 'raft': a flat-bottomed boat, *Int. Journal Nautical Archaeology*, 23/4, 283-8

McGrail, S., 1995. Celtic seafaring and transport, *The Celtic World*, (ed. Green, M.J.) London & New York, 254-81

Macpherson-Grant, N., 1969. Two Neolithic Bowls from Birchington, Thanet, *Archaeologia Cantiana*, 84, 249-50

Macperson-Grant, N., 1980. Archaeological Work along the A2: 1966-1974 *Archaeologia Cantiana*, 96, 133-183

Macpherson-Grant, N., 1989. The Pottery from the 1987-89 Channel Tunnel Excavations, *Archaeologia Cantiana*, 107, 354-7

MacSween, A., 1992. Orcadian Grooved Ware, *Vessels for the Ancestors, Essays on the Neolithic of Britain and Ireland in honour of Audrey Henshall* (eds. Sharples, N. & Sheridan, A), Edinburgh, 259-71

Manley, J., 1989. *Atlas of Prehistoric Britain*, London

Margary, I.D., 1948. *Roman Ways in the Weald*, London

Markey, M., Wilkes, E. & Darvill, T., 2002. Poole Harbour, An Iron Age Port, *Current Archaeology*, 181, Vol. 16, No.1, 7-11

Marsden, B.M., 1974. *The Early Barrow-Diggers*, Princes Risbrough

Masefield, R., Branch, N., Couldrey, P., Goodburn, D. & Tyers, I., 2003. A Later Bronze Age Well Complex at Swalecliffe, Kent, *Antiquaries Journal*, 83, 47-121

Meaney, A., 1964. *A Gazetteer of Early Anglo-Saxon Burial Sites*, London

Megaw, B.R.S. & Hardy, E.M., 1938. British Decorated Axes and their Diffusion during the earlier part of the Bronze Age, *Proc. Prehistoric Society*, 4, 272-307

Megaw, J.V.S., 1970. *Art of the European Iron Age*, Bath

Megaw, J.V.S. & Simpson, D.D.A., 1979. *Introduction to British Prehistory*, Leicester

Mellars, P. & Reinhardt, S.C., 1978. Patterns of Mesolithic Land-use in southern England: a geological perspective, *The Early Postglacial Settlement of Northern Europe* (ed. Mellars, P.), London, 243-93

Mercer, R., 1980. *Hambledon Hill, A Neolithic Landscape,* Edinburgh

Mercer, R., 1981. *Grimes Graves, Norfolk, Excavations 1971-2,* Dept. Environment Archaeological Report, 11, vols I & II, London, HMSO

Mercer, R., 1988. Hambledon Hill, Dorset, England, *Enclosures and Defences in the Neolithic of Western Europe* (eds. Burgess, C., Topping, P., Mordant, C. & Maddison, M.) B.A.R. (Int. Series), Oxford, 89-106

Midgley, M., 1985. *The Origins and Function of the Earthen Long Barrows of Northern Europe*, B.A.R. (International Series), 259, Oxford

Midgley, M., 1992. *The TRB culture, the first farmers of the North European Plain*, Edinburgh

Ministry of Works, 1961. *Ancient Monuments in England and Wales,* London, HMSA

Moir, J.R., 1927. *The Antiquity of Man in East Anglia*, Cambridge

Moir, J.R., 1932. Further Solutré implements from Suffolk, *Antiquaries Journal*, 12, 257-61

Moir, J. R., 1938. Four Flint Implements, *Antiquaries Journal*, 18, 258-61

Money, J.H., 1960. Excavations at High Rocks, Tunbridge Wells, *Sussex Archaeological Collections*, 98, 173-221

Money, J.H., 1962. Excavations at High Rocks, 1954-56: Supplementary Note, *Sussex Archaeological Collections*, 100, 149-51

Money, J. H., 1968. Excavations in the Iron Age hill-fort at High Rocks, near Tunbridge Wells, *Sussex Archaeological Collections*, 106, 158-205

Money, J. H., 1975. Excavations in the Two Iron Age Hill-forts on Castle Hill, Capel, near Tonbridge, *Archaeologia Cantiana*, 91, 61-85

Money, J.H., 1978. Excavations in the two Iron Age Hill-Forts on Castle Hill, Capel, near Tonbridge 1965 and 1967-71, Supplementary Note, *Archaeologia Cantiana*, 94, 268-70

Morrison, A., 1980. *Early Man in Britain and Ireland*, London

Mortimer, J.R., 1905. *Forty Years' Researches into the British and Saxon Burial Mounds of East Yorkshire*, London

Movius, H.L., 1950. A wooden spear of Third Interglacial Age from Lower Saxony, *South-western Journal Anthropology*, 6: 2, 139-42

Muckelroy, K., 1981. Middle Bronze trade between Britain and Europe: a maritime perspective, *Proc. Prehistoric Society*, 47, 275-97

Muckleroy, K., 1980. Two Bronze Age cargos in British Waters, *Antiquity*, 54, 100-09

Newall, R.S., 1928. Two Shale Cups of the Early Bronze and other similar cups, *Wiltshire Archaeological & Natural History Society Magazine*, 44, 111-7

Oakley, K.P., 1955. Fire as Palaeolithic Tool and weapon, *Proc. Prehistoric Society*, 21, 36-48

Oakley, K.P., 1964. *Frameworks for Dating Fossil Man*, London

Oakley, K.P., Andrews, P., Keely, L.H. & Clark, J.D., 1977. A reappraisal of the Clacton Spearpoint, *Proc. Prehistoric Society*, 43, 13-30

Oakley, K.P., Barker, H. & Sieveking, G. de G., 1967. The Skeleton of Halling Man, *Archaeologia Cantiana*, 74, 218-20

Oakley, K.P. & Montagu, M.F., 1949. A reconsideration of the Galley Hill skeleton, *Bulletin British Museum (Nat. Hist) Geology*, L, No. 2, 25-48

Ogilvie, J.D., 1977. The Stourmouth-Adisham Water-Main Trench, *Archaeologia Cantiana*, 93, 91-124

Ogilvie, J. D., 1982. The Hammill ritual shaft, *Archaeologia Cantiana*, 98, 145-66

Ogilvie, J.D. & Dunning, G.C., 1967. A Belgic Burial-Group at Shoulden, near Deal; and a Belgic tazza from Mill Hill, Upper Deal, *Archaeologia Cantiana*, 82, 221-26

O'Kelly, M.J., 1989. *Early Ireland,* Cambridge

O'Malley, M., 1978. Broom Hill, Braishfield, Mesolithic Dwelling, *Current Archaeology*, 63, 117-20

O'Malley, M. & Jacobi, R.M., 1978. The Excavation of a Mesolithic Occupation site at Broom Hill, Braishfield, Hampshire, 1971-1973, *Rescue Archaeology Hampshire*, 4, 16-38

BIBLIOGRAPHY

O'Neil, B.H. St. J., 1948. War and Archaeology in Britain, *Antiquaries Journal*, 28, 20-44

Ó'Ríordáin, S.P., 1936. The Halberd in Bronze Age Europe: a study in prehistoric origins, evolution, distribution and chronology, *Archaeologia*, 86, 195-321.

Oxford Archaeological Unit, 2000. Thurnham Roman Villa, *Current Archaeology*, No. 12, 14, 454-7

Palmer, R., 1976. Interrupted ditch Enclosures in Britain: the use of Aerial Photography for Comparative Studies, *Proc. Prehistoric Society*, 42, 161-86

Parfitt, K., 1984. Reports from Local Secretaries and Groups (Dover), *Archaeologia Cantiana*, 101, 382-83

Parfitt, K, 1991. Deal, *Current Archaeology*, 11, No. 5, 215-20

Parfitt, K., 1993. The Dover Boat, *Current Archaeology*, 12, No. 1, 4-8

Parfitt, K., 1995. *Iron Age Burials from Mill Hill, Deal,* London, British Museum

Parfitt, K., 1998. Neolithic Earthen Long-Barrows in East Kent, a Review, *Kent Archaeological Review*, 131, 15-21

Parfitt, K., 1998. A Late Iron Age Burial from Chilham Castle, near Canterbury, Kent, *Proc Prehistoric Society*, 64, 343-51

Parfitt, K., 2002. A Prehistoric Site off Green Lane, Whitfield near Dover, *Archaeologia Cantiana*, 122, 373-96

Parfitt, K., 2002. Kent's Gold Cup, Finds at Ringlemere Farm, Woodnesborough, near Sandwich, *Kent Archaeological Society Newsletter*, 53, 1

Parfitt, K. & Fenwick, V., 1993. The Rescue of Dover's Bronze Age Boat, *A Spirit of Enquiry, Essays for Ted Wright* (eds. Coles, J., Fenwick, V. & Hutchinson, G.), Exeter, 77-80

Parfitt, K. & Grinsell, L.V., 1991. The Bronze Age Urn from Capel-le-Ferne, *Archaeologia Cantiana*, 109, 334-5

Parsons, J., 1961. Broomwood Bronze Age Settlement – St. Paul's Cray, Kent, *Archaeologia Cantiana*, 76, 134-42

Patten, M., 1993. *Statements in Stone, Monuments and Society in Brittany*, London & New York

Payne, G., 1880. Celtic remains discovered at Grovehurst in Milton-next-Sittingbourne, *Archaeologia Cantiana*, 13, 122-26

Payne, G., 1885. (Bronze Age burial at Sittingbourne) *Proc Society of Antiquaries London*, 10, 29-30

Payne, G., 1893. *Collectanea Cantiana*, London

Payne, G., 1893. Minster Hoard, *Proc Society Antiquaries London*, 14, 309-11

Payne, G., 1900. Celtic interments discovered at Shorne, *Archaeologia Cantiana*, 24, 86-90

Payne, G., 1915. Researches and discoveries in Kent, 1912-1915, *Archaeologia Cantiana*, 31, 275-86

Perkins, D.R.J., 1985. The Monkton Gas Pipeline: Phases III and IV, 1983-84, *Archaeologia Cantiana*, 102, 43-69

Perkins, D.R.J., 1987. The Jutish Cemetery at Half Mile Ride Margate: a Re-appraisal, *Archaeologia Cantiana*, 104, 219-36

Perkins, D.R.J., 1988. A Middle Bronze Age Hoard from a prehistoric settlement site at St. Mildred's Bay, Westgate-on-Sea, *Archaeologia Cantiana*, 105, 243-9

Perkins, D.R.J., 1991. A Late Bronze Age Hoard from Monkton Court Farm, Thanet, *Archaeologia Cantiana*, 109, 247-64

Perkins, D.R J., 1993. North Foreland Avenue, Broadstairs, *Archaeologia Cantiana*, 112, 411-14

Perkins, D.R.J., 1997. A Report on work by the Trust for Thanet Archaeology, 1997-1998, *Archaeologia Cantiana*, 118, 355-7

Perkins, D.R.J. & Gibson, A.M., 1990. A Beaker Burial from Manston, near Ramsgate, *Archaeologia Cantiana*, 108, 11-27

Perkins, D.R.J., MacPherson-Grant, G., Healy, F., 1994. Monkton Court Farm evaluation *Archaeologia Cantiana*, 114, 237-316

Petrie, W.M. Flinders, 1880. Notes on Kentish Earthworks, *Archaeologia Cantiana*, 13, 8-16

Philp, B., 1973. *Excavations in West Kent, 1960-1970*, Dover

Philp, B., 1984. *Excavations in the Darent Valley*, Dover

Philp, B., 2002. *Archaeology in the Front Line, 50 Years of Kent Rescue 1952-2002,* Dover

Philp, B. & Dutto, M., 1985. *The Medway Megaliths,* Dover

Phillips, C.W., 1987. *My Life in Archaeology,* Gloucester

Phillips, P., 1980. *The Prehistory of Europe,* London

Philipot, T., 1659. *Villare Cantianum: or Kent surveyed and illustrated,* London

Piercy Fox, N., 1967. The Ritual Shaft at Warbank, Keston, *Archaeologia Cantiana,* 82, 184-89

Piercy Fox, N., 1969. Caesar's Camp, Keston, *Archaeologia Cantiana,* 84, 185-99

Piercy Fox, N., 1970. Excavation of the Iron Age Camp at Squerryes, Westerham, *Archaeologia Cantiana,* 85, 29-33

Piggott, C.M., 1949. A Late Bronze Age Hoard from Black Rock in Sussex and its Significance, *Proc. Prehistoric Society,* 15, 107-21

Piggott, S., 1931. The Neolithic Pottery of the British Isles, *Archaeological Journal,* 88, 67-158

Piggott, S., 1935. Neolithic Pottery Spoon from Kent, *Proc Prehistoric Society,* 1, 150-51

Piggott, S., 1938. The Early Bronze Age in Wessex, *Proc. Prehistoric Society,* 4, 52-106

Piggott, S., 1949. An Iron Age Yoke from Northern Ireland, *Proc. Prehistoric Society,* 15, 192-93

Piggott, S., 1950. *William Stukeley. An Eighteenth Century Antiquary,* London (2nd revised ed., 1985)

Piggott, S., 1951. Stonehenge Reviewed, *Aspects of Archaeology in Britain and Beyond, Essays for O.G.S. Crawford,* (ed. W.F. Grimes), London 274-92

Piggott, S., 1954. *The Neolithic Cultures of the British Isles,* Cambridge

Piggott, S., 1956. Windmill Hill – East or West? *Proc. Prehistoric Society,* 21, 96-101

Piggott, S., 1957. A Tripartite Disc Wheel from Blair Drummond, Perthshire, *Proc. Society Antiquaries of Scotland,* 90, 238-41

Piggott, S., 1962. *The West Kennet Long Barrow, Excavations 1955-56 London,* HMSO

Piggott, S., 1963. The Bronze Age pit at Swanwick, Hants. A postscript, *Antiquaries Journal,* 43, 286-87

Piggott, S., 1965. *Ancient Europe,* Edinburgh

Piggott, S., 1971. Beaker bows: a suggestion, *Proc. Prehistoric Society,* 37, 80-94

Piggott, S., 1972. Excavation of the Dalladies long barrow, Fettercairn, Kincardineshire, *Proc. Society of Antiquaries of Scotland,* 104, 23-47

Piggott, S., 1973. The First Agricultural Communities, Neolithic Period, c.3000-1500 BC, *The Victoria History of Wiltshire,* 1, Pt.2, 284-337

Piggott, S., 1975. *The Druids,* London

Piggott, S., 1976. *Ruins in a Landscape,* Edinburgh

Piggott, S., 1978. Nemeton, Temenos, Bothros: Sanctuaries of the Ancient Celts, *Academia Nazionale dei Lincei, Quad.,* No. 237, 37-54

Piggott, S., 1981. Early Prehistory, *The Agrarian History of England and Wales* (ed. Piggott, S.), I, Cambridge, 3-5

Piggott, S., 1983. *The earliest Wheeled Transport,* London

Piggott, S., 1983. Archaeological Retrospect, *Antiquity,* 57, 28-37

Piggott, S., 1989. *Ancient Britons and the Antiquarian Imagination,* London

Piggott, S. & Powell, I.G.E., 1949. The excavation of three chambered tombs in Galloway, *Proc. Society of Antiquaries of Scotland,* 83, 103-61

Pitt Rivers, A.H.L. Fox, 1883. Excavations in Caesar's Camp, near Folkestone, conducted in 1878, *Archaeologia,* 47, 429-65

Pitts, M., 1996. The Stone Axe in Britain, *Proc Prehistoric Society,* 62, 311-71

Pitts, M., 2003. Don't Knock the ancestors, *Antiquity,* 77, 172-78

Pitts, M. & Roberts, M., 1997. *Fairweather Eden,* London

Poste, Rev. Beale, 1853. *The Coins of Cunobeline and the Ancient Britons,* London

Powell, A., 1948. *John Aubrey and his Friends* (rev. ed. 1963), London

Powell, I.C.E. (ed.), *Megalithic Enquiries in the West of Britain,* Liverpool

Powell-Cotton, P.H.G. & Crawford, O.G.S., 1924. The Birchington Hoard, *Antiquaries Journal,* 220-26

BIBLIOGRAPHY

Powell-Cotton, P.H.G. & Pinfold, G.F., 1939. The Beck Find, Prehistoric and Roman Site on the Foreshore of Minnis Bay, *Archaeologia Cantiana*, 51, 191-203

Prestwich, G.A., 1899. *The Life and Letters of Sir Joseph Prestwich*, London

Pretty, E., 1863. On the Golden Armillae in the Society's Museum, *Archaeologia Cantiana*, 5, 41-44

Pryor, F.M., 1974. *Excavation at Fengate, Peterborough, England: the First Report*, Toronto

Pryor, F.M., 1988. Earlier Neolithic organised landscapes, The *Archaeology of Context* (eds. Barrett, J.C. & Kinnes, I.A.), Sheffield, 63-72

Pryor, Francis, 2003. *Britain BC*, London

Pugh-Smith, J. & Samuels, J., 1996. *Archaeology in Law*, London

Pyke, J.A., 1978. Danes Trench and Prehistoric land divisions in the Upper Darent Valley, *Archaeologia Cantiana*, 94, 231-37

Pyke, J.A., 1980. Greenhill Bronze Age Site, Otford, *Archaeologia Cantiana*, 96, 321-339

Pyddoke, E., 1961. *Stratification for the Archaeologist*, London

Rackham, O., 1976. *Trees and Woodland in the British Landscape*, London

Rackham, O., 1986. *The History of the Countryside*, London

Radford, C.A.R., 1954. The Tribes of Southern Britain, *Proc. Prehistoric Society*, 20, 1-26

Radley, J. & Mellars, P., 1964. A Mesolithic Structure at Deepcar, Yorkshire, England, and the affinities of its associated flint industries, *Proc. Prehistoric Society* 30, 1

Rady, J., 1991. Extension of the A20: Folkestone to Dover, *Archaeologia Cantiana*, 109, 284-85

Rady, J. & Ouditt, S., 1989. Excavations at Castle Hill (Folkestone), *Archaeologia Cantiana*, 107, 352-54

Ramm, H., 1978. *The Parisi*, London

Rankine, W.F., 1956. *The Mesolithic of Southern England*, Research Paper Surrey Archaeological Society, 4

Reid, Clement, 1913. *Submerged Forests*, Cambridge

Renfrew, C., 1973. *Before Civilisation*, London

Reynolds, P.J., 1979. *Iron Age Farm, The Butser Experiment*, London British Museum

Richardson, A., 2003/4. Thurnham Potin Hoard, *Kent Archaeological Society Newsletter*, No. 30, 1-2

Rivet, A.L.F. & Smith, C., 1979. *The Place-Names of Roman Britain*, London

Roach Smith, C., 1850. *The Antiquities of Richborough, Reculver and Lymne in Kent*, London

Roach Smith, C., 1874. Gold Torques and Armillae discovered in Kent, *Archaeologia Cantiana*, 9, 1-11

Roach Smith, C., 1883. *Retrospections Social and Archaeological*, I, London

Roberts, O.T.P., 1992. The Brigg 'raft' reassessed as a round bilge Bronze Age boat, *Int. Journal Nautical Archaeology*, 21/3, 245-48

Robinson, D., 2003. A Feast of Reason and a Flow of Soul: the Archaeological Antiquarianism of Sir Richard Colt Hoare, *Wiltshire Studies*, 96, 111-28

Roe, D.A., 1968a. *A Gazzeteer of British Lower and Middle Palaeolithic Sites*, CBA Research Report, 8, London

Roe, D.A., 1968b. British Lower and Middle Palaeolithic Handaxe Groups, *Proc. Prehistoric Society*, 34, 1-82

Roe, D.A., 1981. *The Lower and Middle Palaeolithic Periods in Britain*, London

Rook, A.G., Lowery, P.R., Savage, R.D.A. & Wilkins, R.L., 1988. An Iron Age Bronze mirror from Aston, Hertfordshire, *Antiquaries Journal*, 62, 18-34

Ross, A., 1957-8. The Human Head in Pagan Celtic Religion, *Proc. Society Antiquaries Scotland*, 91, 10-43

Ross, A., 1967. *Pagan Celtic Britain*, London

Ross, A., 1968. Shafts, pits, wells – sanctuaries of the Belgic Britons? *Studies in Ancient Europe, Essays presented to Stuart Piggott* (eds. Coles, J.M. & Simpson, D.D.A.), Leicester, 255-85

Rowlands, M.J., 1976. *The Production and Utilisation of Metalwork in the Middle Bronze Age in Southern Britain*, British Archaeological Reports, 31, Oxford

Rust, A., 1937. *Das Altsteinzeitliche Rentierjagerlager*, Neumunster

Rust, A., 1943. Die *Alt- und Mittelsteinzeitlichen Funde von Stellmoor*, Neumunster

Saunders, A.D., 1983. A Century of Ancient Monuments Legislation, *Antiquaries Journal*, 63, 11-33

Scott Robertson, W.A., 1878. Gold Torques from Dover, *Archaeologia Cantiana*, 12, 317-20

Schwarz, K., 1962. Zum Stand der Ausgrabungen in der Spatkeltischen Viereckschanze von Holzhausen, *Jahresbericht der Bayerischen Bodendenkmalpflege*, 1962, 22-77

Shackley, M., 1980. *Neanderthal Man*, London

Shand, G., 1998. A Neolithic Causewayed Enclosure in Kent, *Past, The Newsletter of the Prehistoric Society*, No. 29, July, 1998, 1

Sheldon, J., 1982. The Environmental Background, *Archaeology in Kent to AD 1500* (ed. Leach, P.E.), CBA Research Report 48, London, 1-2

Sherratt, A., 1997. *Economy and Society in Prehistoric Europe, Changing Perspectives*, Princetown

Sieveking A. & G., 1962. *The Caves of France and Northern Spain: A Guide*, London

Sieveking, G. de G., 1960. Ebbsfleet: Neolithic Sites, *Archaeologia Cantiana*, 74, 192-93

Simmons, I. & Tooley, M., 1981. *The Environment in British Prehistory*, London

Simpson, D.D.A., 1968. Food Vessels: Associations and chronology, *Studies in Ancient Europe, Essays presented to Stuart Piggott* (ed. Coles, J. & Simpson, D.D.A.), Leicester, 197-211

Smith, G.H., 1987. A Beaker (?) Burial Monument and a Late Bronze Age Assemblage from East Northdown, Margate, *Archaeologia Cantiana*, 104, 237-85

Smith, I.F., 1954. The pottery: excavation of a neolithic long barrow on Whiteleaf Hill, Bucks (Excavation by Sir Lindsay Scott and prepared for publication by V.G. Childe and I.F. Smith), *Proc. Prehistoric Society*, 20, 212-30

Smith, I.F., 1961. An essay towards the reformation of the British Bronze Age, *Helinium*, 1, 94-118

Smith, I.F., 1965. *Windmill Hill and Avebury: Excavations by Alexander Keiller, 1925-1939*, Oxford

Smith, I.F., 1971. Causewayed Enclosures, *Economy and Settlement in Neolithic and Early Bronze Age Britain and Europe* (ed. Simpson, D.D.A.), Leicester, 89-112

Smith I.F. 1973. *The Prehistoric Pottery*, Philp, 1973, 9-14

Smith I.F., 1974. The Neolithic, *British Prehistory, a New Outline* (ed. Renfrew, C.), London, 100-136

Smith, M.A., 1959. Some Somerset Hoards and their place in the Bronze Age of Southern Britain, *Proc. Prehistoric Society*, 25, 144-87

Smith, R.A., 1911. A Palaeolithic industry at Northfleet, Kent, *Archaeologia*, 62, 515-32

Smith, R.A., 1912. On Late-Celtic antiquities discovered at Welwyn, Herts., *Archaeologia*, 63, 1-30

Smith, R.A., 1915. Origin of the Neolithic Celt, *Archaeologia*, 67, 27-48

Smith, R.A., 1920. *A Guide to the Antiquities of the Bronze Age*, London, British Museum

Smith, R.A., 1925. A Rare Urn from Suffolk, *Antiquaries Journal*, 5, 73-74

Smith, R.A., 1926. *A Guide to the Antiquities of the Stone Age*, London, British Museum

Smith, R.A., 1927. Flint Arrowheads in Britain, *Archaeologia*, 86, 81-106

Smith, R.A., 1931. *The Sturge Collection*, London, British Museum

Smith, R.A., 1933. Implements from a High Level Gravel near Canterbury, *Proc. Prehistoric Society East Anglia*, 7.2, 165-70

So, C.L., 1971. Early Coast Recession around Reculver, Kent, *Archaeologia Cantiana*, 86, 93-97

Spurrell, F.C.J., 1880. On the Discovery of the place where Palaeolithic implements were made at Crayford, *Quart. Journal Geological Society London*, 36, 544-48

Spurrell, F.C.J., 1883. Palaeolithic Implements found in West Kent, *Archaeologia Cantiana*, 15, 89-103

Spurrell, F.C.J., 1884. On some Palaeolithic knapping tools and modes of using them, *Journal Anthropological Institute*, 13, 109-18

Spurrell, F.C.J., 1891. Neolithic implements from Bexley, *Archaeological Journal*, 48, 436

Stead, I.M., *The La Tene Cultures of Eastern Yorkshire*, York

Stead, I.M., 1970. The earliest burials of the Aylesford culture, *Problems in Economic and Social Archaeology* (eds. Sieveking, G. de G., Longworth, I.H. & Wilson, K.E.), London, 401-16

Stead, I.M., 1971. The Reconstruction of Iron Age buckets from Aylesford and Baldock. *Prehistoric and Roman Studies* (ed. Sieveking, G. de G.), London, British Museum, 250-82

Stead, I.M., 1979. *The Arras Culture*, York

BIBLIOGRAPHY

Stead, I.M., 1998. *The Salisbury Heard,* Stroud

Stebbing, W.P.D., 1934. An early Iron Age site at Deal, *Archaeologia Cantiana,* 46, 207-09

Stebbing, W.P.D. & Cave, A.J.E., 1943. Cherry Garden Hill Tumulus, Folkestone: Report on the Human Remains, *Archaeologia Cantiana,* 56, 28-33

Stevens, S., 1975. Dover Sub-Aqua Club, *Archaeologia Cantiana,* 91, 208

Stevenson, R. & Johnson, C., 2004. Brisley Farm, the last Iron Age Warriors of Kent, *Current Archaeology,* XVI, No. 11, 490-4

Stone, J.F.S., 1948. The Stonehenge Cursus and its Affinities, *Archaeological Journal,* 104, 7-19

Stone, J.F.S. & Thomas, L.C., 1956. The Use and Distribution of Faience in the ancient East and Prehistoric Europe, *Proc. Prehistoric Society,* 22, 37-84

Stukeley, W., 1724. *Itinerarium Curiosum, Centuria I,* London

Stukeley, W., 1740. *Stonehenge: a Temple Restor'd to the British Druids,* London

Stukeley, W., 1743. *Abury: a Temple of the British Druids,* London

Stukeley, W., 1776. *Itinerarium Curiosum, Centuria II,* London (posthumous)

Swanscombe Skull, 1938. Report of the Swanscombe Committee of the Royal Anthropological Institute, *Journal Royal Anthropological Institute,* 68 (Jan-June), 17-98

Tatton-Brown, T., 1976. Excavations in 1976 by the Canterbury Archaeological Trust, *Archaeologia Cantiana,* 92, 235-44

Tatton-Brown, T., 1977. Excavations in 1977 by the Canterbury Archaeological Trust, *Archaeologia Cantiana,* 93, 212-18

Tatton-Brown, T., 1977. Beaker from Swalecliffe, *Archaeologia Cantiana,* 93, 212

Tatton-Brown, T., 1988. The Parish church of St. Laurence, Godmersham: a History, *Archaeologia Cantiana,* 106, 45-81

Taylor, J.J., 1980. *Bronze Age Goldwork of the British Isles,* Cambridge

Taylor, K.J., 1996. The Rough and the Smooth: Axe Polishers of the Middle Neolithic, *The Early Prehistory of Scotland* (eds. Pollard, A. & Morrison, A.) Edinburgh, 225-36

Tester, P.J., 1950. Palaeolithic Flint Implements from the Bowman's Lodge Gravel Pit, Dartford Heath, *Archaeologia Cantiana,* 63, 122-34

Tester, P.J., 1951. Three associated neolithic axes from Pembury, *Archaeologia Cantiana,* 64, 57-62

Tester, P.J., 1952. Surface palaeoliths from Standardhill Farm, near Elham, *Archaeologia Cantiana,* 65, 85-89

Tester, P.J., 1965. An Acheulian site at Cuxton, *Archaeologia Cantina,* 80, 30-60

Thomas, K.D., 1977. The Land Mollusca from the enclosure on Offham Hill, *Proc. Prehistoric Society,* 43, 234-39

Thomas, N., 1964. The Neolithic Causewayed Camp at Robin Hood's Ball, Shrewton, *Wiltshire Archaeological & Natural History Mag.,* 59, 1-27

Thompson, F.H., 1955. Excavations at Reculver, Kent, *Archaeologia Cantiana,* 66, 52-59

Thompson, F.H., 1978. Kentish Hill-forts, *Kent Archaeological Review,* 512, 2-6

Thompson, F.H., 1979. Three Surrey Hillforts: Anstiebury, Holmbury and Hascombe, 1972-7, *Antiquaries Journal,* 59, 245-318

Thompson, F.H., 1983. Excavations at Bigberry, near Canterbury, 1978-80, *Antiquaries Journal,* 63, 237-78

Thompson, F.H., 1984. Oldbury, 1983, *Kent Archaeological Review,* 76, 140-44

Thompson, I., 1978. The 'Belgic' Cemetery at Allington, *Archaeologia Cantiana,* 94, 127-38

Thompson, M.W., 1981. *Ruins, their Preservation and Display,* London

Thorpe, J., 1788. *Custumale Roffense,* London

Thurnham, J., 1871. On Ancient British Barrows, especially those of Wiltshire and the adjoining Counties (Part II, Round Barrows*),* *Archaeologia,* 43, 285-552

Tilley, C., 1996. *An ethnography of the Neolithic, Early prehistoric societies in Southern Scandinavia,* Cambridge

Todd, A.E., 1936. Early Palaeoliths from the Summit of the South Downs, *Proc. Prehistoric Society,* 2, 140-43

Torbrugge, W, 1972. Vor- und Fruhgeschichtliche Flussfunde, *Breicht Romisch Germanisch Kommission,* 51/52, 1-46

Toynbee, J.M.C., 1962. *Art in Roman Britain,* London

Trechman, C.T., 1936. Mesolithic Flints from the Submerged Forest at West Hartlepool, *Proc. Prehistoric Society,* 2, 161-68

Trigger, B., 1980. *Gordon Childe, Revolutions in Archaeology,* London

Turner, J., 1928. On an early Palaeolithic workshop site at Stonecross, Luton, *Proc. Prehistoric Society East Anglia,* 5, 299-305

Turner, J., 1962. The *Tilia* decline: an anthropometric interpretation, *New Phytologist,* 61, 328-41

Tylden-Wright, D., 1991. *John Aubrey, A Life,* London

Uslar, von, R., 1956. Der vorgeschtliche Goldbecher von Fritzdorf, Kreis Bonn, *Rheinisches Jahrbuch,* I, 71-79

Vale, J., 1987. Archaeological Notes from the Kent County Museums Service, *Archaeologia Cantiana,* 104, 368-74

Valera, R. de, & Ó Nualláin, S., 1961. *Survey of the Megalithic Tombs of Ireland, I: Co. Clare,* Dublin

Waals, J.D. van der, 1964. *Prehistoric Disc Wheels in the Netherlands,* Groningen

Waddell, J., 1998. *The Prehistoric Archaeology of Ireland,* Galway

Waechter, J.d'A., 1969. Swanscombe, 1969, *Proceedings Royal Anthropological Institute,* 1969 (1970), 83-93

Wainwright, G.J., 1979. *Gussage All Saints, An Iron Age Settlement in Dorset,* Dept. Environment Archaeological Reports, No. 10, London, HMSO

Wainwright, G.J., 1979. *Mount Pleasant, Dorset, Excavations, 1970-1971,* Reports of the Research Committee of the society of Antiquaries of London, 37, London

Wainwright, G.J., 1989. *The Henge Monuments,* London

Wainwright, G.J. & Longworth, I.H., 1971. *Durrington Walls: excavations 1966-1968,* Reports of the Research Committee of the Society of Antiquaries of London, 29, London

Wallace, J.N.A., 1938. The Golden Bog of Cullen, *North Munster Archaeological Journal,* 1, 89-101

Walsh, Sir D., 1969. *Report of the Committee of Enquiry into the Arrangements for the Protection of Field Monuments,* London, HMSO, Cmnd., 3904

Ward-Perkins, J.B., 1938. An Early Iron Age Site at Crayford, Kent, *Proc. Prehistoric Society,* 4, 151-68

Ward-Perkins, J.B., 1939. Excavations on Oldbury Hill, Ightham, 1938, *Archaeologia Cantiana,* 51, 137-81

Ward-Perkins, J.B., 1944. Excavations on the Iron Age Hillfort of Oldbury, Near Ightham, Kent, *Archaeologia,* 90, 127-76

Warnicke, R.M., 1973. *William Lambarde, Elizabethan Antiquary, 1536-1601,* London & Chichester

Warren, S. Hazzeldine, Clark, J.G.D., Godwin, H. & M.E., & Macfadyen, W.A., 1936. An early Mesolithic site at Broxbourne sealed under Boreal peat, *Journal Royal Anthropological Institute,* 64, 101-28

Way, A., 1856. Report to the Central Committee of the British Archaeological Association, *Archaeological Journal,* 13, 404

Webster, D.B., 1991. *Hawkeseye, The Early Life of Christopher Hawkes,* London

Webster, J., 1995. Sanctuaries and Sacred Places, *The Celtic World* (ed. Green, M.J.,) London & New York, 445-64

Webster, G. & Dudley, D.R., 1965. *The Roman Conquest of Britain,* London

Wegner, H.H., 1986. *Koblenz und der Kreis Mayen-Koblenz,* Stuttgart

West, R.G., 1956. The quarternary Deposits at Hoxne, Suffolk, *Phil. Transactions Royal Society,* London, series B, 239, 265-356

Wetherall, D., 1998. The Growth of Archaeological Societies, *The Study of the Past in the Victorian Age* (ed. Brand, V.), Oxbow Monograph, 73, 21-34

Wheeler, R.E.M., 1929. The Roman lighthouses at Dover, *Archaeological Journal,* 86, 29-46

Wheeler, R.E.M., 1943. *Maiden Castle, Dorset,* Research Report of the Society of Antiquaries of London, 12, London

Wheeler, Sir Mortimer, 1954. *Archaeology from the Earth,* Oxford

Whimster, R., 1977. Iron Age Burial in southern Britain, *Proc. Prehistoric Society*, 43, 317-27

Whimster, R., 1978. Harlyn Bay Reconsidered: the excavations of 1900-1905 in the Light of Recent Work, *Cornish Archaeology*, 16, 61088

Whimster, R., 1981. *Burial Practices in Iron Age Britain,* British Archaeological Reports (British Series), 90, Oxford

Whittle, A.W.R., 1977. *The Earlier Neolithic of Southern England and its Continental Background* British Archaeological Reports, Supp. Series, 35, Oxford

Whittle, A., 1991. Wayland's Smithy, Oxfordshire, excavations at the Neolithic Tomb in 1962-3, by R.J.C. Atkinson & Stuart Piggott, *Proc. Prehistoric Society*, 57 (Pt.2), 61-101

Whittle, A.W.L., 1996. *Europe in the Neolithic,* Cambridge

Wickham, H., 1877. Celtic Remains found in the Hundred of Hoo, *Archaeologia Cantiana*, 11, 123-25

Williamson, T., 1987. Early co-axial field systems on the East Anglian Boulder Clays, *Proc. Prehistoric Society,* 53, 419-31

Wilson, D.R., 1982. *Air Photo Interpretation for Archaeologists*, London

Woodcock, A.G., 1975. Mesolithic Discoveries at Perry Wood, Selling, near Canterbury, Kent, *Archaeologia Cantiana*, 91, 169-77

Woodruff, C.H., 1874. On Celtic tumuli in East Kent, *Archaeologia Cantiana*, 9, 16-30

Woodruff, C.H., 1877. An account of discoveries made in Celtic tumuli near Dover, Kent, *Archaeologia*, 45, 53-56

Woodruff, C.H., 1904. Further Discoveries of Late-Celtic and Roman British interments at Walmer, *Archaeologia Cantiana,* 26, 9-16

Woodruff, C.E., 1921. George Payne FSA (obit.), *Archaeologia Cantiana*, 35, 161-66

Woodward, A., 1993. The cult of relics in Prehistoric Britain, *In Search of Cult* (ed. Carver, M.), 1-7

Wooldridge, S.W. & Goldring, F., 1962. *The Weald,* London

Worsfold, F.H., 1927. Observations on the provenance of the Thames Valley pick, Swalecliffe, Kent, *Proc. Prehitoric Society of East Anglia,* 5, 224-51

Worsfold, F.H., 1943. A report on the Late Bronze Age site excavated at Minnis Bay, Birchington, Kent, *Proc. Prehistoric Society*, 9, 28-47

Worsfold, F.H., 1948. An Early Iron Age Site at Borden, *Archaeologia Cantiana*, 61, 14855

Wright, E.V. & Wright, C.V., 1947. Prehistoric Boats from North Ferriby, East Yorkshire, *Proc. Prehistoric Society,* 13, 114-38

Wright, E.V., 1990. *The Ferriby Boats, Seacraft of the Bronze Age,* London

Wright, T., 1854. *Wanderings of an Antiquary chiefly upon the traces of the Romans in Britain,* London

Wymer, B.O., 1955. The Discovery of the Right Parietal Bone at Swanscombe, Kent, *Man,* 55, No. 133

Wymer, J.J., 1962. Excavations at the Maglemosian sites at Thatcham, Berkshire, England, *Proc. Prehistoric Society,* 28, 329-61

Wymer, J.J., 1964. Excavations at Barnfield Pit, 1955-60, *The Swanscombe Skull: a survey of research at a Pleistocene site* (ed. Ovey, C.D.), Royal Anthropological Institute, Occasional Paper No. 20, 19-60

Wymer, J.J., 1968. *Lower Palaeolithic Archaeology in Britain as represented by the Thames Valley,* London

Wymer, J.J, 1971. A possibly Late Upper Palaeolithic site at Cranwich, Norfolk, *Norfolk Archaeology*, 35, 259-63

Wymer, J.J., 1977. *Gazetteer of Mesolithic Sites in England and Wales,* CBA Research Report, No. 20, Norwich

Wymer, J.J., 1982. *The Palaeolithic Age*, London

Wysocki, M. & Whittle, A., 2000. Diversity, lifestyles and sites: new biological evidence from British Earlier Neolithic mortuary assemblages, *Antiquity*, 74, 591-601

Yates, N., 1994. Kent, *English County Histories* (eds. Currie, C.R.J. & Lewis, C.P.), Stroud, 208-15

Zeuner, F.E., 1950. *Dating the Past*, London

Zeuner, F.E., 1959. *The Pleistocene Period* (2nd ed. 1964), London

INDEX

INDEX

SUBJECTS

If you are interested in purchasing other books published by Tempus,
or in case you have difficulty finding any Tempus books in your local bookshop,
you can also place orders directly through our website

www.tempus-publishing.com